QUINN MARTIN, PRODUCER

QUINN MARTIN, PRODUCER

A Behind-the-Scenes History of QM Productions and Its Founder

by Jonathan Etter

Foreword by WALTER E. GRAUMAN

McFarland & Company, Inc., Publishers
Jefferson, North Carolina, and London

The present work is a reprint of the illustrated case bound edition of Quinn Martin, Producer: A Behind-the-Scenes History of QM Productions and Its Founder, *first published in 2003 by McFarland.*

Frontispiece: **Quinn and Muffet Martin at a party for the QM television series** *Banyon* **(1972)**

LIBRARY OF CONGRESS CATALOGUING-IN-PUBLICATION DATA

Etter, Jonathan, 1961–
Quinn Martin, producer : a behind-the-scenes history of QM Productions
and its founder / by Jonathan Edward Etter ; foreword by Walter E. Grauman.
p.   cm.
Includes bibliographical references and index.
ISBN 978-0-7864-3867-9
softcover : 50# alkaline paper

1. Martin, Quinn, 1922–1987.   2. QM Productions—History.   I. Title.
PN1992.4.M373E88   2003   791.45'0232'092—dc21   2002156356

British Library cataloguing data are available

Manufactured in the United States of America

*McFarland & Company, Inc., Publishers
Box 611, Jefferson, North Carolina 28640
www.mcfarlandpub.com*

To my father, Arthur J. Etter,
who got me interested in classic television
and films all those years ago.
Dad, I just wish you had lived to see this.

ACKNOWLEDGMENTS

One of the problems in writing this book was in deciding what material to use. Quinn Martin was such a beloved figure to almost everyone who worked for him, this author was never lacking for information, or for contacts. All of the information in this book, except when noted, comes from telephone interviews. To all of those interviewees who opened doors and provided access to some very hard to reach people, a heartfelt thank you. To those people who were willing to be interviewed, but whom the author could not reach, for lack of time, my apologies. The author hopes to rectify this in the future.

Mom, thanks for supporting and encouraging me throughout this endeavor. Bets, thanks for your support as well. Jane and Bill, thank you for the generosity you exhibited on more than one occasion. Greg Denslow, that goes double for you. A special thanks to Jeremy Rosen for clearing up the author's confusion regarding Jewish holidays. To the rest of my family and friends, thanks for all your support and encouragement.

Marty Martino, everyone should have a friend like you. Thanks for the *12 O'clock High* pictures and *12 O'clock* and *Most Wanted* videos, and for the contacts you gave me. Ray Elliott, thank you for *The New Breed* and *Dan August* videos. Mark Speck, thanks for *The FBI* and *The Untouchables* shows. Dennis Atkins, thank you for the QM television movie, *The Face of Fear*. A special thanks to Jim Benson of Jim's TV Collectibles for providing pictures, and for helping me in other ways. Thanks also to Jerry Ohlinger's Movie Material Store and the Movie Market for making available other photos.

Very special thank yous go to Mrs. Stuart Bowie (Muffet Martin) for her time and patience in granting interviews, and for providing the *Banyon* party picture and hard to find videos, John Wilder for sharing the personal letter Quinn Martin sent him in regards to *Centennial*, William W. Spencer for providing pictures, and many archival materials (cast lists, staff lists, production sheets, etc.), Robert Jeffords for the vast amount of archival materials he sent, and the extra efforts he went to in regards to the *Streets of San Francisco* pilot, and *Cannon* dart-board photo, Robert Day for making available the *A Home of Our Own* video, Walter Grauman for interrupting his schedule to write the foreword, Lynda Day George for providing pictures from one of her *FBI* guest appearances, and finally, Henry "Hank" Simms for the extra time and trouble he went to in sending the QM series main titles poster. A very special thank you to QM production manager Howard Alston for providing so many title cards from the QM television series and television movies.

For the generous amount of time the above and the following willingly set aside for interviews, the author would like to thank: Richard Anderson, Alan Armer, R.G. Armstrong, Don Brinkley, Richard Brockway, Robert Butler, Michael Caffey, James Callahan, Richard Church, Oliver Crawford, George Eckstein, John Elizalde, Robert Forster, Martin Fox, Harold Gast, James Gavin, Kenneth Gilbert, Jonathan Goldsmith, Robert Goodwin, William A. Graham, William Hale, Ken Howard, Robert Huddleston, Debbi Lahr Lawlor, Steven Lodge, Sally Richman Manning, Debbie Yates Marks, Marlyn Mason, the late Gerald Mayer, Lee Meriwether, Meryl O'Loughlin, Barry Oringer, Philip Pine, Michael Preece, Peter Mark Richman, Carol Rossen, Philip Saltzman, Jacqueline Scott, William Self, Ralph Senensky, Karen Shaw, Anthony Spinner, Roy Stork, Sam Strangis, Duane Tatro, Joan Van Ark, Paul Wendkos, David Whorf, William Windom, Lois Winslow, Paul Wurtzel, William Robert Yates, and Efrem Zimbalist, Jr. Thanks to Paul Monash as well for the information he provided, by mail, concerning *The Untouchables* pilot.

If there is any bias in this book, it is towards those, such as the late Adrian Samish, who are no longer here to give their side of the story, and towards those, who, because of their excellent memories, analyses and descriptions of the QM television series, movies, and other productions, are quoted more often and at greater length than others. As the reader will note, there is a generous amount of quotations in this book. The reason for this is quite simple—the author did not know Quinn Martin. He never worked for QM Productions; he never worked on any Hollywood set. Thus, he is not qualified to judge when it comes to the degree of Quinn Martin's talent, and the quality of his company's productions. As the author's intention in writing this book is to provide an objective history of the QM company and its founder, he thinks it best that the people who worked for QM Productions and who knew its founder tell this story.

Jonathan Etter
January 2003

CONTENTS

FOREWORD

A Producer!
Big Q!—Quinn Martin

A man of taste, integrity, talent and courage. Over a span of a dozen years I had the pleasure of directing six pilots and series for Quinn Martin. I must say they were the most fascinating and energizing years of my directing television. Quinn had imagination and tenacity. There were countless times during which he refused to give into network and advertising agency demands to change what he, in his gut, knew was dramatically correct. I can't begin to tell you how much I liked, respected and fought with Quinn. Most of the time his dramatic instincts were right but the few times that I was right he readily admitted his possible fallibility with humor and an infectious grin. When Quinn smiled the whole world smiled and when he died the whole world mourned the loss of "A QM Production."

Walter Grauman

Walter Grauman
Los Angeles, California

PREFACE

> He wanted to get into features but he couldn't because he was ahead of the people who were making features. He couldn't get them to hear what was going to be happening. It's difficult sometimes to reach people in this industry because they are so very for the moment, so very much in this minute they're not thinking about what's around the corner, where does this path lead to, where will we be if we stay on this road? Quinn Martin knew. He was ahead of everyone else. He was ahead of the future.
>
> *QM Player Lynda Day George*

"A QM Production!"

The minute the television viewer of the 1960s and the 1970s heard that from QM announcers Dick Wesson (*The New Breed, The Fugitive, 12 O'clock High, The Invaders*) and Henry "Hank" Simms (*The FBI*, and every other QM series after that), he knew he was in for a good hour-long television show. A show that was well-produced from beginning to end. A show that was well-written, well-directed, well-acted. QM Productions prided itself on having the best repertory company in the business; with a roster that ranged from the very well known—Bradford Dillman, Jessica Walter, Peter Mark Richman, Stefanie Powers—to the lesser known—Judee Morton, Robert Doyle, Nan Martin, Jonathan Lippe—the "QM Players" (as they were called) were certainly that.

The directors—from the greats: Paul Wendkos, Walter Grauman, Don Medford, to the up-and-comers: script supervisors Kenneth Gilbert, Michael Preece—were no less talented. Ditto writers-turned-associate-producers-turned-producers Philip Saltzman and Anthony Spinner. Saltzman was so good he practically ran *Barnaby Jones* for seven out of its seven-and-a-half seasons. Spinner somehow managed to produce (all at the same time) two series: *Cannon* and *Caribe* in addition to the critically well-received QM Players television movie, *Panic on the 5:22*. Thanks to such aforementioned talents, MGM-trained cinematographers William W. Spencer and Andrew

J. McIntyre, David O. Selznick–versed editors Arthur Fellows and Richard K. Brockway, and classically-trained musicians the caliber of John Elizalde and Duane Tatro,
QM Productions consistently turned out television series which were "always much
more advanced than other programs," declares Wendkos. "Quinn always challenged
you to rise above yourself. That made his shows very unusual; there was nothing
like them on television."

Considered a genius by many who worked for him, Quinn Martin "didn't really
put his name on anything that wasn't one hundred percent right," says the producer's
secretary, Sally Richman Manning.

> He could take a look at a show, and, in five minutes, say, "That's good." And
> that was it. It didn't sit on his desk and keep everybody in agony. If he was wrong,
> he would change it quickly. He did very few things by committee. He was the one
> who made the decisions, and he made them quickly.
>
> When I first began with him (in the early '70s), he didn't really do anything that
> didn't have a twenty-six episode commitment. He was so intimately involved with
> his product—that had a great deal to do with the quality that resulted. He had the
> final say on everything. No detail was too small. He had such a good eye, always
> could tell when things weren't right. He was so bright, so intelligent, so creative.
> He could come up with a paragraph about a series, and the networks would buy the
> series just based on that. His reputation preceded him so much in the industry, his
> whole career was so stellar, he didn't have to make any kind of presentation. All he
> had to do was come up with a premise.
>
> The repertory company that he had was like an ensemble because he used the
> same actors again and again. We always prided ourselves on having the best reper-
> tory company in town. We did. Because every time he put those actors in a pilot,
> that series got sold.

The track records of Vera Miles (*The Fugitive, Cannon*), J.D. Cannon (*The
Invaders, Cannon*), William Windom (*The House on Greenapple Road, Landon, Landon & Landon*), Roy Thinnes (*The Invaders, Tales of the Unexpected*) proved Richman's point. With the exception of *Landon, Landon, & Landon* which worked well
enough to generate a second-pilot, *Quick & Quiet* (QM Production's very last production), each of these hour-long or movie-length pilots resulted in a prime-time
television series.

Quinn Martin tried out many of his series ideas on Sally Richman Manning. "I
spent hours and hours with him," recalls Manning, "acting mostly as his ear. He'd
run things off me, not always require a response." Usually, Martin's ideas had merit.
The producer had an uncanny knack for matching the right people with the right
projects. If there was any producer who could keep fresh and believable a series concept as rigid and as predictable, and as unbelievable and contradictory as *The Fugitive*, it was Alan A. Armer. If there was any performer who could work within that
framework week after week, it was title character David Janssen. While Walter Grauman was consistently Martin's choice to establish the format of a QM series, Lynda
Day George was the producer's ace in the hole when it came to series departures
that featured unbelievable and contradictory characters. When George played those

characters, the unbelievable became believable, the contradictions were perfectly natural.

Production manager Howard Alston always gave QM directors less-costly alternatives that maintained the same creative value the director desired. QM composer Duane Tatro guaranteed himself a permanent job at QM with his extraordinary score for Martin's very first television movie, *The House on Greenapple Road*. Co-producing this feature was Martin's assistant, Adrian Samish. The acid-tongued, perfectionist Samish demanded scripts so tight, so in keeping with a series' format, more than one writer assaulted him physically. *Streets of San Francisco* producer John Wilder never had any trouble with Samish. When it came to versatility in pilots, few equaled Wilder. He could do light-hearted mysteries: 1977's *Winner Take All*; westerns: 1976's *Law of the Land*; science fiction/horror anthologies: 1976's *Nightmare*.

Had it not been for *The FBI*'s diplomatic first producer, Charles Larson, and its gracious, cooperative leading man, Efrem Zimbalist, Jr., Quinn Martin's "QM Productions" might have crumbled; had it not been for the changes Martin made to his second QM series, *The Fugitive*, the faith he had in that daring concept, QM Productions might never have influenced the television industry to the degree that it would.

Quinn Martin didn't wait until he set up QM Productions in 1961, or until he started producing the Desilu series *The Untouchables* in 1959, to demand high standards from his people. Those standards were in place when Martin produced his very first television program—an episode of *The Jane Wyman Show*. Wanting the show as realistic as possible, Martin went out on location; he didn't like shooting on the back lot.

"He liked quality," states the producer's widow, Marianne Muffet Webb Martin. "He believed the public deserved more than they were getting, that they were intelligent, and appreciated good production much more than the networks ever gave them credit for." Quinn Martin worked hard to give the public those things. Through the high standards he established from the outset, standards which he insisted on throughout his career, he achieved that goal. In the process Martin did something more—he changed television for the better.

INTRODUCTION

Everybody working in television in the 1960s and '70s was working against this absurd time schedule of finishing a show in seven days. We had to do that in order to survive. I don't think anybody else in the world could do that. Even the Brits— who maybe equaled us on the script level—could not equal us on a production level. It took them ten to twelve days to do a show. We did ours in seven. We did superb work, world class work. It was a miracle, a real testimonial to American know-how, and commitment, and ability, that so much quality emerged. I've always felt that that time was the Renaissance in American television.

QM director Paul Wendkos

No one, arguably, was more responsible for bringing about and sustaining that Renaissance than television producer Quinn Martin. Yet like so many of the most gifted people in his company, Irwin Martin Cohn, better known as Quinn Martin, hadn't planned on a lifelong career in the entertainment industry. The second of two children of film editor Martin Cohn and his wife, Anne, Irwin Cohn, who was born on May 22, 1922, in Brooklyn, New York, and raised in Los Angeles from age four, dreamed of becoming a journalist. Educated at Berkeley, Cohn majored in English. He never graduated.

Like most teenagers, Irwin Cohn defied his parents. "He wanted to go back East, but his parents wouldn't let him," laughs his widow, Muffet Martin. "He showed them. He enlisted in the Army [in the Signal Corps] in 1939 or something." After the United States entered World War II, Cohn and childhood friend, Gordon ("Gordy") Hubbard were moved from the Presidio, in San Francisco, to Europe. Once the European phase of the war ended, Cohn's unit again traveled, this time to the South Pacific. In time, Cohn achieved the rank of sergeant. "He always had that leadership quality," chuckles Muffet Martin. "He was always more of a Chief, not an Indian."

Returning home following V-J Day, Irwin Cohn then joined his older sister, Ruth, in an amateur theatrical production. "It was a funny little business," remembers his

QUINN MARTIN

1041 NORTH FORMOSA AVENUE · HOLLYWOOD, CALIF. 90046

Telephone
(213) 650-2653

October 30, 1978

Mr. John Wilder
Universal Studio
100 Universal City Plaza
Universal City, California 91608

Dear John:

I just got back from London in time to see the
'Levi Zandt' episode Sunday night. It was one
of the most moving experiences I've ever had
from watching television.

I had also seen the opening episodes which were
excellent. As a Michener fan I can tell you that
no one could be translating his characters better.
Photography, music and editing were also outstanding.

Thanks for a memorable experience. I look forward
to seeing the rest. Best to Caroline and the kids.

Warmest regards,

Quinn Martin

QM/dl

Photocopy of letter received by *Centennial* producer John Wilder from his friend Quinn Martin congratulating Wilder on the second installment of that October 1978–February 1979, NBC-TV mini-series.

widow, "a little road-show with a swimmer in a tank; they went around and played at these different movies." During this period, Irwin Cohn became Quinn Martin. "It wasn't because he was ashamed of being Jewish," explains Muffet Martin. "He wasn't raised religiously. He wasn't religious. He wasn't anything. That didn't have anything to do with it. His sister had changed her last name to Martin, and Quinn's nickname was Marty; whenever anybody called him by his last name, they always called him 'Co-Inn.' So he changed his name to Quinn Martin."

Under his new name of Quinn Martin, Cohn applied for jobs at the *Los Angeles Times* and at his father Martin Cohn's place of employment, MGM. Ever practical, Cohn opted for the studio in the end. The studio paid more money than the *Times*. Moving from Metro to Universal Studios, and later to ZIV-TV, as both sound and film editor, it wasn't long before Quinn Martin began following in the footsteps of his father. Like his son, Martin Cohn, editor on such famous motion-pictures as Metro's 1935 adventure *Mutiny on the Bounty*, eventually wound up running his own production company. Martin Cohn made an invaluable contribution to the movies—"he was credited with developing the change-over," states Muffet Martin. "That allowed them to go from one reel to the next when they were showing the movie. They didn't have to stop and change the reels on the projector."

The accomplishments of Martin Cohn's son were to be even greater. In addition to developing his talents as both sound and film editor, Quinn Martin would write for such series as *The Dick Powell Show* and the Desilu Studios' comedy *I Love Lucy*. Martin's marriage to Madelyn Pugh, one of *Lucy's* two head writers, may have helped him secure writing jobs and a position as producer at Desilu, but his wife Madelyn was none too supportive of his future ambitions. "She'd say, 'You shouldn't be doing that. That's too risky,' and so forth and so on," states Muffet Martin. Madelyn Pugh Martin was among the first to learn that one didn't say, "No" to Quinn Martin. She was certainly not the last.

Despite their inevitable divorce, Quinn Martin stayed in close touch with the Martins' one child, Michael Quinn Martin. That was until Madelyn Pugh Martin remarried and moved back to Indiana with her new husband and Michael. During that period Michael grew apart from his real father. Quinn Martin's second marriage to former Pan-American stewardess Marianne Muffet Webb was much happier. Marianne's brother had nicknamed Marianne "Little Miss Muffet" when she was two years old. From then on, everyone called her Muffet.

Muffet Martin first met her future husband at the "small, clubby" Los Angeles restaurant, Dominic's. "It was the kind of place where you could sit and talk to somebody out of the blue," laughs the producer's widow, "but, if you didn't know Dominic, you didn't get in. Well, I had a date with somebody; Quinn was there by himself. At the time, he and Madelyn had separated, but not divorced, and he was going with somebody else. Anyway, the person I was with admired a show that Quinn had done. He started talking to Quinn about it, and he said he wanted to see the show. So Quinn set it up. My date asked me if I wanted to go, I did. After it was over, Quinn asked us out to dinner. Then he asked me out. A year later, we got married." As soon as the couple had children, Muffet quit her stewardess job to raise them. The Martins' marriage produced two children—Cliff and Jill. Both would go on to work in the industry. Jill Martin's acting credits were to include supporting guest shots on her father's series *Barnaby Jones* and *Most Wanted*; Cliff Martin would later find employment as a Warner Bros. executive.

In spite of his busy schedule, Quinn Martin found time for his family. The producer tried very hard to keep his work life separate from his home life. Because of that, and because Martin had to wait until the end of the day to reach various people in the business, he often didn't get home until seven or eight in the evening. After he did, Martin frequently told his children a bedtime story before going out to dinner with Muffet, usually about nine. Muffet's aunt baby-sat for the children whenever the couple went out on weeknights; on the weekends, Martin's mother, Anne Cohn, assumed that chore.

Weekends Martin spent playing tennis on Friday and Saturday; sometimes he and Muffet played doubles with Robert and Rosemarie Stack. On Sunday, the Martins went to the races at Santa Anita, often with their good friends Anthony and Jackie Spinner. Whenever Quinn Martin went to the racetrack by himself, he always took a limousine. That wasn't uncommon—numerous people went to the track in limousines—but in Martin's case, it wasn't for show. The long drive allowed him time to read scripts and handle other business matters. The producer worked all the way down to the track, all the way back. "He didn't have a car phone so that was his quiet time," says his widow. "I think he got a lot done." It wasn't until later that Martin bought his own limousine. Prior to that, he rented one.

By taking a limousine, Quinn Martin also avoided a long drive. Martin hated long drives—he hated the commute, and the traffic he encountered driving to the Warner Bros. studios during the years his company produced *The FBI*. After QM Productions began doing other shows, Martin started going to work much later—usually at nine A.M. Eventually he moved from Warner Bros. back to his less ostentatious home base: the Samuel Goldwyn Studios.

Quinn Martin was no less showy in the houses he lived in during his career. During the first few years, he and Muffet rented a home in Malibu; then they moved to Sunset Boulevard in Westwood. "That was a disaster," remembers Muffet Martin. "We were right above Sunset Boulevard during the sixties, and there were all these problems with the hippies, bottles in the yard all the time. It was just awful." After that, the Martins moved to West Hollywood, then to Beverly Hills. They lived there for twelve years.

"We had rather normal houses," says Muffet Martin. "We'd have a little bit of property because Quinn liked to walk around in the yard, but we didn't have a projection room or anything like that." One home was an old-fashioned two story house with an entry hall, living room, dining room, kitchen, and upstairs bedrooms. Another in Beverly Hills "looked kind of grand from the outside," admits the producer's widow, "but it was a homey house."

In the 1970s, the Martins lived in Bel Air. "They'd used it in *Barnaby Jones* as a practical location," remembers Muffet Martin. "Quinn saw it in the dailies, it had a tennis court, and we'd been looking for a house with a tennis court. Well, he found out it was for sale, we went and looked at it at nine in the morning. At eleven A.M. we bought it." The Martins lived in the Bel-Air home for five years. The little room that faced off the living room became an office with bookcases; there were also bookcases in the den. The bookcases featured historical fiction (James A. Michener, Herman Wouk), mysteries (Dashiell Hammett, Dick Francis), and novels (Hemingway was one of Martin's favorite authors). It was usually not until the annual two-week Christmas vacation in Hawaii, or any other holiday trip, that Martin had time to read such books. Much of his time was spent reading scripts.

Quinn Martin always saw to it that his children received a good education. Both attended private schools, both studied piano, and at one point, the producer had his secretary, Sally Richman Manning, order a set of the classics—Martin wanted his children exposed to good literature. Sally Richman Manning was a close friend of the Martins'—she once took Jill Martin and Jill's friend to an Elton John concert. Another time she chaperoned a high-school party for Jill when Muffet and Quinn went out of town.

Though Quinn Martin socialized with QM series stars David Janssen, William Conrad, and Burt Reynolds during the time those stars' respective series were on the air, though he and Muffet once met Henry Kissinger at a party thrown by neighbor Ed Friendly, most of the couple's friends came from the production side of the business. Friends from QM Productions included life-long friend Walter Grauman, John Conwell, Arthur Fellows, John Wilder, and Howard Alston. In the 1970s, John Wilder was a very special friend. Though he and Martin later had a falling out, the two men remained close. After Martin saw Wilder's 1978 miniseries, *Centennial*, he sent his friend a congratulatory letter. John Wilder has kept that letter to this day. He and Muffet Martin still keep in touch.

As do Muffet and QM announcer Hank Simms. In the early '60s, before Simms became the regular QM announcer of the QM series' main titles, episode titles and guest stars, the Martins were next-door neighbors to Simms, his wife Mo, and what Simms laughingly refers to as the Simms' "three pygmies," their children. Hank Simms was always grateful to his friend Quinn Martin for hiring him as the off-screen announcer of the QM series. Because of that, Simms qualified for membership in the Screen Actors Guild. The Guild had a very good insurance plan. Moreover, since he was part of each QM show, Simms collected on the QM series' residuals. The Martins' other friends from the business included *Bewitched* producer William Asher and 20th Century–Fox Television studio head William Self.

As for Quinn Martin's unique friendship with perhaps his favorite QM Player Lynda Day George, it was always during business hours, whenever the one or the other wasn't busy and had ten or fifteen minutes to chat. George's friendship with Quinn Martin was remarkable. "Quinn was a very shy man who felt uncomfortable around actors because often when an actor befriends a producer, he does it so he can get something," explains George. "Quinn felt comfortable with me because I never tried to take advantage of anybody. I never tried to use anybody for anything. I didn't require anything from Quinn. I never asked him for anything. That wasn't part of my M.O. So he didn't feel uncomfortable when I popped my head in the door and said, 'Hi, got a minute? How you doin'? What's up? How's everything going? How's the family?' All that kind of stuff. It was just a friendship. I never saw him outside of his office. I never saw him as a close personal friend in that way. We never went out to lunch or dinner, or any of that kind of stuff. We didn't need to, we were just friends." Quinn Martin liked Lynda Day George because she was not Hollywood. He wasn't either.

Martin never acted like the stereotypical big-name Hollywood producer. He didn't talk hip; he didn't call people "baby." He and Muffet never attended wild parties where people did drugs or engaged in other illegal or immoral activities. The producer usually managed to find time for his children—every Sunday night, he, Cliff, and Jill would go out to the nearby Chinese carryout to get supper. During the workweek, Martin had two favorite restaurants where he always went for lunch—some days it was Musso-Frank's; other days, Tail of the Cock. Quinn Martin's tastes in food were nothing extraordinary. He liked hamburgers, steak, Mexican food, Italian food. Drinks included old-fashioned Crown Royals, Canadian Clubs, and, occasionally, Mexican beer. At the racetrack, Martin often had a Salty Dog. In Hawaii, it was fruit punches and rum punches. Some days Martin had no drink; some days, no more than two.

Like many people, there were times Quinn Martin drank too much. Like many people, the producer gained—and had trouble losing—weight, especially during his later years. "He went up and down in his weight," remembers his widow. "Sometimes he was one-eighty, sometimes one eighty-five. Periodically he'd go on a diet, go to a spa for a week or two; before you knew it, it was back to bacon and eggs."

From 1962, or 1963 on, the six-foot Martin's personal car was often red—red was the producer's favorite color. The license plates on the one car read QM 1; the license plates on the other, QM 2. "He had a big ego," admits Muffet Martin. "He was kind of bigger than life. When he thought he was right, he would be very positive, but I never found him obnoxious. I only got annoyed with him a couple of times in the twenty-seven years that we were married. Sometimes he'd get a little hyper. It was exhausting trying to keep up with him at times."

Unlike some in the entertainment business, Quinn and Muffet Martin had a very stable marriage. Muffet Martin always gave her husband plenty of support. In addition to discussing different projects with him, accompanying him on business trips, and visiting him at the office, she and her aunt did the Christmas cards for QM Productions year after year. Every Christmas QM Productions gave Christmas baskets to all its employees. They sent presents out to the series stars. There was always a Christmas party at QM, always an end of the season wrap party, too. Particularly good at throwing parties were *Barnaby Jones* series stars Buddy Ebsen and Lee Meriwether. Guest stars from the season were often invited to such parties.

The people who did *Barnaby Jones* felt as if they were a family. The family feel on the *Barnaby Jones* set was not unique. It existed on the set of *The Fugitive, The FBI, The Streets of San Francisco, Cannon*, and numerous television movies and television pilots, especially on the set of the 1974 television movie, *Panic on the 5:22*. Without that family feel, without such gracious series stars as David Janssen, and such considerate series producers as Philip Saltzman, QM Productions might never have been as successful as it was. Quinn Martin established the key to the company's success in the way he treated every one of his employees. At QM, everyone was important, no matter what his or her position.

"They were a very classy group of people," declares QM Player Lynda Day George, "a very compassionate and straightforward group of people. It was always important to them to do a good job. They were very careful about the things they did. There was always a high level of integrity and quality concerned. Those were high priorities to the whole company. I would have done anything for Quinn Martin. If I had something else in the works and Quinn Martin called, I would go for that. I would never pass up an opportunity to work for him. I respected him intensely. He was a man who was in touch with the future. Far more than the times. He just automatically knew. He had a really good sense of what was."

Quinn Martin proved that with a new ABC TV Thursday night television series that had its first telecast on October 15, 1959. The series was an outgrowth of an April 1959 special which Martin had produced for ABC's network rival, CBS. Involved in that special was a set decorator by the name of Sandy Grace. Grace would move with Martin to this new series, and then to QM Productions when Martin established the company in 1961. Producing episodes of the new company's first series, *The New Breed*, was a young director by the name of Walter Grauman. "If that's entertainment, then I can do a hell of a lot better" was Grauman's philosophy going into television. Quinn Martin shared that same philosophy, as Walter Grauman learned on the set of *The Untouchables*.

Chapter 1

THE UNTOUCHABLES

Watch this guy Quinn Martin. He's gonna go far in the business.
Untouchables *director Vincent McEveety to
script supervisor Michael Preece a short time
before Martin launched* The Untouchables

Contrary to popular opinion, Quinn Martin wasn't that involved with *The Untouchables*. True, the series did launch Martin's career, introduce the Martin style (low angles, shooting night scenes at night, etc.), have an off-screen narrator (former newsman and columnist Walter Winchell), and true, it did guest star such future QM players as Richard Anderson and Anne Francis, but the October 15, 1959, to September 10, 1963, ABC series was produced by Desilu Studios.

Quinn Martin produced only the first season. After that, Jerry Thorpe, Leonard Freeman, and future QM producer Alan A. Armer assumed that chore. During the first year, Martin set the standards for the series' subsequent producers. Those standards impressed first season director Walter Grauman. "They were massive productions," remembers Grauman, "done like small features. Most of the scenes used night exteriors—we had to shoot practically all night, and they were tough stories because we were doing a period piece with period costumes, period automobiles, and so forth. It was a very difficult show to do, but it was very gratifying." "The hours were unbelievable," adds script supervisor Michael Preece, who would go on to work as script supervisor, and later director, for QM Productions. "They were trying to do too much. You'd start a show in the morning, work fifteen hours. We spent all night long on the back lot. The mechanic was always running around with a kit, fixing cars, the machine guns wouldn't work. It wasn't always a pleasant experience."

Writer Paul Monash had set the series on the right course prior to its premiere episode. Hired by Desilu and Martin to write a one-hour pilot that was based on the Oscar Fraley novel, *The Untouchables*, Monash thought the company could do the concept "more justice by doing it as a two-parter." He wrote the pilot in three or four weeks. Producer Martin was quite satisfied with the completed script. Then he and Desilu began looking for an actor to play the lead character, Treasury agent Eliot Ness. They settled on MGM star Van Johnson. "I was unhappy with the choice," recalls Monash, "and suggested Robert Stack for the role." As events proved, Monash made the right suggestion. *The Untouchables* would bring both television series stardom and an Emmy to Robert Stack.

Despite that stardom and the long hours he put in on the job, Stack never let his success go to his head. "His wife, Rosemarie, would pack a beautiful picnic basket and bring it to the set maybe three times a week," remembers Grauman, "and they would invite me to share the lunch. It was better than the location food." Robert Stack liked Grauman. In the actor's opinion, Grauman was the best of all the series directors. "He says that to people all the time," reveals Grauman. "He felt I had more sense of the sinew and the muscle and the bizarre quality of the series than any other director who worked on the show." Given the talented directors who were to work on the series—Paul Wendkos, Robert Butler, Stuart Rosenberg—that was quite a compliment.

Quinn Martin had similar feelings regarding Grauman, especially when he learned that quality was so important to the director that he'd risk being fired by the production manager. To Grauman, producing shows cheaply often resulted in "a piece of crap." It was this yearning for quality which drove Grauman into the business; he went through a number of jobs: candy-store owner, real estate broker, before settling on a directorial career. But Grauman also produced—his first series was *Lights, Camera, Action.* Later he would do the dramatic half-hour series, *Felony Squad, The Blue Light,* and *The Silent Force*; among his big-screen productions: *Lady in a Cage, 633 Squadron, Rage to Live;* among his television movies: *Dead Men Tell No Tales, Paper Man, The Old Man Who Cried Wolf.*

Walter Grauman's versatility as a producer, director, and writer made him very valuable to QM Productions. After seeing a show the director had done on the 1950s anthology, *Alcoa-Goodyear Theatre,* Martin sent Grauman the *Untouchables* script "Noise of Death" by Ben Maddow. He wanted Grauman to direct the show. Grauman did. "The script was absolutely brilliant," enthuses the director. "It was so fascinating I read it twice in one night. That show was the beginning of my relationship with Quinn. I did about twenty percent of *The Untouchables* shows. The series was probably the most difficult show I ever did in my life. We worked maybe sixteen, seventeen hours a day. That show was the best of its type; it was head and shoulders above all the others in terms of casting, story, production value, style." Series producer Quinn Martin was the reason why. "He was a very fine producer," declares Grauman. "Very hands on, instinctively correct in most areas."

Quinn Martin thought just as highly of Walter Grauman. Grauman was to direct the pilot episodes, and or pilot films of *The Fugitive, The Streets of San Francisco, Barnaby Jones, The Manhunter,* and *Most Wanted.* He would direct numerous episodes of the three former series, a few episodes of *The FBI, Tales of the Unexpected,* and *12 O'clock High.* He would also produce numerous episodes of Martin's first series, *The New Breed*. In fact, Walter Grauman's tastes were so similar to Quinn Martin's, at one point the two men had identical blue blazers, which resulted in a rather humorous situation following an extraordinarily long casting session during which the two men had removed their blazers. "We finally settled on Harry Guardino as our leading man," remembers Grauman, "and by then it was after ten o'clock. Now, Quinn was a big man—he was about six feet, maybe two hundred pounds, and I'm rather short. I was about five foot seven, one-hundred-and-fifty pounds in those days, so I pick up my jacket, put it on, and I'm thinking, 'Geezus. I've shrunk!' I'd put on Quinn's jacket. He got so hysterical laughing—he said the expression on my face was incredible."

Quinn Martin had a good sense of humor. At times he used it in a rather clever way, such as when he informed *Untouchables* series regular Jerry Paris he would be dropped from the series at the end of the first season. "For some reason Quinn didn't like Jerry's character [Agent Martin Flaherty] and he wanted to change casting," explains Grauman. "He called Jerry into his office about two or three shows before the end of the season. He says, 'Listen, Jerry, I just want to ask you something. When you get killed on the show, do you prefer to be killed on camera, or just have us talk about you?' And Jerry looked at him, and he says, 'Oh, no. I wanta be killed on camera!' And he was. I don't think there were any bad feelings about that. [Paris later guest-starred on *The Fugitive*.] It was just a business decision."

Unfortunately, there were bad feelings between Martin and Desilu. Martin wanted to do quality shows. Desilu wanted them done as cheaply as possible. That resulted in numerous disagreements between their production manager, Marvin Stewart, and directors like Walter Grauman. "One time I wanted Victor, the stunt guy who was doubling the heavy, to run this car into a building and knock down its support," recalls Grauman. "Marvin told him not to; he said it would be too expensive. Eventually the guy came to me. I said, 'Which way do you want to do it?' He says, 'Your way.' I said, 'Then do it. And fuck him!'" Quinn Martin's attitude towards Desilu was similar. That was one of the reasons future QM producer Alan A. Armer assumed Martin's position at the beginning of the second season.

"Quinn had executive produced the first year of the series," explains Armer, "and, depending on who you talk to, either he quit or he was fired. My guess is that Desilu fired him. Quinn was the person who made *The Untouchables* a success—he spent a fortune—he did night for night shooting, went extra days, and Desilu was having catfits. Night for night shooting is really expensive—you have to light everything; it just takes so long."

The violence in the series was another problem—at one point there'd even been a congressional investigation. Remembers Armer, "We had this two or three hour meeting with the guys in network practices, talking about what they would and would not allow, so we had to be especially careful. We had to cut down the violence in our shows. Well, the next day, we had a meeting with the executives at ABC. They said, 'Look we know you had a meeting yesterday with the guys in Standards and Practices, and we know that they told you to cut back on the violence, but just between you and us, the violence is what brings in the audience. Put in as much violence as you can. If you have trouble with the people in Standards and Practices, call us. We will help you fight your battles.'"

Thanks to head censor Dorothy Brown, there weren't that many battles. "She was a very gutsy lady," states Armer, "who liked the show, liked us, and she worked very hard to keep the things in that were important. So when we were writing the script, I'd tell her, 'Dorothy, we have to kill these six people. What can we get away with?' She'd always help us get the show to a point where it would get past the censors."

Coming up with last names for the gangsters was another problem. "Most of the heavies in real life were Italian-Americans, and during the first year all of the bad guys had Italian surnames," explains Armer. "Well the Italian-Americans didn't like that. So we tried German, Hungarian, Greek, all those groups were offended. But you can't have a bad guy whose name is John Smith. It just doesn't work. You gotta put in some colors, some chemisty."

While Alan Armer was struggling with such problems, Quinn Martin was in the process of forming his own production company. Thanks to the great success he'd had with *The Untouchables*, Quinn Martin had become invaluable to the executives at ABC. The struggling network needed hit series. Thus new TV producer Quinn Martin was just the person they needed. Under the terms of the exclusive contract Martin signed with ABC, the producer was guaranteed a series pilot, perhaps two pilots, for a number of years. Years later the terms of this contract, which kept Martin from working at any place but ABC, would be broken. In the late 1960s, ABC filed a lawsuit against Martin claiming Martin had not honored his contract. As it turned out, it was ABC who had not honored the contract. After that, Quinn Martin had the opportunity to work at other networks. *Cannon* was to begin his long association with CBS. Eventually Quinn Martin would leave ABC. The producer would have no regrets in leaving the network. Nor did he have any regrets in cutting his financial ties to *The Untouchables*. In order to get out of his *Untouchables* contract, Martin agreed to have his ownership of the series reduced to five percent.

Finding a home base for his new company, QM Productions, was his next concern. "He went around and looked at what was available, and ended up at Goldwyn," remembers Muffet Martin. "Sam Goldwyn kind of liked Quinn. We went to his house for dinner before we were married." After one dinner, Goldwyn took Martin in his private projection room and showed him (the Barbara Stanwyck classic) *Stella Dallas*. Then Goldwyn asked Martin if he'd like to remake the picture. Martin didn't want to—a 1960s remake of the 1930s Stanwyck feature wouldn't be right for the times.

Quinn Martin didn't like doing remakes. The producer wanted to do original things in television. The first two series pilots ABC offered Martin satisfied that urge. One was a World War I aviation drama. It was called *The Skyfighters*. The other starred a young actor by the name of Leslie Nielsen. It was called *The New Breed*.

Chapter 2

THE NEW BREED

We were just sort of setting our own agenda when we made that show. A lot of companies were making shows in five or six days; we did ours in seven. That became a pattern for all the series we made.
New Breed unit production manager Howard Alston

On September 18, 1964, Quinn Martin launched his first, and only successful, war series, *12 O'clock High*. It was not the first time Martin produced a war drama. Three years earlier, the producer made the half-hour World War I series pilot, *The Skyfighters*. Unlike *12 O'clock High*, *The Skyfighters* lacked genuine actual combat footage. "It was good that it didn't sell," states Muffet Martin. "To film just a few biplanes in dogfights—the production costs would have been outrageous."

The show that Martin did produce—the October 3, 1961, to September 25, 1962, hour-long drama *The New Breed*—was a perfect first series for the new producer. Not only did its contemporary setting save on production costs; there was the benefit of topicality. A short time before the series' premiere, a new branch of the LAPD's Metropolitan Squad had been created. It was called "The New Breed."

Created by Hank Searls, *The New Breed* was what series writer Don Brinkley calls "a very honest police show which did stories with heart, not blood and guts." Quinn Martin's next series, *The Fugitive*, had stories of a similar nature. That made *The New Breed* something of a trial run for that series. Serving as *The New Breed*'s production manager was Fred Ahern; acting as his assistant, his brother-in-law, Howard Alston. Previously Ahern had been production manager for Alfred Hitchcock; prior to that he'd worked at Selznick on classics like *Gone with the Wind*. Alston's film credits included being the assistant production manager on RKO's *The Thing*; at Universal, he'd been location auditor on films like *Winchester '73*. In contrast to Ahern, Alston had also done both live and filmed television—Art Linkletter's *Life with Luigi* among the former; *Gunsmoke* and *Have Gun, Will Travel* among the latter. "They needed somebody who had experience in series," reveals Alston. "I did. So Fred hired me as an on-set unit production manager."

"We averaged no less than fourteen hours a day shooting the show," recalls *New Breed* assistant director Sam Strangis. "That was an easy-going show. It was like a family show. Everybody worked together. That was uncommon. Quinn started that on *The Untouchables*. He was the first one to come around and create a family feel among the crew. He worked us a lot, but he treated us well. I can't say the same for Howard Alston and Fred Ahern. I think I worked three Christmas Eves in a row because of them. They liked to work on Christmas Eve. I don't know what they had against life."

Strangis put in such long hours on the show he never went home. He slept in his car in the parking lot. "We always slept there," says Strangis. "We worked all night. The only person I ever had trouble with about that was Sherry Jackson. I parked my car one morning, and I parked in the guest star's parking lot. She got mad. She claimed I was in her spot, and raised hell. So I told her to go to hell." Strangis got along much better with series director Joseph Pevney. "Joe Pevney was one of the nice guys," says Strangis. "We used to call Joe 'Nice Guy' because he always smiled. [Series director-producer] Wally Grauman we called 'The Bantam Rooster.' He was always huffing and puffing, had a little cigarette hanging out of his mouth all the time." The series' other directors included Quinn Martin's friend, Virgil W. Vogel, and Allen H. Miner. "Allen was a very talented man who thought he should be bigger than he was," laughs Strangis. "He thought he was gonna be a partner with Quinn. It never quite happened."

Because QM was an independent company, the series always shot on location. Filming on location caused all kinds of problems, especially when thirty camera setups a day was the norm on a QM show. "You never saw the location till the day of filming," reveals director of photography William W. Spencer, whom Alston brought to QM three years later on *12 O'clock High.* "You confronted the problem then. You were constantly adapting, constantly sacrificing and letting things go. You had to shoot very large areas of streets and buildings. That was more common on *The FBI* than on the other shows."

Howard Alston had a talent for resolving on-location dilemmas. He developed much of that during his time on *The New Breed.* "We filmed on county roads and highways," remembers Alston. "Nobody had ever required that before. There were no provisions, no permits for that kind of thing. So we improvised—we'd put up signs like 'Men Working,' and pretend we were with the gas company. That way we could close the highway." As a result of such innovations, Howard Alston's stock rose quickly at QM. In time, he replaced Fred Ahern as the company's production manager. Directors like Paul Wendkos enjoyed working with Howard Alston. "Most of those guys came out of accounting, so they were number-crunchers," says Wendkos, "but Howard had a filmmaker's precocity and concern. He was very helpful to the directors, the producers, the writers. Howard was as conscious of quality as anybody else. If you wanted another camera, if you wanted a crane, he'd suggest these things (to Quinn

Martin). That always contributed to the style and the look of the show. Howard was there to help you, not fight you. I always considered him a very strong asset of the team."

The locations Alston found for the many productions he made at QM proved Wendkos' point. During Alston's years at QM, the company shot in hospitals (Glendale Memorial, Queen of Angels), the L.A. County Museum, USC, military bases, gas stations, real hotels, real houses. The latter required permits and often much furniture moving. Consideration of the home owner and his property was always a top priority. "Having thirty-five people in your house at seven o'clock in the morning, people who are there all day, was asking a lot of the people who let us shoot in their homes," notes Alston. "We'd treat the house like it was our home; nobody took food into the house or smoked in the house. Before we took in our cameras, we put down rubber mats and lots of covering to protect the floors." "We frequently shot in very cramped quarters," adds Spencer. "The lamps were often so close to the actors, they almost got burnt. We had to do a lot of cheating and fudging things. You'd hide lamps behind desks, things like that. You were constantly improvising. Sometimes it took forty minutes to light a scene, sometimes three minutes." Often the company invited the home owners to join them for lunch. Once shooting finished, everyone thanked the owners for loaning them the house. The actors were very good at that—particularly *The FBI*'s Efrem Zimbalist, Jr., and *Barnaby Jones*' Buddy Ebsen. Both men were always happy to sign autographs or talk with fans whenever any approached.

If the on-location filming was something new, the practice of night-shooting was not. That tradition, begun on *The Untouchables*, continued throughout QM Productions' history. Laughs assistant director David Whorf, "We had this motto: 'A.M., P.M., Q.M.' That meant we worked day and night." "We'd start setting up at five o'clock in the evening, work from seven till one in the morning," adds Alston. "After one o'clock, half of the crew disappeared." Unless the company was filming in a casino. Then they worked from two till seven A.M. "Those were the only times they'd let us shoot," reveals Alston. "They didn't want us interrupting their flow of gamblers."

What made the casts and crews amenable to such unpleasant conditions was the esprit de corps established by Quinn Martin. "There was no snide attitude towards the actors," explains *Fugitive-Invaders* director Robert Butler. "There often was with other producers. That wasn't the case with Quinn. The air was very clear and fresh on his shows. Everybody was given the respect and credence to do whatever they did." "After we finished a show, everybody would say goodbye to the guest actors," states Alston. "It was our way of thanking the guest people who came in to work for the show."

As the opening credits of every Quinn Martin series made clear, guest stars were held in very high regard by Quinn Martin. *Fugitive* star David Janssen shared that regard. To him, the guests Martin gave him were the series' "only saving grace. That's saved my life," Janssen once told guest James Callahan. "They're so good to work with." Janssen had a similar respect for *The Fugitive* crew. "David cared very much about the crew," states QM Player Lynda Day George. "He spent a lot of time with

Lynda Day George (as nurse Carol Grant) and Henry Silva (as "Top Ten Fugitive Macklin") take time out during the shooting of the November 26, 1967, third-season ABC-TV *FBI* episode "Line of Fire" to create some good public relations for QM Productions.

the crew, had a great time with them. The crew were very important to David as people. He wanted to make sure they had fun. That was very important to me, too. The crew make the performances possible in the first place. They're the most important people in this business."

Quinn Martin had the same attitude. The producer knew all of his crews, all of the names of their wives and children. In the early years, Martin took pains to get down to the set at least once a week and visit. In Quinn Martin's opinion, everyone's job at QM was important, including receptionist Debbie Yates Marks'. Remembers Marks, "He once said to me, 'Whenever you answer the phone, always find out who's on the other end. Remember, you're that person's first contact with the company. That first impression is very important.'" Unlike other producers, Quinn Martin protected his crew people. More than once, a series star threatened to fire a crew member. That was as far as it went. "I make the decisions as to who gets fired," Martin would tell the star. "If there's anyone around here who's going to get fired, it'll be you, not them."

Martin went even further than backing up his employees. Recalls *New Breed* contributing writer Don Brinkley, "I was writing one show when I got married. Quinn wanted me to finish the script before I left on my honeymoon. I did, turned it in, waited three, four days, then asked if he needed a rewrite. He says, 'No. It's great. Go on your honeymoon. Enjoy yourself.' He sent me a wedding gift, and a check for the full script. I left for Spain for about a month, came back, then asked him how the show went. He says, 'We never did it. It's the worst script you've ever written.' I said, 'Well you paid me. I owe you another script.' He says, 'Absolutely not. Now come on in so we can do another show.' I wound up writing about five, six shows for him. That was one of the best things about Quinn. He always treated you well."

"He was my hero," enthuses post-production supervisor John Elizalde. "I'd been working for him for several years, and during that time I was not contributing to the Motion Picture Health and Welfare System. Well, when my first wife got sick and was in the hospital, he personally wrote a check himself on his own account to make up for all of those years that I hadn't contributed. I didn't even know about it until it appeared. During that last four, five months of my wife's life, I was almost never in the office. Despite that, he paid me every week. I just can't express enough love for this man. He was supremely generous, always paid the bills whenever he took people out, was never afraid to compliment his people."

Production mixer Dick Church learned that working on the 1971 television movie, *Incident in San Francisco*. "It was the first show I did for him," recalls Church, "the first time they'd ever used radio mikes, and as lousy as they were, we saved a lot of the dialogue. Well, after it was over Quinn, Arthur Fellows, and Howard Alston came up to me. They said, 'Thank you very much. We're very impressed. We thought we'd have to loop the whole picture.'"

From that point on, Church, who'd previously run the sound department for director Robert Aldrich's company, had a guaranteed future at QM. Predecessor John Kean hadn't fared as well. "Kean thought very highly of himself," laughs QM assistant director Paul Wurtzel. "The two of us got into a fight one time on *The New Breed* [the Robert Redford guest shot, "Ladykiller"]. It was one of the first things Redford ever did. We were on the beach in Malibu, running out of daylight, and Kean was having trouble recording Redford; we'd buried the microphone cable in the sand. I said, 'Do you want the audience to hear it or see it?' We didn't get along too well after that." "John was in love with anything that showed him to good effect," laughs

Sam Strangis. "But he was a good sound man. Redford talked real low and we weren't used to that; they couldn't stick the mike close to him because the camera would see it. We didn't have good walking mikes at that time so we couldn't solve the problem that way. The walking mikes used to have static to them. So John kept searching for a way we could record Redford. He couldn't record him because we were real close to the ocean."

While Sam Strangis left QM Productions in 1963 to work on other series, like *Mission: Impossible,* Paul Wurtzel continued with QM practically till its end. The blunt, no-nonsense Wurtzel, whose father Saul helped William S. Fox establish 20th Century–Fox Western Studios, and whose own pre–QM credits included the Fox classic, *A Tree Grows in Brooklyn,* did a lot to keep what William Spencer calls the "artsy-fartsy" people at QM in check. During their years at QM, Wurtzel and Spencer became friends. Like many of the people who worked for the company, the two men are still in touch.

"The production team was like a family," states *FBI* lead Efrem Zimbalist, Jr. "We were all like a family, and of course, that family moved from show to show as Quinn did different shows. The crews liked Quinn. Quinn was very loyal to them. He was extremely loyal to actors and directors unless they did something he didn't like—then he just wouldn't have 'em back." One thing Martin didn't like was having an actor thank him for giving him work. After Jonathan Goldsmith (formerly Jonathan Lippe) did that at a company party, he never worked for Martin again. Quinn Martin wasn't comfortable around actors. He wasn't too comfortable with most of his employees.

"He always came to the parties," remembers script supervisor Michael Preece. "He never stayed long. He'd be there for maybe ten, fifteen minutes. He was very friendly, but not real sociable; he never interacted with you. A lot of people didn't even know who he was. One wardrobe lady worked for him for eleven years, but never saw him." "In all the time I was there, I probably saw Quinn about three or four times," believes Dick Church. "He was a very hands off producer."

Martin's experience with *The New Breed* was why. "He was very immersed in its day to day operation," explains Alston. "He decided on every costume, read every script, selected each guest star." Martin's involvement didn't save the series from cancellation though. According to Muffet Martin, that cancellation came as "a shock." After a slow start, the series' ratings had improved considerably. "It had good ratings and everything," reveals Sam Strangis. "ABC didn't have the confidence in it that everybody else did. It was an excellent show. A well-done show." So, Martin assumed the series would be picked up for another season. Ironically, the producer's high standards might have brought about the series' cancellation.

"It was going to be renewed when Richard Pinkum, the head of advertising for the agency that bought the show told Quinn he wanted some kind of change," reveals producer-director Walter Grauman. "Quinn felt Pinkum was trying to dictate the production of the show. He told Tom Moore [president of ABC] to tell Pinkum to go fuck himself. Moore says, 'I can't tell him that!' Quinn said, 'Tell him exactly that.'

So Moore did. He went to Pinkum, he says, 'Quinn Martin says for you to go fuck yourself. It's his show. He's going to do it the way he wants.'" Pinkum withdrew the advertising from the show. The show was gone. "Quinn was so involved with the show, he didn't realize he didn't have anything else until we were canceled," laughs Alston. "So he decided, that's enough of that. I'm not gonna have that much hands-on control again. I'm gonna turn it over to someone else, and let them run it. That way I can make sure we've always got a series going."

The only way to ensure this was through establishing what QM producer Philip Saltzman calls "a (hand-picked) cadre of specialists." With Howard Alston and Fred Ahern, Martin already had his specialists in production; with Arthur Fellows, his specialist in editing. Fellows' pre–QM credits included *For Whom the Bell Tolls* and *Citizen Kane*. Fellows had been with Quinn Martin since the days of *The Untouchables*. The two men were good friends. They had a number of things in common — among these, a love of thoroughbred horse-racing. To John Elizalde, Fellows and Martin "were almost interchangeable in their functions. There was an implicit, deep trust between them," declares Elizalde. "Quinn used to call Arthur 'Kato'; Arthur called Quinn 'The Green Hornet.'" "Quinn held Arthur in very high esteem," agrees Fellows' replacement Richard Brockway, whom Fellows brought to QM in the late '60s. "Arthur was a tough little guy. You couldn't fool him. He was kind of abrasive, off-putting. He never minced words. If he didn't like something, he'd tell you." "Arthur could be very humorous, but he could also be very short," adds QM assistant director/unit production manager Bob Jeffords. "He had a level of professionalism he expected. If someone didn't meet it, he let them know. Some people didn't appreciate that."

Such as the writers. Often when Fellows read a script, he'd decide, "We don't need that scene." A few years later the job of reading and editing scripts fell to Martin's script specialist, Adrian Samish. Fellows didn't like that. He didn't like Samish period. "He thought he had no talent," says Brockway. "Whenever Adrian came in the editing room to look at our final cut, he just stayed for a couple of minutes. He never said a word." Acerbic and rarely pleasant, Samish was one of the most disliked people at QM. Especially among the writers. To many, he was just "a suit."

John Elizalde knew better. "Adrian was one of the good guys," asserts Elizalde, "brilliant, and very creative, but a victim of his own devices, because he wanted the very best. Adrian was the major-domo for Quinn in the writing department, the boss when it came to scripts, motivation, all that stuff. He had very strong opinions, and he stuck to those opinions. Generally people do not like working under someone like that. He was a perfect gentleman at all times except when he was fighting with the writers. He had a very good sense of what Quinn wanted. Quinn trusted him. If Quinn trusted you, you'd have to be pretty far afield to get any opprobrium."

"Adrian was a perfectionist," adds Lynda Day George.

> In all our conversations, he would describe to me what was needed. He wanted to ascertain whether or not I could agree with that, and make my performance work within the script. Adrian was very concerned that a show maintain its

integrity. He wanted to be sure that characters were understood, that what was wanted by the production was understood. He was concerned that an actor and a director could communicate, that their lines of communication were open. He was there to bridge gaps between actor and director, to bridge gaps in interpretations. Adrian did brilliant work. Yes, he was forceful. Yes, he was domineering. Because this was important work to him. He wanted it to be right. When people are like that, when they have that intense passion in them, where they have to have things right to the point where it becomes an obsession with them, it's very frequently misunderstood. There were people who were frustrated by that. That doesn't mean they were inaccurate in their assessment of Adrian. Because Adrian was not an overtly welcoming person. But if you took a few minutes to get in there and know Adrian, he was a very dear person.

"Nobody could have ever really put a job description to what Adrian did," elaborates Martin's secretary, Sally Richman Manning. "Adrian was so in tune with the quality that Quinn expected. He was wonderful. He saved Quinn endless hours in getting something to the degree so that when Quinn read the script, he'd say okay. Adrian really knew the things that were not gonna fly, so Quinn trusted him to be his voice when it came to scripts. Quinn didn't second guess anybody when he trusted them. Adrian, Arthur Fellows, Howard Alston, John Conwell would not have been given the carte blanche that they had, had Quinn not felt that their taste was his taste. He could never ever have handled as many things as he did if he didn't have people whom he trusted."

Martin was particularly fond of executive casting director John Conwell. Most everybody at QM liked Conwell. "John Conwell was a super guy," raves David Whorf. "He was kind of like the keeper of the zoo. He maintained that coterie of characters from Brad Dillman to all of the people who worked the QM shows." It was New York stage actor Conwell who brought to QM Productions such future big-name stars as Robert Duvall (*The Fugitive, The FBI*), Cicely Tyson (*The FBI*), Gene Hackman (*The FBI, The Invaders*). Nor did the standards waver when it came to the supporting guests. "For every part on *The FBI*, [series casting director] Dodie McLean had to come up with six, seven, eight people, and find out if they were available," remembers Elizalde. "Just making sure they were available—that was a Herculean task."

If Quinn Martin was fond of John Conwell, John Conwell was no less fond of Quinn Martin. To Conwell, Martin was "Big Daddy." The nickname was a reference to the producer's paternalistic operation of QM Productions. Conwell and Martin frequently lunched at either Tail of the Cock or Musso-Franks. (It was right outside the entrance to the latter where Martin later had his star installed on the Hollywood Walk of Fame.) Conwell's secretary, Lois Winslow, remembers the "mind game" Martin played on his employees one time when he took them to Musso-Franks. Laughs Winslow, "He kept going on about the salads. He says, 'They have these great salads. They're just so great. You've got to try them.' He went on and on and on until finally everybody ordered one of the salads. Then the waitress took Quinn's order. He ordered something else."

Given Martin's love for "mind games," it's easy to believe the producer might have carried this over into the constant variety displayed in his series' opening credits. The billing guest stars received sometimes seemed to be a "mind game." The first season *FBI* episode, "The Insolents," certainly misrepresented the importance of guest Eileen Heckart. Though Heckart received "Special Guest Star" billing in the episode, she didn't appear until the fourth act. There was no intention to deceive however. "The 'Special Guest Star' billing was kind of a goodie awarded to certain people even if they had a very small part in order to entice them to come on a show," states Elizalde. "It wasn't always true. There were a lot of 'Special Guest Stars' who really weren't all that special."

Another reason actors did QM guest shots was the money. Unlike other producers, Martin paid his guest stars more. As always, the producer wanted the best. "When he went to ABC," reveals Elizalde, "he told them 'If I'm gonna have guest stars, I'm gonna have the very best ones in the business. One of the ways we can get them is to acknowledge them at the beginning of our shows. Depending on how many we might have, to your advantage, I might add, we're gonna need more time for our opening credits.'" ABC-TV gave Martin that time. "They had a lot of confidence in him," says Elizalde, "they gave him a lot more leeway than other producers, and a lot more privileges. But he earned them. The guy was brilliant. He was a very prescient man when it came to knowing his audience."

Martin also performed a courtesy for his audience. Thanks to his identification of his series at the beginning of every Act, the channel-switching viewer didn't have to consult the TV listings to see what series he had just tuned in, nor did he have to wonder how much longer the program would last. When the viewer saw that *12 O'clock High* had just started Act III, this meant the show was halfway over. "We thought that was a pretty keen idea," says Alston. "We started that on *The New Breed.*" Contrary to the producer's detractors, not every QM show honed to this four acts and an Epilog formula. The 1976–77 Robert Stack drama, *Most Wanted*, had five acts; *Barnaby Jones* had four acts, but no Epilog. *Cannon* had four acts as well, but it broke one of them in two. Which one was anybody's guess. The pattern varied from week to week. Just as did the opening credits of every QM series.

"We had varying lengths of titles," discloses Alston. "We shot various backgrounds, various mattes so we could change things from week to week." "We recorded several versions of the main title for every show," adds Elizalde. "We restructured the main titles every week." Critics of Quinn Martin's series never noticed the difference in the main titles. To them, a QM series' opening credits were just as bland and predictable and formulaic as the stories. The people who worked for Martin knew the shows weren't formula, yet very few in the company caught the weekly changes in the credits. Lynda Day George was one of the few who did.

"There was nothing predictable about Quinn Martin, or his shows," states the actress. "You only have to look at his work, at the shows that he did, to see that. Quinn Martin was the most innovative and creative of his kind. Generally speaking, his characters were not stereotypical characters. His production methods were not stereotypical either. He was unique in a number of ways, in the ways he created his shows and put them together and put them out there on the screen. For example, the opening titles, the way he introduced the series stars and guest stars, that was something that they used to do in the early days of film. In the early days of film, one of the things that they did was introduce all the characters up front. Now the television audience at that time, the adult audience at that time, had grown up watching those films. By bringing that back, by bringing back something that was familiar to the audience, something that felt good, Quinn connected with his audience. That was a stroke of brilliance on his part. That's one of the reasons why he was so successful, one of the reasons why his shows did so well."

Hiring perceptive, versatile performers like George, who, in the words of *FBI* series star Efrem Zimbalist, Jr., "always brought qualities to a production far in excess of those expected or even hoped for," was another reason. "I liked working with Lynda Day George a lot," says QM director Robert Butler. "She had a good perspective on what all of us were doing. At the same time she had the ability to do a really wonderful job in her work. That's a very rare quality. It's very unusual to find someone who is very natural and very real. It's even harder to find someone who is smart and sane and natural. Those are high marks—to be smart and sane and natural, that's very different, it's very exceptional. Lynda was that way. Bob Stack was that way too. David Janssen was like that as well. The guy had a sort of tortured ... it wasn't self-sorry, but you knew he was carrying some kind of a load. With that kind of actor, you believe immediately, you lean forward. You want to believe that person, you want to go with that person. Clark Gable had that. Some people just have that thing where you want to believe, and Lynda Day George definitely had it. You believed her. You leaned forward. You pulled with her. That's a huge thing."

Quinn Martin agreed with Butler. During her fourteen-year association with QM Productions, Lynda Day George was to do more series pilots and more special episodes than any other QM player. Unlike David Janssen and Robert Stack, Lynda Day George was never offered a QM series. Quinn Martin knew from his conversations with George that the actress wasn't interested in playing the same character week after week, he knew that the only kind of series George would enjoy doing was one like *The Silent Force* or *Mission: Impossible*, where she got to play a different character every week. Having seen both series, having seen the actress' TV movies like *The Sound of Anger, Fear No Evil,* and *The Trial of Chaplain Jensen*, Quinn Martin could not understand why Lynda Day George was doing television when she could be doing motion-pictures. He told the actress she should be doing film. George didn't want to be on the big screen. She wanted to be on the small screen. That way she could come into people's homes, connect with them on an intimate and personal level, and, with any luck, give them some insight into themselves through one of the characters that she played. That was the main thing Lynda Day George wanted to do in her career. At QM Productions, she always had that opportunity. In addition to the many shows she did for the company, the actress was also offered *The Streets of San Francisco* (two or three times), *Banyon, Tales of the Unexpected*, a couple more *FBI*s besides the four she did, and at least one more *Barnaby Jones* after she'd done two.

QM post-production supervisor John Elizalde was another who was treated very well at QM. Brought in by his good friend Jeff Alexander as music editor for *The New Breed*, the Paris-educated, classically trained Elizalde was given "tremendous latitude" when it came to the music. "Quinn left it completely up to me," reveals Elizalde. "He put me in charge of the dubbing rooms, let me select all the composers. He really was a wonderful man. He gave me a lot of opportunities that aren't ordinarily there. I was in charge of scheduling all of the scoring, all of the dubbing. I selected all of the composers, recommended them on the basis of their style, how that style compared to the subject we were doing."

In the case of *The New Breed*, Quinn Martin wanted a hip, jazz score for the series theme. Freelance composer Dominic Frontiere gave him one. Frontiere was hired as the series' regular composer. "Jeff Alexander was kind of put out by that," remembers Elizalde. "He'd expected to do the whole show. But Dominic was more of a swinger. Dominic was a genius. He could do anything. He'd studied at Yale under Paul Hindemith, and at Fox studios had worked with some of the finest orchestrators in the world like Eddie Powell and Conrad Salinger. He loved using the orchestra. He could produce a score in two or three days. Sometimes that was all the time we had. Dominic was always saying to Quinn, 'Do you want it good, or do you want it now?' Quinn wanted it good. Dominic always gave him that. The guy was a melodist supreme. He often quoted himself. He could turn out reams of stuff just on that basis."

Quinn Martin was very pleased with Frontiere. The composer went on to write music for such QM series as *The Invaders* and *The FBI*. For *The New Breed*, Frontiere wrote close to an hour's worth of music. That included both the main and end titles. The rest of the series was totally tracked. John Elizalde selected all of the tracks. Unlike Frontiere, who eventually had a falling out with Martin, Elizalde and Martin got along very well."

"It was kind of like love at first sight," laughs Elizalde. "We talked for about four hours that first day I met him. We were so closely aligned in regards to our preferences, in what was wrong with television at that time." The work of producer-director Lee Sholem offered the perfect example. "His nickname was 'Roll'em Sholem," chuckles Elizalde, "because every show he did, it was just 'Wham bam, thank you, ma'am, write 'em up, shoot 'em. Get 'em done. Cut! Print. Okay, that's good enough.' Quinn didn't like that. He wanted to do things with care. He looked for quality."

Martin had high standards when it came to making shows. That reminded Richard Brockway of his former boss, David O. Selznick, as Brockway told Martin. "He liked that because he admired Selznick," states Brockway. "He'd say, 'Oh, really? You really think so?'" No one at QM would have viewed Brockway's comments as idle flattery. "Quinn wanted the best," declares Elizalde. "He wanted everything as real as possible. He didn't like Foley [sound effects for footsteps, etc.], didn't like voice-overs [someone off-camera talking over a scene], didn't like looping [actors coming in to re-record dialogue which the sound people missed the first time]. He didn't want to loop at all. He was a bear on coverage, on production look, on sound.

He could tell if something was out of sync, or if it was a frame off. Every sound effect was singularly cut. The sound effects editors really worked hard. It's tough to do those things without falling into a pattern. They never did."

At QM even the smallest detail was important, including the noises during a car chase. "It wasn't like an Aaron Spelling show," notes Lynda Day George. "Whenever Aaron Spelling did car chases, they always had the same car chase noises. It didn't matter if they were on gravel, or on country roads, you always heard those same car chase noises." "Quinn always wanted things realistic," adds Brockway. "If the characters were up in an airplane, and Quinn didn't hear that engine outside, you'd have to go back and put that engine sound in, so that the viewers knew the characters were in an airplane."

"Everything with Quinn was top quality," agrees QM director William Hale. "He was the best producer in television. He was one of the people I really wanted to work for. He always went for quality. He hired the very best actors in the business. Everything with him was top quality. That's why I liked working for Quinn so much. It just was the absolute best. He gave you a day more if you needed it. Other producers wouldn't do that." Like Walter Grauman, William Hale was one of Martin's favorite directors. Hale had worked as an assistant director for George Stevens on the all-star epic, *The Greatest Story Ever Told*. The low angles he used for his first QM production, the fourth-season *Fugitive*, "Approach with Care," greatly pleased Martin. "That's what made *The Untouchables* a success," the producer told Hale. After that, remembers Hale, "Quinn offered me practically every show he had."

Don Medford, Virgil Vogel, Robert Day, and Walter Grauman enjoyed similar opportunities. Each directed at least one QM television movie. Other directors like Paul Wendkos, whom Hale calls "a superb director who is head and shoulders above most television directors," and Harvey Hart were saved for special projects. "Harvey Hart was a little bit like Walter Grauman," believes Bob Jeffords. "He almost demanded obeisance. He was very very bright, very aware of what was going on. He was good for almost any show, so well prepared, so specific. Both he and Walter were very intense. Both were excellent with actors. I think that was true of most directors Quinn used."

None was used more than Walter Grauman. Like his fellow *New Breed* directors Allen H. Miner and Joseph Pevney, Grauman enjoyed a very special privilege on that series—he always produced the episodes he directed. Grauman was always Martin's first choice when it came to a series pilot. "I did about seven pilots for him that made it to series," remembers the director. "He wanted me to do the pilot for *12 O'clock High* too. I couldn't. I was going to England to do a picture called *633 Squadron*. I think he was pretty pissed off about that."

"Walter always busted his butt for Quinn," notes Michael Preece. "He was very sharp, innovative, bright. You had to be on your toes when you worked with him." Knowing exactly what Martin wanted, Grauman almost always completed a show in seven days. "Walter would go faster than hell through dramatic stuff," laughs David Whorf. "But it took him forever to do a huge drive-up—one car coming around a corner, up a road, and up into a driveway. He'd go four, five, six takes." "All of them got carried away and wanted to do grander things at some point," agrees Muffet Martin. "Even Walter." Sometimes Martin went along with his directors; sometimes he fired them. Harvey Hart almost was when he did his first *FBI*, "Nightmare Road." Hart hadn't given Martin and Arthur Fellows the coverage that they'd wanted. When the two men looked at the film, they realized they didn't need it. That was the exception, not the rule.

"Quinn didn't like camera-cutting," states Efrem Zimbalist, Jr. "He wanted to have masters (the entire scene). He wanted to have over-the-shoulders. He wanted to have close-ups so that he could cut the whole thing together the way that he wanted. He didn't want to be put in a corner where he had to take what the director gave him, so he insisted on having that kind of freedom. And God help a director who didn't give him that. If he camera-cut a scene and Quinn couldn't get his scissors on it, very likely that director would never work for Quinn again." "Quinn hated going from two shots or long-shots to direct, zoom-in cuts," adds Richard Brockway. "He didn't like going from over the shoulders to big head close-ups. He never liked that. He always liked to have you cut away, then go to a close-up. He didn't like any jarring or shocking cuts. He wanted everything smooth as glass."

"He looked at every single foot of dailies," continues Howard Alston. "Sometimes it took three or four hours to watch all the dailies." "Quinn always knew if something wasn't there, or if the dialogue had been changed," adds Brockway. "It was remarkable." "He had a great memory," agrees Alston. "When Arthur Fellows was editing the picture, Quinn would sit with him and say, 'There's a two-shot here that I'd really like to have. Then we can eliminate this whole minute.'"

Martin's standards regarding coverage extended to a character's appearance. "He didn't like seeing people with beards, or chewing gum," states Brockway. "Anybody chewing gum, forget it. He would go out of his mind." People with toothpicks or matchsticks in their mouths were another annoyance. Ditto certain suit fabrics. *FBI* producer Philip Saltzman remembers, "One time Efrem was wearing this suit which had kind of a nailhead fabric, and it gave off this sheen. When Quinn saw that in the dailies, he said, 'Oh, I hate that! I hate that!' He sent the production manager down to the set to tell Efrem to 'Kill the suit. Get rid of the suit. Wear the other ones!' Efrem got so insulted. He said, 'Tell Quinn Martin I don't like his suits! He's not such a marvelous dresser!'"

Martin rather wisely conceded to Zimbalist on that occasion. When it came to fashion, Efrem Zimbalist, Jr., was very conservative in his dress. To Martin, reveals Michael Preece, conservative dress was very important. "He didn't want skirts too long or too short," Preece explains, "didn't want wide ties, glasses, didn't like leisure suits. He didn't want anything that wouldn't endure. That's because he wanted reruns — reruns were where he felt the money was. So the hair-stylists had to get traditional hairstyles, and it was up to wardrobe to keep everybody dressed in Brooks Brothers fashion." Adds Lynda Day George, "One of my first conversations with Quinn was about wardrobe and he said, 'In the reruns that you see now, the clothes may look dull and conservative, but think about when people see the show years from now. Because the clothing is conservative, because it's classic, you won't be able to tell when the show was made.' I said, 'Ahhh yeah! That's right! You're right!'"

Editor Richard K. Brockway shared Martin's tastes when it came to a character's appearance. Apprenticing at Selznick Studios in the '40s on such features as *Duel in the Sun, Portrait of Jennie,* and *The Paradine Case*, Brockway joined QM as a supervising editor under the aegis of his old friend from Selznick, Arthur Fellows. "I started out doing pilots," Brockway remembers. "*The Streets of San Francisco* was the first one I did. I put in many hours working on those things. I'd work till three, four o'clock in the morning trying to get something ready for Quinn. I knew exactly what Quinn wanted. I saved him an awful lot of time. He'd take one look at the completed film, say, 'Yeah, that's fine. Ship it.'"

After Fellows left QM a few years later to form his own company, Brockway moved up to executive editor, then vice-president in charge of post-production. "I saw every show that we made there," says Brockway. "I'd go to dailies maybe three, four hours a day. If there was any time left, I'd be in the cutting room." Brockway found amusing Martin's solution for keeping the directors out of the cutting rooms when the editors were working on the shows. (It was part of a director's contract that he always had the first cut.) "If a director had two or three series," chuckles Brockway, "Quinn would sign them up for those so that when they finished one show, they had another one to prep. That way they didn't have time to sit down at a moviola and cut the picture."

By the time Richard Brockway joined QM Productions, the company had obtained almost all its regular production staff, almost all its QM Players. *The New Breed*'s Leslie Nielsen had the honor of being one of the earliest QM Players. The hard work Nielsen invested in *Breed* guaranteed his future as a QM Player. Leslie Nielsen would make more than one guest appearance on Martin's next series, *The Fugitive*. He would also guest on *The FBI, Barnaby Jones, The Streets of San Francisco*, and *Cannon*. During the course of *The Fugitive*, QM Productions was to obtain its specialists in casting (John Conwell) and scripts (Adrian Samish). Both men would play a vital part in the company's success.

No one knew it at the time, but *Fugitive* series narrator William Conrad would be a great help to the company too. Conrad's series, *Cannon*, would give QM Productions its first big hit of the '70s. In so doing, it would change the shape of television. *The Fugitive* was to do that in the 1960s. Had it not been for Quinn Martin however, that might never have been.

Chapter 3

THE FUGITIVE

David Janssen was the character. He was Richard Kimble.

Fugitive *producer Alan A. Armer*

Perhaps it was good that ABC rejected *Darrow*, the series Quinn Martin pro-posed to the network in 1962, because Martin had a "pay or play" deal in his con-tract. That meant ABC either paid him for a rejected series or offered him another project. The network did the latter. They gave Martin *The Fugitive* (September 17, 1963–August 29, 1967).

The story of Dr. Richard Kimble (David Janssen), a man unjustly convicted of murdering his wife, Quinn Martin's *Fugitive* was not *The Fugitive* of series creator Roy Huggins. "Roy Huggins received $1500 a week for the 'created by' credit, but he had absolutely nothing to do with the show," declares Muffet Martin. "The series people saw was Quinn's doing." Though Quinn Martin wanted David Janssen to play Richard Kimble, he had trouble working out a deal with the actor's agent, until Janssen interfered. Janssen wanted to play the character. "Make the deal," the actor told his agent. Narrator William Conrad—who usually described Kimble's current situation to the series audience—was the program's only other regular. "Bill Conrad had this voice that shook the world," states *Fugitive* associate producer George Eckstein. "In the pilot, Bill tells you Kimble's innocent. You can't deny anything Bill Conrad says, he's so authoritative." "I could always hear Conrad's voice when I wrote the narra-tions," says series producer Alan Armer. "I wrote most of them. That was my fun. I'd done the same sort of thing years earlier in radio."

To write *The Fugitive* pilot, "Fear in a Desert City," Martin hired *New Breed* writer Stanford Whitmore. To direct, he picked *Breed* producer-director Walter Grau-man. After Grauman re-shot one scene in "Fear" to make Kimble's pursuer Lt. Philip Gerard (Barry Morse) "less overtly psychotic," the completed pilot was then flown to New York for an ABC network preview. The network executives didn't care for the

31

QM favorite Vera Miles (as piano-player Monica Welles), David Janssen (center, as Dr. Richard Kimble), and Brian Keith (as rancher Ed Welles) in the September 17, 1963 ABC-TV *Fugitive* premiere, "Fear in a Desert City."

show; nonetheless Martin's contract committed them to a pick-up. No fan of Quinn Martin, ABC president of programming Tom Moore was happy to add the producer's new series to ABC's 1963-64 prime-time schedule. "The show will be gone in thirteen weeks," crowed Moore in the letter he sent to Martin. "It will finish your career." Martin was so proud of proving Moore wrong, he later took Moore's letter, had it framed, and mounted it over his desk.

Even series writers Don Brinkley and Oliver Crawford were skeptical concerning *The Fugitive*'s chances. Crawford didn't see why a man facing a death sentence would keep risking his life to perform good deeds. Brinkley considered the concept a "one-joke" idea. "Which shows how much I know," laughs Brinkley. Both Don Brinkley and Oliver Crawford would go on to write a number of *Fugitive*s. Brinkley's "The Good Guys and the Bad Guys" was to give the series one of its most comic episodes. Crawford's "There Goes the Ball Game" would stun David Janssen. It was to present the star with the one *Fugitive* story-line he thought he'd never do.

Once Quinn Martin got the green light for *The Fugitive*, which he always considered a modern-day retelling of Victor Hugo's *Les Misérables*—The Dr. Sam Shepard case was purely coincidental—he hired *The Untouchables'* still-active producer Alan A. Armer as his producer. Shuttling back and forth between Desilu and Goldwyn Studios during *The Fugitive*'s early stages, Armer worked very closely with Martin defining both the character of Richard Kimble and the types of stories that would work on *The Fugitive*. "By the textbook, the protagonist is supposed to make things happen, but by its very nature, that couldn't be," reveals Armer. "Because the Fugitive was running from the people, that made things happen." Despite that problem Don Brinkley found the series "really easy to write. Unlike any other cop show, or cowboy show, where you always had to find reasons to emotionally involve your hero, the protagonist was involved just by waking up in the morning," explains Brinkley. "He was involved just because he was in trouble. That helped in plotting. That way you could bring on a new facet of the Kimble character—something that would be consistent, but was new to the show. By dredging people up out of his past, things like that, we were able to tell more about him. That was the fun of the show. You could always add to the character. He wasn't a stilted, one-dimensional TV protagonist."

"It was a very smart show," adds *Fugitive* director Robert Butler. "Smart in the gimmick, the device, the story, the character, the way the various hours could be presented and unfold. It was very nimble, believable, and just plain good. It had legs." "The premise allowed for a great variety," agrees George Eckstein, "but you had to spend your first act justifying why Kimble didn't get just the hell out of town. You had to get him emotionally engaged so that he'd stick around and do what a hero usually does." One way to do so was to have the doctor visit his family ("Home is the Hunted"), or in-laws ("The Survivors"), present a new detail concerning the Kimble case (future QM producer Philip Saltzman's "Trial by Fire"), meet someone from his past ("Taps for a Dead War," "World's End"). Other solutions were: arrest him for another crime ("Middle of the Heatwave," "Passage to Helena"), witness another person's crime ("Glass Tightrope"), encounter someone needing medical assistance ("Never Stop Running"). The latter, directed by William A. "Billy" Graham, was one of the better first-season shows.

As was Graham's "Never Wave Goodbye," the series' first two-parter. In "Never Wave," Kimble tries to convince Gerard he's been drowned at sea. "Quinn was dead set against shooting on a real boat," chuckles Graham. "He thought it'd be expensive, wouldn't look good. We used my boat. Turned out so well, Arthur Fellows later said to Quinn, 'Well, for once, we listened to somebody.'" Towards the end of the first season, Graham shot another at sea *Fugitive* ("Storm Center"), this time on director Walter Grauman's boat. "We did it on Walter's boat so he could deduct it on taxes," explains George Eckstein. "It wound up being the most expensive episode of the series."

Being a yachting enthusiast and "madly in love with [guest star] Susan Oliver," William Graham says his favorite *Fugitive* was "Never Wave Goodbye." "Bobby Duvall played a Norwegian sail-maker," laughs Graham. "He had the worst Norwegian accent. I should know. Both of my sisters live in Norway. They're married to

Barry Morse (center, as Lt. Philip Gerard) is "tried" for assault by moonshiners Sandy Kenyon (second from left, as Kyle), Bruce Dern (second from right, as Cody), and QM favorite R.G. Armstrong (foreground, right, as Tully) in the February 9, 1965, second-season ABC-TV *Fugitive* episode, "Corner of Hell."

Norwegians." Equally unrealistic was the story's hurricane sequence. "We shot it in a tank at Goldwyn with big Ritter wind machines," recalls Graham. "I thought it turned out pretty well." As for the Los Angeles County courthouse and jail scenes, while the interiors were filmed in Santa Barbara (the location for most of the story) the exteriors were shot at the actual building. Quinn Martin always wanted things as real as possible.

That meant shooting in real railroad yards and in a real boxcar ("When the Bough Breaks"), working with real tigers—guest Laurence Naismith did in "Last Second of a Big Dream"—flying in a real helicopter—guest Peter Mark Richman did in "The Last Oasis." "[Helicopter pilot] Jim Gavin had me leaning over the side of the copter, and the doors were off, so I was strapped in," remembers Richman. "As we banked, I was looking straight down at the ground." The freighter in Oliver Crawford's "Ticket to Alaska" (the one *Fugitive* to use narrator William Conrad for all four acts plus the Epilog) was real too. "We rented it, brought it up from Ensenada, Mexico, painted it, and had to exterminate because it was full of rats," laughs assistant director Paul Wurtzel. "We never got rid of all the rats, so nobody wanted to go board on the damn thing. That whole production was a disaster. We had a Mexican skipper, a Mexican crew. We'd tell them to go left, they'd go right. Go right, they'd go left."

The on-location filming of "Not with a Whimper" at an Orange County sugar factory had its problems too. "We did a lot of work around the factory," recalls guest Lee Meriwether, "and the white sunlight and the white sands and the white sugar and the white buildings … Oh! Our eyes just paid for it for weeks. It was not an easy show for David, or for me, or for the little boy. It certainly wasn't easy for [guest] Laurence Naismith. Everybody was just dying. Breathing was very difficult." Director of photography Meredith Nicholson had his problems as well. "That poor man," sympathizes Meriwether. "Trying to film that white on white on white. He had his hands full."

Director Alexander Singer had plenty of problems during the third season's "This'll Kill You." All of his own making! "We were talking about who to cast," laughs George Eckstein, "and Mickey Rooney was mentioned. Somebody said, 'Yeah, but he can be trouble on the set.' And Alex said, very grandly, as Alex was wont to say, 'Listen, whether or not I'm a good director, that's up for grabs, but as far as being in control of the set, just don't worry about it.' Two days later into shooting, he was on the phone, trying to get off the show, Rooney was driving him crazy."

No one seemed to be in control during the filming of the bus sequence in the first year's "Come Watch Me Die." "We spent half a day shooting that sequence," recalls Armer, "and behind the bus, we had a process screen which showed the road going away behind the bus. Well, we get to dailies the next day, and the bus looks like it's going backwards! Somehow they'd loaded the process plate backwards. It was absurd because on the stage there were maybe seventy people. I'm talking about carpenters, electricians, camera crew, the director. It got away from all of them. It's hard to believe that a process plate with seventy people watching could keep running backwards. But that's what happened." The sequence had to be re-shot.

Expenses like that resulted in the second season's "Fun and Games and Party Favors." "We told the director [Abner Biberman] he had to do it in six days, because we needed to save some money," admits Armer. "It was mostly interiors. It wasn't a very good show, but he did it and by God we saved some money." Erecting a "green set" for the night sequences in the Grand Hotel on a bus episode, "Detour on a Road Going Nowhere," also kept down costs. "The 'green set' was the bus," explains director Ralph Senensky. "They decided that rather than going up and shooting in the mountains at Franklin Canyon at night, they'd do all of the night bus scenes on stage. That way we avoided late hours because we could shoot the night stuff in the daytime. The breakdown of the bus was the only thing we shot up in the hills."

Finding music for each episode of the series was certainly no problem. Thanks to the efforts of post-production supervisor John Elizalde. "I had established a very good rapport with Lud Gluskin at CBS," reveals Elizalde, "and negotiated permission from Lud to use their library despite the fact that this was an ABC show. CBS had the finest library of music at that time. All the shows were being tracked with libraries. Ken Wilhoit (the series' musical arranger) was a master at that. He took that package and used it throughout the series."

Keeping the show's plot-line fresh was much more difficult. "That was the toughest thing," states Don Brinkley, "coming up with new concepts, new ways to get Kimble in trouble." Revisiting the classics was one way. During the third season, in "The Chinese Sunset"—*The Fugitive*'s take on *Pygmalion*—Dr. Kimble found himself educating a gangster's hillbilly girlfriend (Laura Devon). During the second year, in "Nicest Fella You'd Ever Want to Meet," murderous sheriff Pat Hingle tracked the doctor in a "countrified" version of the classic short-story, "The Most

Dangerous Game." "I love that story!" Martin enthused when Armer broached the subject to the executive producer—"Do it!"

Guest star R.G. Armstrong and director Robert Butler were no less excited concerning the same season's "Corner of Hell." In "Corner," Gerard is put on trial for assaulting a young woman—by a bunch of moonshiners! "That was pretty extreme," laughs Butler, "kind of theatrical. At one point they sat Gerard in this chair and put him up on this table. The irony of Kimble saving Gerard was fun." As was staging the lieutenant's temporary escape from the hillbillies. "When anyone is given that script, you have to play into the irony of Gerard compared to Kimble," notes Butler. "So, where possible you'd stage similarly and mount similarly just to underline that irony. That show was very bizarre, a little larger than life."

The same couldn't be said for Butler's second *Fugitive*, "World's End," featuring David Janssen's long-time friend, Suzanne Pleshette. "It was a talky show with lots of interiors, and no interesting locations," recalls Butler. "I found it an unexciting gig."

Alan Armer was very disappointed with Christian Nyby's direction of the episode, "Nightmare at North Oak." "He didn't get the values out of the show that were there," feels Armer. "That should have been an excellent show." Armer was also dissatisfied with the following season's Kimble develops amnesia entry, "Escape into Black." At least when he viewed the show in English. Later the producer had the opportunity to see the episode in Spanish. "It was much better in Spanish than in English because one of the performers that I didn't like in the English version was just wonderful in the Spanish version," says Armer. Featuring Ivan Dixon as a black doctor who treats Kimble, "Escape" made it clear that Quinn Martin and ABC president Tom Moore had gotten on a better footing when it came to such subjects. The first year the two men clashed over the black prizefighter story, "Decision in the Ring." Moore was against airing the show.

Despite such progress when it came to black roles, not to mention the chronic worries of perfectionist Alan Armer, and the high standards of executive producer Quinn Martin, *The Fugitive* had its flaws. "In the opening credits, you always saw this picture of Kimble with a bottle of hair dye," says fourth-season director William Hale. "That was the label on the bottle, 'Hair Dye.' That is so cliched, so corny. It should have been called 'Dr. Reddy's Hair Dye,' something like that, not 'Hair Dye.'"

Perhaps David Janssen's performance as The Fugitive explained why nobody caught this cliché. "David's instincts were superb," praises George Eckstein. "He could make things work that I thought had no business working. He was the definitive television actor. He could take a line that was not very well written and somehow make it credible. There was something in his acting make-up that prohibited a false move. Once in a while, you'd wish he would show a little more emotion, but he never crossed the line. He was never over the top, or missed a value. There were so many layers to that character. So many that he had to embody and play. You never saw a performance that wasn't real."

Which was a good thing. For in every episode, Richard Kimble encountered (and often created) a situation that threatened to expose his true identity. By the end of the story, he'd somehow escaped. To put it mildly, that premise strained credibility. Making the premise believable was a great challenge for David Janssen, one which guest Lynda Day George states, the actor welcomed. "He had such great perception where scripts were concerned," explains George. "He was very good in judging scripts, and he had taken great care in his career to do things that were interesting and exciting. He never did anything that was boring. We had a lot of conversations when I did the show. He would talk about the demands of the series, the hours, the character. He was very concerned about keeping the character fresh."

"He always rehearsed with me," recalls semi-regular Jacqueline Scott. "He told me that he didn't rehearse with a lot of people because he was doing the show every week, doing basically the same thing every week, and one thing he had going for him was the spontaneity of the takes. A person who does a series week after week like that, they find their own rhythm, their own style." Adds George, "He didn't learn the dialogue until it was time to memorize, because the truth was, and the truth is, that's a good way to keep a character fresh."

David Janssen's characterization as the perpetually do-gooding Richard Kimble was not an act. Years later, during the filming of the Gregory Peck–Laurence Olivier war drama, *Inchon*, Janssen gave his co-star James Callahan three of his suits, and twenty-five of his white shirts. For the next few years, James Callahan had no worries concerning wardrobe. "Janssen was just a regular guy," says William ("Billy") Graham, "very easy to work with, very courteous to the other actors. Once in a while, he might not like the way a scene was staged, but most of the time he did whatever you asked him. He treated everybody as an equal." "Part of David's charm was that he could make everybody feel a part of the show," adds script supervisor Kenneth Gilbert. "The guy, Solly, who made the coffee, he felt just as important in what he was doing, he felt that he was as much a part of the show as everybody else."

By bringing these same qualities to his characterization of Richard Kimble, Janssen established a strong bond with TV viewers. "The reason audiences so strongly identified with the guy was that he was a very human, good-hearted person, by a lot of old-fashioned standards," explains Alan Armer. "We had more empathy with this character than any show I can remember. We loved him. We rooted for him, and I will never forget the night that [actress] Ann Rutherford's mother called me. Now this is a woman whose daughter was in the business, who knew the realities of show business. She called me about ten o'clock one night, kept pleading with me to give Kimble another trial. I said, 'Don't you realize that if we do that, the show is over?' She says, 'Yes, but this poor guy…' She went on and on. This from a sophisticated woman."

"He was a sympathetic character," says Don Brinkley, "and David played that very well. He had a wounded quality; you always felt sorry for him." "It was just amazing the way people were drawn to him, and wanted to help," adds Kenneth Gilbert. "They wanted to support him in any way they could. He just had a quality about him. You just were for him." James Callahan realized the truth of that when driving home one evening Janssen accepted his dare to run into an office building and ask for a hiding place. Laughs Callahan, "He came running back out and jumped in his motor home, and as we were driving away, fifty people came running after the bus shouting, 'David! David!' It was really cute." As Richard Kimble's sister, Donna Kimble Taft, Jacqueline Scott (who only appeared in four of the series' one-hundred-and-twenty episodes) also encountered situations which demonstrated to her the impact of the show. "I'd go to these movie premieres," says Scott, "different things around town, and people would come up to me and ask, 'How's your brother? How's your brother?' I'm thinking, What is this? I don't have a brother. Then it finally hit me."

Barry Morse (Kimble's pursuer, Lt. Philip Gerard) and Bill Raisch (the one-armed killer, Fred Johnson) had similar experiences. Morse's tended to be amusing. Raisch's were not. "Sometimes he'd come out of the supermarket, and there'd be a police car parked nearby," reveals Alan Armer. "The cops would look at him. They'd know he was wanted for something. They'd take him down to headquarters. He'd say, 'Look, I'm just a guy. I'm just an actor…' They'd say, 'Sure you are.' Eventually it would get straightened out. That happened to him two or three times."

Playing the real killer of Richard Kimble's wife, Helen, Raisch had a plum role. But when the one-armed man made his debut in the first-season's "Search in a Windy City," Quinn Martin was stunned. "Quinn had always thought of the one-armed man as kind of a mystic, unreachable character, and he was shocked, absolutely shocked," explains Armer. "We sat down. We talked. I said, 'Look, as you go on, you need to develop new story areas. This gives us a whole new area.' Quinn finally agreed." The job of finding a real one-armed man fell to assistant director Paul Wurtzel. "We found this extra," remembers the a.d. "We didn't know he was gonna be in more episodes; we thought it was a one-shot deal. But they kept putting him in more pictures, so naturally he wanted more money—after all he was the only one-armed guy." The character became even more important after the late third-season entry, "Wife Killer." In that episode, needing medical assistance from Kimble, Fred Johnson confesses to murdering the doctor's wife. Fortunately for Johnson, his confession is worthless. Unfortunately he now has a man very determined to catch him. In his next appearance—in mystery author Howard Browne's hard-edged, "A Clean and Quiet Town"—Johnson puts out a contract on Kimble. It was not the only time he tried to kill the doctor. *Fugitive* costumer Steve Lodge saw the increased use of Johnson as a positive development. "I was happy when they gave Bill Raisch more to do," declares Lodge. "People got to see just what an evil guy Johnson was. It led to the finale much better." More importantly, it eased the pressure on David Janssen.

"They shot such long hours," remembers Jacqueline Scott, "and David was there so long. When I did my first show, he was scheduled for a shot at noon and the last shot of the day. That's impossible. Sometimes he was sitting around the set for eight or nine hours." "One or two nights of that is one thing," adds Ralph Senensky, "but to do that day after day after day—that is mind numbing. I would get burned out directing those stories; I can only imagine how David felt. They always wrote that show around him. He was in everything." "It wasn't like the half-hour comedies," agrees casting director Meryl O'Loughlin. "That's the good life. They come in at ten, go home at six. But the hour shows—you leave home at five, shoot well into the night. That's very exhausting." "I don't think David ever fully recovered from doing that show," states returning guest Richard Anderson. "I think that show might have killed him."

Janssen's heavy drinking certainly didn't help. "Nobody blamed him," says Armer. "It was one way to relieve the terrible pressure of being in almost every scene. But it aged him. He didn't look like quite the same guy in the later years. He didn't look quite as vulnerable." That made using first-year stock footage of the actor very difficult. "That's why he wore the same outfits so many times," explains Armer. "So we could use the same endings." That allowed Janssen a break. As did any scene of Richard Kimble in long-shot; in time, the actor's photo double, David Greene had captured Janssen's rather distinctive gait. Giving the show to someone else (like Richard Anderson in the third-season's "Three Cheers for Little Boy Blue") further eased the pressure. That was a guarantee whenever Barry Morse did the show. "I think the shows with Gerard were the better shows," feels Steve Lodge. "I remember watching the show the first two years, being just terrified of that guy."

One of the best Gerard shows was the Walter Grauman directed third-season two-parter, "Landscape with Running Figures." "That's the one where Kimble hit bottom," states Armer. "He'd reached the very bottom, and was working as a dishwasher in an all-night restaurant. He had to get out of town because he'd given his employers his real name. I gave Tony Wilson the concept for that show. I said, 'Tony, what if we do a story about a relationship between Kimble and Gerard's wife?' He says, 'That's interesting. Let me think about that.' He came back with this story so clever, so ingenious, of how to get these two together." Yet Wilson's script was too long for an hour-show. Quinn Martin solved that problem by telling Wilson to write the show as a two-parter. The result was one of the series' best episodes, marred only by what Armer believed was an at times too over the top performance by Barbara Rush as Gerard's temporarily blinded wife, Marie. David Janssen himself cast Rush. "David wanted to have dolls, and adorable girls that Kimble could have sex with," laughs Armer. "We kept giving him women he considered less than attractive. That was one of our running jokes. So, this time we let him do the casting."

Says Walter Grauman, there was certainly no dearth of attractive women on *The Fugitive* set. "Whenever you shot and gathered a crowd on the street," remembers the director, "it was always women. I remember one girl—good-looking girl—she was there all the time. Even late at night." That didn't please Janssen's then wife, Ellie. Nor was Ellie Janssen happy when her husband's long-time friend, Suzanne Pleshette, did the show. Like Janssen, Pleshette had a good sense of humor. Naturally, she figured in the prank Quinn Martin played when he presented Janssen with his new motor home, "The Silver Bullet," during the shooting of the third-season's "Not with a Whimper."

"They drove it to the set," laughs Kenneth Gilbert, "and somebody says, 'Oh, there's your new trailer, David,' and David's 'Oh, my God,' and 'Geez,' and things like that. So he goes inside and walks into the bedroom and Suzanne's back there on the bed, sprawled out. She says, 'Quinn said he wanted this to come equipped with everything.'" "They wouldn't let me go in to see it when they first drove it up," remembers guest star Lee Meriwether. "I thought, Okay, let him have it all to himself. The next thing you know we're hearing all these screams and howls of laughter from inside the trailer. They even rocked it so that the people outside would think there was something going on. I said, 'You know I think somebody's in there with him,' and everybody who was on the set looked at me like I was a stupid bumpkin. Anyway at that particular moment, nothing else happened. I mean we were still filming. So David was out of there in five minutes. He didn't come out disheveled."

David Janssen was very flattered to be one of the very first stars in Hollywood to receive his own trailer. "It made him feel important and special," says Armer. "That really meant more to David than money. Quinn always gave David more than David ever really asked for in terms of perks. He always made sure David Janssen was the star with a capital 'S.'" Which was not to say the two men never clashed. "One time," remembers Paul Wurtzel, "David was drunk at this big important party in Malibu and was bad-mouthing Quinn to some people. Quinn happened to be standing there at the time. Later he called him into his office. He says, 'If I ever hear you talking like that again, I'll fire you, and I'll replace you. If they shut this series down, you'll be the one who's to blame. You'll be the one they sue.' Well, that straightened him out." Despite this unpleasant incident, Quinn Martin and David Janssen were quite friendly throughout the series' run. The producer took an almost fatherly interest in his star. He was greatly concerned about his heavy drinking. "David's drinking didn't become a problem until the last year," says Muffet Martin. "By that time, David was bored with doing it. So he'd have a few drinks at lunch. They had to be careful how they filmed him in the afternoon."

"Janssen was easy to work with," recalls the series' most frequent fourth-season director, Gerald Mayer. "but he was bored stiff. If there was a shot where there was some movement, some kind of action, it was not easy to get him to do it. Boredom was the whole thing. Everything he did, he'd done before five times." "He didn't spend much time with the guest stars the last year," elaborates Kenneth Gilbert. "They always liked to rehearse; he just didn't have the energy to do that anymore."

Knowing that he would be out of *The Fugitive* after its fourth year was the one thing that kept Janssen going. *Fugitive* fan Lynda Day George was very disappointed when Janssen told her this news. "I said that that was a shame," remembers the actress, "because the show was an institution and it was a really wonderful show. I said that from a viewer's point of view, not an actor's point of view. As an actor I would think he'd be looking for ways to kill himself on camera. Just anything. So that he could finally get the hell out of there."

In fact, Janssen was so tired of *The Fugitive* that the third season could very well have been the program's last. "The show was still a success, but it was kind of a comedy of errors," says Armer. "It went back and forth, two or three times with David saying 'No' to a fourth year, then changing his mind and saying 'Yes,' at which point

ABC would change its mind and say, 'No.'" "David just got burned out on the show," states Kenneth Gilbert. "He got out of it by agreeing to guest star on Quinn's other series and do some movies of the week." Jannsen had a hard time keeping the news of the series' cancellation from *The Fugitive* crew. Eventually he told them.

New producers Wilton Schiller and John Meredyth Lucas had an even harder time coming into the show. "At that point," declares Armer, "the show needed a fresh mind. We had covered all the bases that I could think of. Coming into that last year was very difficult. It's very tough coming into a series without knowing what patterns work and what patterns don't. I'm sure that was a challenge. But Will was, and is, a good writer. He and Jack Laird (who moonlighted under his wife's name for a few scripts on *The Fugitive* during the Armer years) wrote some *Broken Arrows* for me when I was producing that series. Will's a bright guy. I have nothing but respect for him." George Eckstein, who had remained with the series following Armer's departure, held a similar regard. "I had a very pleasant working relationship with Wilton Schiller," says Eckstein. "Once the new writers became familiar with the series, there were no problems. The quality may have gone down in the beginning. But I really didn't sit back and compare seasons." Unfortunately *Fugitive* fans and historians did. They didn't like the new ideas and concepts Schiller and Lucas were introducing—among these an increased use of the one-armed man, a $10,000 reward for the doctor's capture, an increasingly harder-edged Richard Kimble. Casting director Meryl O'Loughlin didn't share the fans and historians' opinion. "The format of that show was so limiting, they had to take it in a different direction at that point," says O'Loughlin. "I think that was good." "Those two guys were kind of riding a dead horse that last year," adds Steve Lodge, "but they managed to get another season out of the show. It wasn't a bad season." "It was the best season," asserts Lynda Day George. "Certainly the most realistic season. Kimble got to be more human that last year. He was allowed to make mistakes; he was allowed to get angry and upset. He wasn't perfectly wonderful all the time. The character blossomed in that last year into a more cynical person. That was appropriate because at some point he had to turn. He had to turn the corner from optimistic to doubtful and cynical, to be very certain that it was never gonna end. That he was not going to make it."

"When Wilton started doing *The Fugitive*," elaborates fourth-season writer Oliver Crawford, "he wanted to get away from the standard approach as much as possible. He wanted to do something, see something, that was new and refreshing." Director William Hale's QM debut, "Approach with Care," was certainly that. In "Approach," Kimble showed little sympathy for newly acquired, mentally retarded friend Denny Miller. That was quite a change from the way he'd treated mentally backward June Harding in the same season's "Ten Thousand Pieces of Silver." As its title implied, that was the episode in which a reward was offered for Kimble. That made the doctor's temporary blindness in the soon to follow "Second Sight" all the more unnerving. "I can guarantee you David put his soul into that," states Lodge, "because that was a show where he got to do something different. That was one of David's best performances. He was very very good in that show."

Janssen was positively heart-breaking in the February 21, 1967, episode, "The Ivy Maze," in which, thanks to the sleep-deprivation experiments of Kimble's college-professor friend William Windom, the doctor temporarily obtains a taped murder confession from Fred Johnson. "I had a fight with the one-armed man in that show," chuckles Windom. "His stump packed quite a wallop." Written by Edward C. Hume, who would go on to develop Quinn Martin's three most successful series of the 1970s—*Cannon, The Streets of San Francisco*, and *Barnaby Jones*—"Maze" was of further interest thanks to the casting of David Janssen's half-sister Jill as a college coed. Jill Janssen's first *Fugitive* role as an extra came in "The Sharp Edge of Chivalry." "When the extras stepped off the bus, all the young guys were watching them," laughs Steve Lodge. "When Jill stepped off the bus, everybody's going, 'Wow! Who's that?' 'David's sister,' somebody says. 'Stay away.'" Lodge didn't. When Jill Janssen returned to play a biker girl in "The Devil's Disciples," "that's really where I got to know her," says Lodge. "We were sitting in the bar one night having a few drinks. Before you knew it, we were dating. We got married after the series ended. The marriage lasted about eight months. We're still good friends."

Wilton Schiller was that with Oliver Crawford and Gerald Mayer. When all three men came together for "There Goes the Ball Game," the result was the season's most extraordinary episode, without question the entire series' most realistic, and arguably the best *Fugitive* ever. The episode certainly ranked high on David Janssen's list. "Ball Game" presented the actor with a true challenge—make viewers hate Richard Kimble. The scenario he'd been given allowed for such an opportunity. Despite facing no threat to his safety on this particular occasion, Kimble was not the least bit eager to help newspaper publisher Martin Balsam rescue his kidnapped daughter Lynda Day George. The only possible explanation as to why seemed to have been provided in the doctor's brief meeting with the young woman in the episode's opening sequence moments before her abduction. In contrast to every other *Fugitive* woman past and present, Lynda Day George's character showed not the slightest romantic interest in the doctor. "I had to show disinterest," says George, "in order for the rest of the story to work. I really felt honored to be doing that show. When they handed me that script, I knew I'd been given something special."

"David really was excited when he read that script," continues the actress. "He really had a great time shooting that." The way George and Janssen approached their characters added to the fun. "I played Kimble," reveals George. "David played Gerard. We both decided to do that. We took on some of their characteristics." But what really excited both actors was the fact that Oliver Crawford's script never explained to the audience why Kimble kept refusing to help George. The doctor's behavior was baffling. Unlike all those other occasions, there was no danger to Kimble this time—which was why Kimble couldn't help George. Having spent the last four years of his life performing good works in the face of danger, the doctor had established a connection in his mind that the one could not exist without the other. Thus the only way he could help George was to have his own life threatened.

"That was the underpinning of the show," says "Ball Game" writer Oliver Crawford. "You don't say it in so many words, but after all that running, running, running, sure, he had to save face in a sense by being threatened. That was a subtlety that I think Gerry Mayer caught, and brought out in the performances." "That was exactly how David felt," exclaims George. "He had not expected to do that show. It was a departure for the character. It was something new for the character." "It was the kind of show Wilton always wanted to do," adds Crawford. "I'm sure that 'There Goes the Ball Game' was one of Wilton's favorites."

It certainly was a favorite of its leading lady's. "If you had watched the show all the time, it was fairly clear how 'Ball Game' fit into the context of the other shows," explains George. "I enjoyed being in that place at that time on that particular series. It meant a lot to me. I thought it was an important show." But had it not

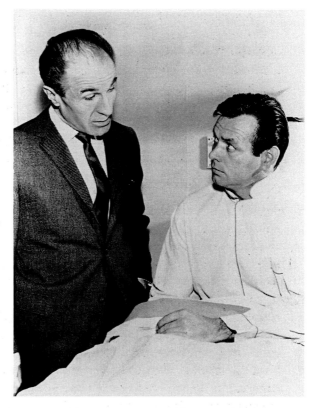

Barry Morse (left, as Lt. Philip Gerard) catches up with David Janssen's injured "Dr. Richard Kimble" in the March 16, 1965, second-season ABC-TV *Fugitive* episode, "May God Have Mercy."

been for the intensive examination Lynda Day George received at the hands of Adrian Samish, the actress might never have received the opportunity to do the episode. "I only had a couple of days before I actually started working on that show," remembers George. "As I had not done a lot of stuff with QM at that time, Adrian wanted to know whether I was clear enough about how the series operated, about how it was put on screen, about how this particular series worked. Adrian was very clear, very forceful, very intense about making it right. Almost exclusively he concerned himself with whether or not the integrity of the show would be maintained. That was desperately important to him."

"There Goes the Ball Game" was not the only clever idea writer Oliver Crawford fashioned for *The Fugitive*. Unfortunately, Crawford's other idea never made it to film. "It had a religious theme," says Crawford, "having to do with the Jewish holiday Passover, where you leave the door open when you sit down for dinner so that the spirit of Elijah the Prophet or any needy person may join in the meal. Well, we opened with Kimble running. He's been spotted. He's ducking in and out of buildings, goes up to this tenement building and sees this open door. So he dashes right in and sits at the table. Then the police come by. But the patriarch, who's presiding at this religious observance, sends them away. Naturally Kimble feels some sense of gratitude; somehow he gets involved with the family. It was a hell of an idea, Wilton wanted very much to do it, but Quinn or the network objected. There wasn't any bias; they just were leery of religious themes in those days."

Martin was just as leery of concluding *The Fugitive*; contrary to most series' histories, however, he had very little to do with that conclusion. The producer had more important things on his mind. His sister Ruth was dying of cancer. "The writing of the thing was all Wilton Schiller," reveals Gerald Mayer. "Schiller's writers, Schiller's staff. Quinn wanted to go a certain direction in that last episode. Wilton thought that a complete cheat, and not very good. He convinced Quinn that Quinn's way was not the best way. It was Wilton's idea for the final episode which attracted all the attention. The ending of the show was all Wilton Schiller." Director Jesse Hibbs was another whose contribution to the series finale was underrated. "He and Don Medford [who received sole credit for "The Judgment—Parts 1&2"] were really kind of opposite in the way they worked, but they both did the final show," states Kenneth Gilbert. "Don had everything exactly diagrammed out. He was very precise on where everybody would move, on what line, all that type of thing. He got sick partway through the final two hours so Jesse came in and took over."

"I was pregnant when they started planning that show," remembers Jacqueline Scott. "When they started filming it [in early spring '67], my baby was just three and a half weeks old. I told them I'd love to do those last two shows, but if they needed me to do anything too difficult, forget it. My first concern was with my baby. So they got me a suite of rooms on the set, or on the lot, and whenever we had a lunch break, I'd go tearing down the street, so I could nurse my baby. Fred Ahern had a grandbaby just about the same age. He'd go tearing down the street with me. That was the kind of affection and sweetness and care that we showed for one another on that show. A lot of that had to do with David. David was the sweetest man there ever was."

Despite his sister Ruth's poor health, Quinn Martin involved himself to some degree in the series' long-awaited conclusion. "He wanted me to do the final show, but I was going over to do this show in England called *The Strange Report*," recalls Don Brinkley. "It was a mystery show—an American series shot on location in England. So when I came back from England, he punished me. When I came back, I was planning to pick up my work on *The FBI*. He wouldn't let me do any of them for a while."

Considering the importance of the series' last episode, the decision to delay "The Judgment—Parts 1 & 2" until the month of August (one of the worst months for television viewing) was an enormous risk for all concerned. Yet, as the ratings proved, that risk paid off. For years *The Fugitive*: "The Judgment—Part 2" was to hold a record as the most watched television program of all time. "It was one of the biggest things that ever happened," remembers Scott. "They announced it at St. Louis during the baseball game. They announced it on ships at sea, at army bases." Of course, everyone knew who the real killer was, but in spite of that, other characters were suspected—

among them Richard Kimble's brother-in-law Leonard Taft (Richard Anderson). "The bets were on all over the country," laughs Anderson. "The heavy betting in Las Vegas was I killed her." The decision to cast Anderson as Leonard Taft was Quinn Martin's own idea. It was one of the few contributions the producer made to the series' last episode. If anyone had any doubts that David Janssen wasn't by then tired of the program, the actor dispelled those during an interview with *Tonight Show* guest host Joey Bishop the night of the series' conclusion—August 29, 1967. "I killed her, Joey," Janssen cracked to Bishop. "She talked too much."

Given his star's attitude, Quinn Martin knew *The Fugitive*'s end was inevitable, but he "later admitted he didn't want to end the show," remembers George Eckstein. "He was afraid the conclusion would hurt syndication sales." The series' great popularity since that time proved Martin's fears to be groundless. Unfortunately, the program the producer launched one year after *The Fugitive*'s premiere didn't fare as well in syndication. It didn't do that well in prime time either. That series was Muffet Martin's personal favorite. The United States Air Force thought very highly of it too. The series was *12 O'clock High.*

Chapter 4

12 O'CLOCK HIGH

Bob Lansing was the glue that people liked. When they took off the glue, the thing fell apart.

12 O'clock High *production manager Howard Alston*

Whatever doubts ABC president Tom Moore may have had concerning Quinn Martin during the first year of *The Fugitive* had definitely disappeared by the time Martin launched his next series, the 1964–67 World War II adventure, *12 O'clock High* (September 18, 1964–January 13, 1967). In fact, it was because of Martin that Moore decided to do the series, which starred Robert Lansing as General Frank Savage, squadron commander of the U.S. Air Force's London-based 918th Bombardment Group. Moore certainly hadn't felt that way when 20th Century–Fox Television studio head William Self presented him with the project. "I'd assigned Paul Monash, whom I'd brought in as head of dramatic development at Fox, to write it," remembers Self. "Then I submitted it to ABC. They turned it down. Then one day Tom Moore said that Quinn Martin had expressed great interest in doing the series, but instead of having General Savage at the same base all the time [as was the case in the Self pilot and the 1949 20th Century–Fox Gregory Peck feature], the character would be going to a different base every week and straightening out their problem. Well, when the new script came in, Quinn decided, 'You know something. Your script's better; your idea's better. Because if you've got the general going to a different base every week, you've got to redo your set every week. You'd need a different cast too. That's too costly.' So we went back to Tom Moore. We said, 'We tried Quinn's idea, but we think the original concept's better.' Tom said, 'Okay. Let's go with that.'"

William Self also provided *12 O'clock High* with its first producer, former publicity man Frank Glicksman. "I had a lot of respect for Frank," declares Self. "He was a very solid story guy. He was my story editor when we did the pilot; he worked on the original script with Paul Monash." "Frank Glicksman was a wonderful pro-

ducer," states contributing writer Don Brinkley, who later co-produced with Glicksman television's longest-running medical drama, *Medical Center*. "He was very story minded, had great respect for writers, and a great sense of humor. He was always at odds with Quinn. Frank was very opinionated. Quinn was too." At the end of the first season, Frank Glicksman left. So did the series' other producer, Charles Larson. Quinn Martin needed Larson for his next series, *The FBI*.

Director Ralph Senensky enjoyed working with Larson on

Title card from the third and final season of the September 18, 1964–January 13, 1967, ABC-TV series, *12 O'clock High*.

that series. Ditto *12 O'clock High*. "Charlie was wonderfully flexible," says Senensky. "He could write in so many different modes. Charlie was always amenable to any changes. So many times a script was written without going out to find locations. Charlie would rewrite the script to fit what you found." "Charlie Larson was terrific," agrees Howard Alston. "He was the guy who made *12 O'clock High* work. He loved that time period; he knew how to write in the stock footage; he was fanatical about making sure everything was in accordance with the characters from the Peck feature." "We adhered to the movie a lot," elaborates Self. "We felt we had a built-in audience. We just couldn't do a totally different series. We felt that would alienate the audience." "Before we made the pilot, 'Golden Boy Had Nine Black Sheep,' Quinn had us look at the Peck movie several times," remembers director Billy Graham. "We talked at great length about how we'd shoot the series. Quinn wanted it to look like the movie, but he wanted it to be done with more style. I thought that was pretty arrogant, because the director of the movie was Henry King."

What Martin meant was the cinematography of the series. Howard Alston's bringing in his *Richard Boone Show* co-worker, the MGM-trained William W. Spencer, as the program's director of photography fulfilled Martin's wants. Like Martin, Spencer loved the film noir look. His preference for shadows and for dim lighting "really established the style of the show," believes John Elizalde. Hiring Spencer solved another problem. "There was so much process photography, so much rear-projection work in *12 O'clock*," declares Howard Alston. "Billy had great experience and expertise in rear projection; they'd done that frequently at MGM. He was able to overcome any problems matching the stock footage (which came from both the United States Air Force and the BBC) with new footage. He did it with as much speed and as much quality as anybody. He was the best black-and-white photographer in the business." Considering the working conditions under which the rear-projection process footage was shot, the quality and speed Spencer achieved was remarkable.

"We had this B-17 which was cut up into different sections, and they were all about ten feet off the stage on different platforms," recalls Spencer. "That way you could be squared up with the center of the projection machine whenever you were filming rear projection. You had the camera on a platform (or sometimes on a crane) so you could be eye level with the people in whatever section of the aircraft you were filming. Whenever they flew through cloud formations, we'd use wind machines on platforms and smoke blowing past the windows to simulate that." The cockpit scenes showing General Savage, and later Colonel Gallagher (Paul Burke), leading the squadron were the most frequently filmed of all the rear-projection process scenes. "The process stage where we shot the cockpit stuff was one of the smallest stages," reveals Senensky. "The camera was back in a corner; there was just enough room for the operator to slide in and sit there. It was all compressed. It was like a large closet."

Obtaining stock footage was never a problem. The Air Force was more than happy to provide that. "They wanted us to do the show," explains Alston. "The Department of Defense gave the series its blessing; all of our stock footage came from the Air Force. The plane blowing up—that was all stock footage; the squadron landing and approaching was all stock. Some of it came from the library of 20th Century–Fox; Fox got a lot of footage from the Air Force when they'd made the Peck feature. A lot of the footage was on 16mm film; a lot came from gun cameras. The military had wanted to keep a filmed record of everything that had happened during World War II; every time there'd been a major combat, several film units had accompanied the troops. And there was always somebody filming on the bases. We had a lot of stock footage of whole squadrons landing on fields so we always had a shot of the airplane landing in the distance, but we only had one airplane that could really taxi."

"They did a good job in solving the problems, because logistically, that was a difficult show," declares William Self. "They only had three planes, two of which could taxi; only one could fly. They had to make that look like an entire squadron." "We were always going out to Chino [Airport] and filming the plane that could taxi," reveals Alston. "We'd bring the B-17 up to the hard-stand—i.e., the cement platform built for the plane—and taxi it around. To make it look like the plane had just landed, we'd cut from the shot of the plane landing in the distance to this shot of it taxiing up to the hard-stand and turning around to stop. Then they'd cut the engines, and Bob Lansing would slide out of the pilot's seat before the engines were dead. That wasn't normal, but it was very exciting. Everything was quick action on that show. It was always physical because there was always something happening with the airplanes; trying to do that for the amount of money we had, well, everybody had to be quite inventive in making it work, in making it believable."

A perfect example of this inventiveness concerned any sequence where the 918th's runway at Archbury (their home base in England) was bombed. "If we wanted it to look like the bombs were hitting the tarmac, we'd build a ramp, paint it the same color as the tarmac, and show it in the distance," explains Alston. "You couldn't see the ramp leading up to the tarmac—we always put something in front of the camera to hide it. Then we'd set off a gasoline bomb because gasoline always gave you a bright flame. If we wanted a big explosion, we'd set off a fifty gallon drum of gas. If we didn't get as big an explosion as we wanted, the optical house later added flames to the picture. They'd take the picture, make a dupe of what we'd shot, then super-impose an explosion over our explosion. They did that quite often."

The company didn't always have to invent however. "We found this air-field in Chino with a row of trees that sort of matched the trees in our stock footage," remembers Alston. "Eventually the city cut down the trees; they were becoming a hazard to the airplanes. That drove us crazy for a while, but in time we got around that." The show even presented an episode around the loss of the trees—the first season Dana Wynter guest shot, "Cry of Fallen Birds." Finding ways to incorporate such environmental changes into the dramatic framework was par for the course on the series: case in point, the first-season Glenn Corbett–Sally Kellerman guest shot, "Those Who Are About to Die"—a sequel to the pair's earlier appearance, "The Men and the Boys." In "Those," tensions run high when a heavy blanket of fog descends on the 918th, thus postponing one of the squadron's most important missions. "Sometimes the fog was so bad that when the [crew] bus arrived outside the airport, you had to get out of the bus and literally lead it into the airport," laughs Alston. "If you didn't, the bus might drive right onto the runway." Director Billy Graham welcomed the fog. "We were shooting the show on location in Ontario, California, and there was a mountain range in the background," states Graham. "On clear days, you had a hell of a time avoiding that mountain range. The fog hid that, which was good. Supposedly all of the action was taking place in England."

Which, because *12 O'clock High* was a period piece, thus required a great deal of set construction. The 918th headquarters was built at Fox Western. The street on its back lot became a London street for the squadron's favorite pub, The Star and Bottle. The company also used streets at MGM and Universal. Pinetree, headquarters for General Savage's superior, Brigadier General Wiley Crowe (John Larkin), was built on the stage at Fox. Art director George Chan made the stands for the wall-sized, plexi-glass maps so often seen at Pinetree. "George was the art director Quinn liked best," notes Alston. "Quinn selected George for *12 O'clock High*. George worked for Quinn till the company shut down."

Chan had nothing to do however with the mock-up of the B-17. The Air Force gave QM Productions an old fuselage. The company took that fuselage and cut it up into different sections. As a result, they were able to shoot in different sections of the plane, like the ball turret, and focus on different members of the crew, for example the navigator. Obtaining an air-worthy B-17 took some time though. "When we began the series," recalls Alston, "we had problems because a lot of the B-17s were being used for water-dropping, for fire-fighting purposes." Eventually Alston and company discovered a usable B-17 at the Ontario, California, Air Force Museum. "The fella there rented it to us for a season," reveals Alston. "We used it on the ground, but when you run an airplane on the ground all the time it doesn't take long to ruin the engines. So, in order to make the plane capable of flight, we had to rebuild all the engines. We had a helicopter when we were doing that show, and once we had the plane in the air, we went up in the copter and photographed the plane landing and taking off. It was good we did that because after the plane became unlicensed, we could no longer use it."

Thus, the company had even more footage. Using that which was provided by the Air Force raised the costs of production. "We had a lot of film expense in that series," relates Alston. "We made process plates, and prints of the stock footage, so we could use our own prints." It was assistant editor Jim Miller who came up with the solution for depicting the aerial battles between the Americans and the Germans. "In the stock film you couldn't tell if the guns were firing," says Alston. "You didn't see the flash of their guns. Well, Jim took the rear-projection film, scratched each frame with a pin, and (when the scratched film was run through the rear projection projector) that made it more believable. Because now what you had were the airplanes coming at one another with flashes of light. It looked like they were firing bullets. Jim was the first one to try that. It worked very well. But we had to keep making prints of all the stock footage so we could keep doing that. That cost money. There was a lot of film expense in that series. That was very unusual in a television series." One thing the stock footage lacked was sound. "So we recorded start-ups on the B-17," explains John Elizalde. "We recorded a bunch of stuff, the rest we got from our vast sound-effects library. We had some unique sound effects, one of them was 'plane-shake.' We used that, and some hydraulics that made the plane move, for the scenes where they were flying through the flak. The 'plane-shake' stuff came in handy for a lot of things later. We used that particular sound effect for various stressful situations, car chases, and such."

Helping QM Productions obtain stock footage from the Air Force was the series' technical adviser, James Doherty. Former Air Force sergeant Doherty, who later worked on the Jack Webb series *Adam-12*, had flown in B-17s during World War II. "Jim would read the scripts, and if he thought there was something that made the Air Force look bad, he'd go to the producers and tell them," says Alston. "All of our requests were funneled through Jim. If we needed special uniforms, or special equipment, he had the authority to go to the various departments and order that. The Air Force knew they could trust him." QM had no difficulties obtaining regular uniforms, equipment, or vehicles—the uniforms were provided by Western Costume Company; the equipment and vehicles came from a company in the San Fernando Valley specializing in such items.

Acquiring aircraft other than B-17s was fairly easy as well. "The person at the Ontario Museum was very aware of the [World War II airplane] clubs that were around town," explains Alston. "We never had to advertise; there was always a private collector who had the planes that we needed. We made several trips down to the Monith and Davis Air Field in Arizona too. They had hundreds of these old fighter planes— P-38s, P-47s, B-17s, P-51s. All this old aircraft was just sitting there in the desert.

None of them could fly. Most of the engines had not been mothballed properly." Other sources for aircraft were the "Planes of Fame" located out at Chino and QM's own airplane and helicopter pilot, James W. Gavin. Gavin had begun working for QM during the first season of *The Fugitive*; he had very little to do with *12 O'clock High*, much more to do on Quinn Martin's next series, *The FBI*.

Finding period aircraft was rarely a problem, finding ammunition pieces was. "The government had all these machine guns and belts for the fifty caliber guns and blanks," remembers assistant director Paul Wurtzel. "We bought tons of that for the show. It was very expensive. Every cartridge was fifty cents or something. The machine guns were very hard to buy. The government had decided to destroy all the gun parts left over from World War II. They worried some might get into the wrong hands."

Series star Robert Lansing's characterization of General Frank Savage created additional frustration. Not that Lansing was trying to be difficult. "Bob took the role very seriously," explains Alston. "He wanted to make it very strong. I think he drove Charlie Larson and Frank Glicksman nuts because of that, but he was always there, he was always on time, he always knew his lines. He worked very hard." "Lansing was ideal," elaborates William Self. "Physically he was perfectly right for that part. He looked like a man of stature, looked like a relatively young general in the Air Force." "He was a very good actor," agrees Billy Graham, "kind of low-key and under-stated, but he could be a real pain in the ass. David Janssen pretty much went along with anything you asked him to do, but Lansing, you had to cajole him more. You had to listen to him run on about the script and his character." "He wasn't satisfied with the scripts," adds Self. "He felt his character needed to be more diversified." "Bob was a perfectionist," explains *12 O'clock High* guest Lee Meriwether. "He wanted things to be right. He worked very hard for that. His work shows what intense focus and concentration can do. He had a wonderful sense of humor, but that only came out if all was going well. It always bothered him when actors would come and use the rehearsal time to learn their lines. That just blew his mind."

Lansing's perfectionism caused considerable trouble for the sound department. "He was a mumbler," states John Elizalde. "If you had a scene where the flak was bursting around him, you could never hear him." "That was part of his style," explains Billy Graham. "He was a very understated, low-key actor. So sometimes the sound people had trouble picking him up. When we asked him to speak louder, he'd say he couldn't, because 'the scene would lose its quality.'" "Bob really cared about what he was doing," points out Ralph Senensky. "I really liked Bob. When we were doing 'The Threat' [featuring Laurence Naismith as an English barber who is actually a German spy assigned to murder Savage] Bob offered to pay Larry's salary so that I could shoot with Larry another day." The night before Naismith's last day on the shoot, Senensky had very meticulously laid out a long scene where Naismith was shaving Lansing. Unfortunately the professional barber the company had hired found Senen-sky's shaving scene totally inaccurate. The director had to restage the entire sequence. By that time, it was too late to shoot the scene. Robert Lansing never had to make good his offer. QM Productions paid Naismith for the extra day.

Robert Lansing (as Brigadier General Frank Savage) plotting out a mission in a first-season episode of the September 18, 1964–January 13, 1967, ABC-TV series, *12 O'clock High*.

In the Josef Leytes directed episode, "The Clash" (where General Savage and his German enemy Albert Paulsen struggle for survival on a raft), Lansing really went the limit. "We had these long shots with him swimming," remembers Wurtzel, "and it was physically exhausting because he was in his high altitude flight gear with this sheepskin lining, and it got all full of water. He almost sank. That thing must have weighed about seventy pounds. We had to use his double when we were doing the close-ups. Lansing was so exhausted. The double really didn't look like him." "It was very difficult for Joe Leytes to do that show," adds William Spencer. "We were working at the beach in Malibu, had the raft in the ocean; then it started to rain very heavy. Paul Wurtzel called Howard at the studios. He says, 'Howard, it's raining like hell. What are we gonna do?" Howard says, 'It's not raining here.' In other words, keep shooting." Which Wurtzel figured on doing in the Ralph Senensky–directed "The Hero." "I'd set up this two-shot with Bob Lansing and Jimmy Whitmore," chuckles Senensky, "then suddenly Billy Spencer says, 'We can't shoot anymore.' Paul says, 'Why?'" Spencer pointed to a sheet of water coming right off the wing of the plane. "It looked like Niagara Falls," says Senensky.

William Spencer always enjoyed working with Ralph Senensky. Directors like Sutton Roley were another matter. "Sutton Roley was a hell of a nice guy but the minute he got on the set, he went screwy," laughs Wurtzel. "He wanted to be the star of the show; he always wanted to shoot a hand-held camera. He was always trying to do extreme things, always trying to get something different with the camera. He pushed everything to the limit. He was always asking the cameraman to do stuff the equipment couldn't do. If the special equipment wasn't there, it just slowed everything down. He did everything on the spur of the moment. He got some unusual stuff though." "He was absolutely the most hyper guy," adds Alston, "very energetic, and he had his own way of working. He liked tight shots, always wanted to shoot it himself. He was all over the place. He wasn't an easy director for Billy Spencer."

Nor was Don Medford. "Don liked to get Bob Lansing out of the airplane before the engines stopped," remembers Alston. "Bob would come out of the airplane right behind the wing. Don liked to time that as close as he could. He wanted that energy, that movement. Don was very meticulous, very detailed. He'd come to work every morning with a shot-list of set-ups he wanted to make; give everybody a copy of that list who was interested. Sometimes he had more work outlined than we could possibly do in one day. Don always knew what he wanted. If you had four people in the master, he'd select a two-shot on two of them, have singles on the other two. It would all be written out ahead of time. A lot of that came from his work in live television. Don was a highly regarded live television director. Quinn always liked using Don. He juiced up the actors. Everybody had more energy with Don. Don was never satisfied with having people walk when they could run." The highly intense Medford had a peculiar habit. Whenever he saw a discarded match-stick on the floor, he'd pick it up and tear it. Paul Wurtzel remembers the day one of the assistants on the show decided to have some fun with Medford. "He got tons of these matches," laughs Wurtzel, "and laid down this trail, dropped them on the floor, dropped them in circles and 'U's and 'H's, took the trail right outside the stage door. Don started picking these things up, followed the trail right out the door. We all watched. We got absolutely hysterical."

Which could easily have happened to anyone watching the make-up artists apply the "blood" to an actor's face for those sequences in which the co-pilot or pilot was shot. "The first two seasons," says Lee Meriwether, "the show was in black and white, so whenever anybody was shot, they smeared this dark chocolate syrup all over their face. That seemed so ghoulish! It wouldn't have been so bad if the stuff had been red, but to have this dark chocolate syrup all over your face, uhhhh. That was so icky. That was so yucky." Peter Fonda was none too comfortable either when he portrayed a rather clumsy bomber in the first season's "The Sound of Distant Thunder." Whenever the series shot scenes in the plane all the characters were in high altitude flight gear. Fleece-lined leather flying gear. "It was heavy stuff," explains Wurtzel. "The Air Force guys always wore it because it was below freezing when those B-17s got up to 20,000 feet or something. Well Fonda rode a motorcycle, and during the weekend he'd gone out on his bike and wiped out and peeled himself like a grape. When he came into work on Monday we were doing this scene in the airplane, on stage where it's hotter than hell. So, he'd sweat and the sweat ran into where he'd scraped himself all up. He never squawked though. He just did it."

Frequent guest Robert Drivas didn't possess the same patience. "Robert was always intense," says Alston. "He was intense in real life. The minute he walked on the set, you knew everybody was gonna have their hands full. Robert was a fine, fine actor, but he had his own method of doing things. The directors had to work hard to keep him in line. He had so many strange mannerisms. There were a lot of things that bothered him. When we were doing "The Albatross" [in which aspiring actor Drivas' face is damaged in an explosion aboard Savage's plane, *The Piccadilly Lily*] he kept complaining about the burn make-up we were putting on him."

Complaining was something returning director Josef Leytes never did. "When we were doing the stuff with the Nazis, it wasn't easy for him," remembers Wurtzel. "Josef had been a very well known director in Poland before the Germans invaded. Then he and his sister were taken to Auschwitz. He saw the Germans beat his sister to death at Auschwitz. Later on he managed to escape, went over the mountains and got out. He didn't do a lot of shows. I loved working with him. I'd say, 'Josef, you want a lot of people in this scene; the budget only gives us this.' He'd say, 'Okay, I understand.' He used to say, 'If you don't get what you like, like what you get.' After what he'd been through, making a TV series really didn't mean too much."

The sudden death of series semi-regular John Larkin during the filming of "The Threat" didn't seem to mean too much to the people who arranged the actor's funeral service. "We were two or three days into shooting," recalls Ralph Senensky, "when the revised pages were brought down. I noticed a scene on the first page was a scene I'd already shot. So I just put it away. Then, a few minutes before we finished shooting, Frank Glicksman and Charlie Larson were suddenly on the set. They told us John Larkin had died. John had been in this show; they'd rewritten it so they could re-shoot the show with Harold Gould. Well, the next day or so, there was to be a memorial service held for John over at some chapel in Beverly Hills. So a bunch of us, including Billy Spencer and myself, went to the service. The service was less than satisfactory. Nothing was mentioned of the family; there was no religious connotation. John had been involved in this small theater group; the service was almost something of an audition. They did scenes that John had performed with the group, putting forth the idea that he was a true artist, which he was, putting forth the idea that his true love was their group, not the commercial world of television and film. Well, we'd all been wondering how we could go to this service, then go back to work at the studio, and when we got out of there, and went back to the studio, to the soundstage where we shot process, it was almost like a sanctuary. We were so relieved to be back there in the sane world. What we had thought would be a difficult thing to do—to go back to work after that service, really turned out to be our salvation."

In addition to "The Threat," Senensky had good memories of "The Trap." In "The Trap," General Savage, a pregnant woman and a few other people are buried alive in an underground bomb shelter. Unfortunately for them, the bomb that has fallen is still ticking. "'The Trap' was a wonderful show," says Senensky. "We didn't even go on location. We just used this street on the other side of [Fox's] Western Avenue. Most of the story took place on this one small set. I had five days to shoot on that set, and it was wonderful. [The series' other art director] Dick Haman designed it. It was incredible that in that five days, I never ran out of angles." For the sequence in which Savage and the others run through the shelter's doorway after hearing the air-raid, Senensky expected just a "partial set." "Dick gave me this alley with a big arch over it," enthuses the director. "He had it arranged so that when you heard the explosion, all this debris which had been rigged would come down and seal off the doorway."

"That show was a character study," continues Senensky. "It was like *Key Largo*,

Petrified Forest. It was like a stage play. That was one show where you really had acting scenes. The show that aired was not the show we'd started with. That was because of Charlie Larson. Charlie just kept writing these wonderful scenes that revealed character and interwove character. He just rewrote and deepened the interactions between the people. Charlie Larson was very good at that."

The art department and special effects personnel were very good in the Americans-in-a-German-prison-camp first-season entry, "Decision." Guest-starring Tim O'Connor as an old friend of Savage's who sacrifices himself in order to help destroy a German munitions factory, "Decision" climaxed with a spectacular bombing of that factory. "The location was out in Chino very near where we had the airplane," recalls William Spencer. "There was this abandoned winery that had been out there for many many years. They built an extension of that winery, then blew up that part. We had three cameras going; those kinds of scenes you can't go back and redo."

Yet the company could redo actors' dialogue. With Swedish actor Gunnar Hellstrom, that was a necessity. "He was playing this German commander, and he had this very heavy Swedish accent," chuckles John Elizalde. "In this one scene, he's asking his people what they found; one of them says, 'Well, all we found was a bunch of wire,' and Gunnar says, 'Yew foool. American prescription [precision] bombers use vire.' Well that broke everybody up when we ran the dailies. We had to redo it." As mentioned earlier, Robert Lansing's delivery of his dialogue also often had to be redone. Quinn Martin had a hard time understanding Lansing. Somebody on the show told that to Lansing. "So, Lansing did this scene," explains casting secretary Lois Winslow, "and at the end of the scene, he turned and looked right into the camera. He says, 'Did you understand that?' That enraged Quinn. He didn't have a lot of patience with actors."

"Bob was giving Quinn a lot of trouble," elaborates William Self. "And finally Quinn got fed up. He came to me. He said 'I want to get rid of Bob Lansing, but I have some reservations about that. The show is doing okay.' Quinn had to have my approval to replace Lansing; *12 O'clock High* was a Fox property. Fox had written the original script; Fox had financed it. We were not a passive partner. So, when Quinn said he wanted to replace Lansing, I said, 'If you do, I haven't approved it yet, but, if you do, it's got to be somebody who I feel can carry the show.' He came back with Paul Burke. I said, 'Okay.'"

Naturally Lansing was disappointed to learn he was being replaced, but, says Paul Wurtzel, he handled it like a pro. "We had three or four episodes left when they told him," remembers Wurtzel. "I was surprised they did. But he did his job. He didn't cause any problems." Like Wurtzel, most everyone from the series' first season thought firing Lansing a terrible mistake. "After that, the show grew less serious," feels Ralph Senensky. "It was like the Rover Boys go to war." "It became a completely different show," agrees Muffet Martin. "When Lansing was doing the show, he was too serious, too dour. They were always trying to get him to loosen up. With Paul Burke, we went to the other extreme. He was too light, too flip. He didn't take it seriously at all." "I think the show might have lasted longer if Bob hadn't been

From the left: **Frank Overton (as Major Harvey Stovall), Robert Lansing (as Brigadier General Frank Savage), Lew Gallo (as Major Joe Cobb), and John Larkin (as Major General Wiley Crowe) in a first-season publicity shot for the September 18, 1964–January 13, 1967, ABC-TV series, *12 O'clock High*.**

replaced," states Alston. "Nobody understood why Bob was let go. Paul Burke was a nice man, but he was walking into a situation that was well established with everybody. I don't know how happy Paul was playing that role. It wasn't right for him." "He was in an awkward position," adds Self. "He did a good job, but I think the public liked Bob Lansing more. We never overcame that. It didn't work after Lansing left. Quinn later admitted he'd made a mistake." "We got stacks and stacks of mail when they dropped Lansing," remembers casting secretary Lois Winslow. "It was just amazing."

Not everybody objected to Burke though. Certainly not Lee Meriwether. "I was very friendly with Bob Lansing, but I don't think the show went downhill," states the actress. "I thought Paul Burke did a wonderful job. I thought he was awfully good. He held up his end very well. He never seemed ill at ease. He was a good actor. He always seemed to be right there and on top of everything." In a way, Burke's casting as the squadron's new commander, Colonel Joe Gallagher, enhanced the series' realism. During the course of the first season, viewers had seen returning guest Burke's Captain Joe Gallagher advance to the rank of major. When the series began its second season, Gallagher was now a colonel.

Third-season semi-regular Richard Anderson (Brigadier General Philip Doud) was another who thought very highly of Burke. "He had a wonderful, vulnerable quality about him," says Anderson. "He showed that in his eyes." "Paul was a terrific actor," adds second-season story editor and, later, associate producer, Philip Saltzman. "He was an easy guy to be around, a very hard worker. I'd always admired him on *Naked City* [Burke's previous series] and I'd worked with him on *Five Fingers* [Burke's series prior to *City*]. Paul enjoyed doing *12 O'clock High*. It was a step up from where he'd been on *Five Fingers*. He was the second banana there. On *12 O'clock*, he was the star of the show." "I liked Paul a lot," adds *12 O'clock High* series director Walter Grauman. "I used him in the first film I ever did [1957's *The Disembodied*]. It was a ridiculous picture, but Paul was very good. I liked Paul in *12 O'clock*; he liked that character. I liked him a hell of a lot better than Bob Lansing. Lansing was an asshole, very difficult, very introverted, sort of sullen. He was very good in the role of the general, but he was very difficult to work with."

In addition to a new series star, the show had a new producer, William D. Gordon. Perfectionist Gordon spent a lot of time at the studio, often staying there all night, constantly working on the scripts. "He seemed to take it upon himself to do all the writing," remembers Lois Winslow. "We had all these wonderful writers, but he just wouldn't delegate anything. He always looked worn out. He seemed to think no one was as competent as he was. He acted like only he could write the show, and he had this organ in his office; every once in a while, you'd hear this organ music wafting through the halls. It was kind of irritating." Adds Howard Alston, "Bill had this very comfortable, soft, easy chair; he'd sit before his typewriter, write, fall asleep, wake up, write, go back to sleep, wake up, write some more. When we came in the next morning, we'd have part of a script. Then, under the door, we'd see more pages coming out. Bill was always keeping us on pins and needles. We never knew when we were gonna get a script. You needed the script at least seven days in advance to prepare. Somehow Bill hated to give up the script until the last minute."

"He was impossible," declares Don Brinkley. "He was so ponderous about everything. It always took him about forty-five minutes to make up his mind. He was a pain. If you were married to the guy you wouldn't want to be involved with him. He just couldn't let go of the scripts. He was very strange. He had that organ, and he always used to wear a paratrooper outfit. I remember, when the show was canceled, they still had four shows left to write. So Quinn called me. He says, 'We have four scripts here that need a rewrite. I can't get them away from Bill Gordon. Can you rewrite 'em?' I said, 'I'll try.' The plan was, Quinn would give me the script, I'd look it over, come in with my notes, look at Quinn's notes, then write the thing, and send it to Quinn. Then he'd put it through, and circumvent Gordon. Well, at the last minute Quinn decided not to do that. He didn't want to make Gordon look bad. So he turned my rewrites over to Gordon. I got notes on these things that were longer than the scripts themselves—eight to ten page single spaced notes. It drove me crazy. There were phone calls, meetings, breakfast meetings, nighttime meetings. I finally went to Quinn. I said, 'I can't take this.' Quinn says, 'I don't blame you.' So I went home. Quinn paid me for all four scripts."

Philip Saltzman had experienced similar problems the year before. Martin brought Saltzman in to help Gordon get the scripts out faster to Alston and the others. He didn't. "Bill was very hands-on in the script department," says Saltzman. "He couldn't deal with story until it was on paper. He couldn't see the problems in the script until he himself rewrote it. That created a logjam; Quinn hired me to break the log-jam. There was no way I could other than to take over some of the scripts Bill had been assigned, or was currently writing. I just did the rewrites; Bill often went over my rewrites."

Which resulted in a lot of dart games. Laughs Saltzman, "We had this great set for the Officer's Club, and a dart board in the club; so while we were waiting for Bill to finish the script, we'd get into these wild dart games. We got very good at it—all of the crew. There was kind of a standing dart game almost every day." "We spent maybe fifteen, twenty minutes at the end of the day playing darts," chuckles Howard Alston's hand-picked second-season replacement, production manager Robert Huddleston. "I'd win a dollar once in a while." Joining in the games was the series' aforementioned Air Force liaison and technical adviser—former master sergeant gunner Jim Doherty. By the second season, Doherty was offering more than technical advice. He was helping develop the stories. Remembers Saltzman, "The two of us would sit around and shoot the breeze. After a while a story would suggest itself." "The technical stuff was very accurate," adds series writer Anthony Spinner. "We would sit with Jim, ask him 'If you were staging this kind of raid, what would the language be? Who would do what?' That way, it didn't sound like science-fiction."

12 O'clock High marked the beginning of Anthony Spinner's association and friendship with Quinn Martin. Martin was very impressed with Spinner's first script. "When I went to work for Quinn," says Spinner, "I had to come up with a show in a hurry because they were short on scripts. I wrote this one ["I Am the Enemy" with William Shatner] about a guy who really hates the Nazis. He was born in Germany. I wrote a couple of others. I wrote about three shows in two weeks. Then Quinn took me to lunch. He offered me associate producership. I said 'No thanks.'"

Anthony Spinner was one *12 O'clock High* talent who definitely appreciated the perilous circumstances under which real World War II airmen had fought. "We had this [B-17] Flying Fortress at Chino which could taxi," recalls Spinner. "I went on it once with the pilot. Taxiing was no great pleasure. That I can tell you. I would never have wanted to be in those planes when they were airborne. If you got hit, you couldn't have gotten out of the pilot or copilot's seat in time." *12 O'clock High* presented its audience with such situations from time to time. What with scripts by Beirne Lay, Jr., and Sy Bartlett (authors of the novel on which both the 1949 Gregory Peck feature and the 1964–67 series was based), and direction by such World War II fighter-pilots as Walter Grauman, Don Medford, and Robert Douglas, those situations were quite realistic.

Nor did series semi-regular, and future California congressman, Robert Dornan have any difficulties in portraying Colonel Gallagher's co-pilot, Captain Fowler; Dornan had flown in the Korean War. "He was the biggest ass-kisser I ever met," growls Spinner. "He was a politician then. I remember I was on the set one day; I had written a couple of shows, and he came up to me. 'Oh! You're the man that wrote the… Oh! I really love it. This is a great show. My name is Bob Dornan, and I was actually a fighter pilot,' and he's telling me all this stuff. I said, 'You know something? The old joke about how dumb the Polish actress was? She slept with the writer.' I said, 'That's what you're doing. You're sleeping with the writer. I have no power in this show.'"

Nor, as he discovered, did series star Paul Burke. "One time Paul Burke was tired, and he wanted to lie down in the back of the limousine," remembers Lois Winslow. "Bob Huddleston said, 'No, we only have seats for a certain amount of people.' Burke said, 'I'll have your job,' and he went to Quinn. Quinn said, 'It'll be your job, not Bob Huddleston's.'" "Quinn was terrific," enthuses Huddleston. "He treated me just unbelievably well. He supported me one hundred percent. Not many producers will do that. Working on that series was a great experience. Between Quinn and Bill Gordon, I had it made." Paul Burke's irritation at Huddleston was understandable. Burke was exhausted when he began *12 O'clock High*. He'd just finished a long-running role on *Naked City*. Like his good friend David Janssen, Burke sometimes drank too much. "He wasn't always on time," remembers Alston. "We'd have to pick him up at home. That meant an hour or an hour and a half drive out of Chino to get him."

There were no such problems with continuing regular Frank Overton (Major Harvey Stovall), new regular Chris Robinson (Tech Sgt. Sandy Komansky), or new semi-regular Andrew Duggan (Brigadier General Ed Britt). To one World War II veteran Duggan played his role so convincingly the veteran was sure Duggan had really served in that rank. But it wasn't just American soldiers who were affected by the series' realism. "We always had an Epilog," explains Philip Saltzman, "a little closing scene, and on one show, we did the bombing of Cologne. The night that aired, I was still at work—it was about five-thirty or six in the evening, and back East, it was about nine or so. The show had aired by then. Well, a call came in to the studio from a bar back East; I picked up the phone. It was from some German Luftwaffe pilots, or some German citizens, and they were very angry. They said, 'How dare you!

Your men have just bombed the most beautiful city in Europe. You've got them coming back smiling and laughing.'"

Despite such realism, its new series star, its dedicated new producer, and its no less talented associate producer, *12 O'clock High* never regained the ratings ground it had lost following the firing of Robert Lansing. "ABC had given the show a very bad time slot," remembers Saltzman. "It was always in trouble when I was doing it. Once it finished the second season, ABC didn't pick it up right away. We waited and waited, and while we were waiting, all the other shows were being staffed. Quinn kept saying, 'Don't worry. We're gonna get picked up.' Well, while we were waiting, Walter Grauman asked me to come over and do [Grauman's series] *Felony Squad*. I asked Quinn if he'd let me out of my contract. He didn't want to at first. Eventually, he did. Then, about two weeks after I left, the show was picked up. It was for a short run though. It was just for about sixteen or seventeen episodes."

That late pick-up hurt the show. "When the networks give you a late pickup, there's not time to get stories and stuff together," explains Howard Alston. "You can't buy stories. You can't hire writers until you know you have a pickup." Fortunately, thanks to perfectionist producer Gordon, his talented new assistant producer Don Ingalls, and the rest of the *12 O'clock* team, the series overcame such creative obstacles. That made no difference in the ratings. Still, no one expected mid-season cancellation.

"When we started the third season," says Huddleston, "we believed it was going to be a full season. We thought it was definitely set for the whole time. We had to go to color because all of the shows were being done in color, we didn't have any problems shooting in color." "We had a surprising amount of footage that we were able to colorize," adds John Elizalde. "We had some striking stuff on that series." "Whatever problems they may have had in the third season I felt very confident Quinn would solve," asserts William Self. "Quinn produced a very good series. Working with him was a great experience."

That was exactly how John Elizalde felt when it came to the music of series composer Dominic Frontiere. "Dominic always had a romantic outlook on things," muses Elizalde, "and the theme for that series was a love song really. When the squadron got into formation, then the full sweep of the theme would come in. Dominic did some beautiful things with that show. He did as many as six or seven scores out of the twenty-six or so shows that we made each year."

Along with the change to color came new series semi-regular Richard Anderson playing the role of Brigadier General Philip Doud. Anderson had the distinction of doing something no other *12 O'clock High* series regular or semi-regular had ever done. "First job I ever had was in the movie, *12 O'clock High*," reveals the actor. "I had one scene in the very beginning. I played a wounded officer, came off the airplane, hallucinating. If you blinked, you'd have missed me. When I started doing that series, I didn't have a contract with Quinn. I just came in for one segment. Then they asked me to come back and do some more. They'd written one show where Andy Duggan and I were to clash. We were anxious to get together and do it. Unfortunately, I couldn't.

I'd started work on another job. I think it was *The Fugitive*. I regret that. I would've liked to do that particular *12 O'clock High*."

Unlike *The Fugitive*, *12 O'clock High* concluded on a rather ambiguous note. In the Epilog of the series' last episode, "The Hunters and the Killers," Paul Burke's Joe Gallagher was temporarily out of commission and therefore off-screen; as always the outcome of the war was just as uncertain as it had been throughout the series. Three days before the January 13, 1967, broadcast of "The Hunters and the Killers," Quinn Martin launched his new series, *The Invaders*. Like *12 O'clock High, The Invaders* was destined for a short run. Like *12 O'clock, The Invaders* concluded rather cryptically.

Such was not the case with the other series Quinn Martin launched in between these two. That program was to keep the producer's company alive until Martin finally hit upon a string of successful series which would continue to make him an important force in television throughout the 1970s. This show was to enjoy a longer run than any other Quinn Martin series. It was to feature some of the most literate scripts ever presented on television and, one of the finest guest casts ever assembled for any long-running television series. The series would anticipate the reality based shows of the late 1980s like *America's Most Wanted;* more importantly during its lengthy run, QM Productions was to obtain most of the talents who helped make the company such a great success in the years to come. Unfortunately, this program never achieved the popularity of other QM shows like *The Fugitive*. Its connection with the real-life organization it portrayed, and the man who founded it, have had much to do with that. Because of this connection, the program came in for frequent criticism. Much of this criticism was unwarranted. Much of it was also inaccurate. The people who made *The FBI* knew that.

Chapter 5

THE FBI

The show was absolutely, superbly produced by Quinn Martin. He was the best TV producer of his time. *The FBI* was his star show. I was just delighted to be into that. The production values were always of the highest quality. He never stinted. He put his money where it would show, which was on the screen, and to that end, he was lavish with it. It was wonderfully produced. Nothing wasted, but nothing withheld at the same time. We had wonderful casts and wonderful directors. It was a great pleasure to be on such a prestigious show.

FBI *series star Efrem Zimbalist, Jr.*

Considering those factors which were against it from the outset, the same factors which lasted with the program throughout its run, it was amazing that *The FBI* (September 19, 1965–September 8, 1974, ABC) lasted a full nine seasons. It was even more amazing that the show was as entertaining as it was. FBI director J. Edgar Hoover wanted technical accuracy in the series. He got it. He wanted the program to portray the bureau in a favorable light. It did. As long as these conditions were met, as long as the *FBI* "agents and employees" had no dark secrets in their past, as long as the guest stars were not politically left-leaning, or connected in some way to the Communist Party, the FBI director had no problems with an FBI series. During the program's nine seasons, Quinn Martin and his people didn't always meet these requirements. Often that caused problems. The series started out with an even bigger problem. They didn't have a producer. Quinn Martin was not the first choice.

In 1959 Warner Bros. had released the James Stewart feature, *The FBI Story*. J. Edgar Hoover was very pleased with the film. No surprise—his friend Mervyn LeRoy had produced and directed the picture. Thus, when Warners decided to do an FBI TV series, they came to LeRoy. "But Mervyn said, 'I don't do television!'" relates *FBI* producer Philip Saltzman. "So now they were stuck. They'd sold this idea of doing *The FBI*, but they didn't have a producer. Well, Hoover was a good pal of [*Untouchables* narrator] Walter Winchell. Now supposedly Hoover said, 'What about that Quinn Martin fellow who did *The Untouchables*? I didn't ever watch it, but I understand he did a good job.'" "I think it was in January [1965] when they asked Quinn if he'd do it," recalls Muffet Martin. "We got on an airplane [for Washington], arrived in a snowstorm, met with Hoover [and Hoover's third-in-command] Deke DeLoach, and sort of made the agreement to do the show."

"The biggest problem in setting the show up was to arrive at a budget," remembers *FBI* production manager Howard Alston. "I negoti-

Title card for Quinn Martin's biggest hit, the September 19, 1965–September 8, 1974, ABC-TV series, *The FBI.*

ated a deal with [Warner's production manager] Charlie Greenlaw as to how much we'd pay for stage rental, equipment rental, costumes, offices, how many hours they'd give us on the dubbing stage, how many editing rooms we'd get, and so on. You had to cover every facet of movie-making when you were making that kind of deal." QM made a very good deal with the studio. Warners would handle all the below-the-line costs (set design, crew, transportation, post-production, etc.); QM Productions all the above-the-line (actors, producers, directors, writers, etc.). Quinn Martin's good relations with studio head Jack Warner were also a great help. "Quinn respected Jack," states Muffet Martin. "Jack respected him. Quinn used to eat in Jack's private dining room all the time." Thanks to this strong rapport, "for the first three years, we pretty much had the run of Warner's thirty stages," recalls Alston. "Often we were the only company shooting on the lot." The series also had a guaranteed sale. That was very unusual in television. Quinn Martin's production methods were too.

"Quinn did everything he could to make the show the best," declares series star Efrem Zimbalist, Jr. "He'd fly in guest stars from Europe, people like Estelle Winwood, Maurice Evans [*James Bond* actress], Karin Dor." "We got a lot of very famous people on the show," says Saltzman. "Quinn believed in good actors and top people; he upped the [fixed TV] guest-star salary from $2,500 to $5,000. He paid more than anybody, so people like Louis Jourdan ["Rope of Gold," "Wind It Up and It Betrays You," "The Minerva Tapes"] and Gene Tierney ["Conspiracy of Silence"] were willing to work on television for $5,000 top." "Quinn was the only television producer who ever topped his own price," *FBI* guest Carol Rossen says with admiration. "Every time I worked for him, he paid me more than the last time."

Complimenting the series' impressive guest casts were its motion-picture–like, big-budget productions. The show filmed episodes in national forests, on Coast Guard cutters, on cruise ships. Many episodes featured a helicopter usually flown by helicopter pilot James W. Gavin. Throughout the 1960s and 70s, Gavin, whose first Hollywood production was the 1961 Clark Gable–Marilyn Monroe feature, *The Misfits,* had a rather lucrative career. In the mid–1960s, helicopter and airplane pilots who were able to work in film were in short supply. After Quinn Martin began filming on location using real helicopters and airplanes, however, James Gavin suddenly found himself in great demand by other film and television production companies. James Gavin worked quite frequently at QM. Usually once a week. No QM series made greater use of Gavin than *The FBI.*

"I did a lot of work with Efrem in the chopper," recalls Gavin, "usually on location, though sometimes we'd fly the helicopter to the studio, and put it up on stage or on a parallel, so that we could pretend we were moving. In most cases, we'd do some filming that would actually establish Efrem's being up in the copter. Zimmy was one of the nicest people you could ever work with. He was always saying, 'Is that okay with you, Gavin?'" James Gavin's first *FBI* was the series' third aired episode, "A Mouthful of Dust." "We shot that in the Mojave Desert," remembers Gavin. "It was so hot on that show. It was like an oven. Billy Spencer developed heatstroke. We shot in all kinds of locations when we were doing that series. We shot at Lake Arrowhead, Big Bear, in the Angeles forest, on Catalina. We were all over the place."

"We were on location in every show," agrees Zimbalist. "We did a couple of shows in Oregon, a couple in Colorado, but most of the time we were in California. We certainly went the length and breadth of California [Sausalito, Pasadena, Sonora, San Diego, etc.]." By doing that, the episodes always looked as if they were taking place in the Midwest, or Northeast, or down South, which was a necessity. After all the FBI was a national organization with branches in every state of the country. During the course of the series, Zimbalist's FBI Inspector Lewis Erskine and his associates, Special Agents Jim Rhodes (Stephen Brooks—'65–'67), Thomas Colby (William Reynolds—'67–'73), and Chris Daniels (Shelly Novack—'73–'74) visited almost every state. Finding locations that would pass for those states was difficult. The job of finding these locations usually fell to assistant director Paul Wurtzel.

"I put in longer hours on that show than any other," remembers Paul Wurtzel. "When you went out on location, you'd go out real early. You traveled for an hour to the place, worked till the sun went down, spent another hour getting home." Thanks to the real FBI's involvement, Wurtzel and the other location people had little trouble obtaining permission to shoot on Army bases, or at other national or local institutions. "Just about everyone cooperated because at the time we were doing the show, the reputation of the FBI was pretty impeccable," explains series director Ralph Senensky. "People always seem to forget that it wasn't until after Hoover died, that all of the negative stuff came out." Not too surprisingly, much of this "negative stuff" was directed at the series. All kinds of charges were made against the program— among them that the show was a publicity vehicle for the FBI.

"Quinn never felt that way," replies Muffet Martin. "He wasn't making the series to make them look good. He was just doing a dramatic show." It was a show that almost always focused on the criminals targeted by the FBI. "The FBI gave us a lot of material, all of their closed cases. There were about a thousand or so cases, but the cases weren't very exciting," recalls Alston. "The writers used to mumble and grumble, 'Who cares about somebody stealing a pack of cigarettes?' That's an exaggeration, but those were the kinds of cases that were in the files." The FBI's description of how they solved the cases was about as exciting. "When they told how they captured the criminal, it was dull," continues Alston. "Because the FBI was dull. When you read the reports, they'd tell you that they went from Point A to Point B, did such and such, and filled out the forms, and that was it. If you'd tried to do those reports and cases as an interesting hour drama, you'd have really been in trouble. We had to do something to spice it up. We did that through the 'heavies.' The 'heavies' were the ones who did all the crazy things. The back-story of the 'heavy' was complete fiction. It was never in the report from the FBI."

Producer Charles Larson seemed to have anticipated the benefits of focusing on the heavy from the very beginning. In the Larson-written premiere episode, "The Monster," the series' first villain, Francis K. Jerome (Jeffrey Hunter), strangled women who had long hair. With their own hair! According to Hoover biographer Curt Gentry's *The Secret Life of J. Edgar Hoover*, this premiere episode so infuriated the director he was ready to cancel the series. Like Francis K. Jerome, Hoover had been reared in an effeminate environment. "I don't even remember that coming up," states Muffet Martin. "They couldn't have canceled the show if they wanted to; the sponsors would have objected."

Adds Ralph Senensky, "The people who said that stuff obviously never talked to the people who did the show. I mean people always thought that each show was based on an FBI case. That was bullshit! We were just remaking those old Warner pictures. At least that's how I felt." The series certainly had the film noir look of the Warner pictures—thanks to the stylish photography of William W. Spencer. "Billy Spencer!" raves *FBI* guest star Lynda Day George. "That guy was an artist! He was just brilliant. I loved what he used to do. His lighting was so wonderful. He was so fast, so bright. He knew what he wanted all the time, how he wanted to set it up, how it would be dramatically correct." "He was a painter," adds Senensky. "He painted with light. With light and shadow. When I did that episode, 'The Assassin,' there was a scene with Rhys Williams, when you first learned that Rhys was the villain in the show. The way Billy lit that, that was Billy Spencer at his best!" William Spencer loved the film noir look. The offbeat villains who populated *The FBI* allowed him a perfect opportunity to create film noir pieces. Spencer loved shooting the scenes with the villains. Everybody on the series loved those scenes. "The villains were the ones who made the show go," declares Saltzman. "Only by heightening the villain could we make the show more fascinating to the audience. You had these wonderful villains, then you had these strait-laced, square-jawed, FBI people going after them. The more difficult that became, the more interesting the show became."

Not that the show wasn't interesting in its technical detail. Thanks to the presence of its technical advisers—FBI Inspector Ed Kemper for the first two years,

Lynda Day George (as nurse Carol Grant) examines the wound of her abductor Henry Silva (as "Top Ten Fugitive Richard Macklin") in the November 26, 1967, third-season ABC-TV *FBI* episode, "Line of Fire."

special agents Dick Douce and Dick Wolf for the remainder—that detail was always accurate. The FBI agents were very impressed with QM Productions' duplication of the FBI headquarters in Washington, D.C.; wanting the show's FBI headquarters to be true to life, J. Edgar Hoover had allowed the company to take photographs and make sketches of the bureau's real offices, hallways, and labs while they'd been in Washington. "When the FBI guys came to the set, they thought they were back in Washington, D.C.," laughs assistant director Paul Wurtzel. "They thought it was the real thing. We had to quit using those FBI sets though. They were just too difficult to light." That was just fine with William Spencer. Spencer hated shooting scenes in the FBI labs and headquarters. He found these sets' "sterile, antiseptic, and bland." "Well, yeah," chuckles Wurtzel. "That's the FBI." J. Edgar Hoover's detractors found something rather sinister in the fact that the director kept hidden from the public the presence of real FBI agents on the *FBI* set. "He did that because the FBI guys were government employees," laughs Wurtzel. "Their salaries were paid by the taxpayers. Hoover didn't want the public knowing these guys were doing a TV series instead of working on a case."

Everyone who worked on the series got along well with the FBI agents, including the series' last producer, Anthony Spinner. Spinner was certainly no fan of the real FBI. For him, doing the series was not "a creatively fun experience." Despite that, Spinner found FBI agents Douce and Wolf "very sweet." Series director Ralph Senensky liked the agents as well. Senensky was friends with both Ed Kemper and Dick Douce. To this day Paul Wurtzel and William W. Spencer remain friends with Dick Wolf. Had the real-life agents interfered with the show to the degree critics have so often claimed, such friendships seem rather unlikely.

"Kemper and Douce were on the set to show actors playing FBI agents how to behave," explains Efrem Zimbalist, Jr., "how to hold a gun, things like that." "They were there as consultants when you needed them," elaborates Senensky. "Their only involvement concerned the procedures of the FBI. When we did stuff in the FBI lab, that's where Dick or Ed could help with procedure. They helped us get props and equipment." "They were not there when the criminal side of the show was being shot," continues Zimbalist. "Which was seventy-five percent of the show," notes Senensky. "When the scripts came to them, they might, out of their own experience, make some suggestions to forestall clichés, but they weren't there to dictate the dramatic values. They weren't equipped to do that. They didn't even have to be on the set. All they had to do was go to the dailies. If they didn't like something they saw in the dailies, they'd tell us, 'That's not acceptable.'" "Whenever the FBI tech advisors were watching the dailies," explains assistant editor Martin Fox, "one of us would sit with them. We'd take notes, writing down when they liked a shot, and when they didn't." "There'd always be somebody in on the very last cut of the show to make sure the show was correct," adds supervising editor Richard Brockway, "but they were pretty cut and dried by the time we got them, they'd been through so many people."

Despite the bureau's involvement, Quinn Martin usually found a way to get around their interference and make the stories the way he wanted. The series' opening credits and theme practically guaranteed that. The FBI was very happy with the Bronislau Kaper theme. "I knew Bronnie would be perfect for the show," states postproduction supervisor John Elizalde. "Bronnie was a wonderful composer, a wonderful pianist. He'd written some things I admired. He'd composed for a lot of movies [*Green Dolphin Street, The Swan, Lili*], and his style always had sweep and grandeur. His theme for the series said power and integrity." That was exactly what Quinn Martin wanted. "When I came in to do the announcements for the show for the first time," remembers series announcer Henry "Hank" Simms, "I identified the show as 'The FBI.' 'No, No, No.' Quinn and Arthur Fellows told me. 'Don't do it that way! We want you to say it slower, draw it out, say it this way, "The F B I!"'" So that's what I did."

The FBI marked the beginning of Hank Simms' long-time position as the QM series announcer. Simms enjoyed doing *The FBI*. "I thought it was a superbly produced show," says the announcer. "I think all of Quinn's shows were superbly produced." "It was one of Quinn's best shows," adds guest Peter Mark Richman. "It wasn't repetitious, like *The Fugitive*. It was consistently good, top of the line in every way; the stories were interesting. Sure, it showed the FBI in a good light; sure, there was a little flag-waving here and there. I don't think that was a bad thing." The audience seemed to agree. Throughout the majority of its run, *The FBI* enjoyed strong ratings, especially among those viewers with a higher education. "We appealed to a more educated audience," explains Philip Saltzman. "We tried to do a real classy show, and real drama." "It was the same kind of theatrical drama that you saw in *The Untouchables*," elaborates guest Richard Anderson. "They got your attention right away with sharp music, good cuts, good openings and all of that." "We were all very proud of the show," states Howard Alston. "Quinn was very proud of the show. He never understood why the show never won any awards." Ralph Senensky never understood why the show didn't play in syndication. "It should have," believes Senensky. "I mean the name values alone. That series was a true anthology. The guest stars in that series were always the meat of the show."

Ralph Senensky enjoyed working on *The FBI*, as did composer Duane Tatro. "I could be experimental on that show," reveals Tatro. "I could be much more radical on that series than on other shows. The FBI never worried about the music. I did all kinds of strange, inventive music. One time I did a show called 'Tower of Terror.' I used some unusual instruments on that one. I used coat hangers." "Tower of Terror" aired in the series' last season. By that time, the FBI was comfortable with the way QM made the show. During the first season, very few people on the series were comfortable. It took some time to learn the ground rules when it came to portraying the bureau. Series producer Charles Larson and FBI Inspector Ed Kemper had no idea of what they could and could not do that first season. J. Edgar Hoover had already let pass two infractions in the portrayal of FBI agents. One was Quinn Martin's decision that Efrem Zimbalist, Jr., wear no hat (all FBI agents wore hats). The other was Zimbalist's decision to leave his jacket unbuttoned when he was carrying his gun. (Hoover wanted the jackets buttoned all the time.) But when Zimbalist buttoned his while carrying his gun, "it looked like I'd had a colostomy or something," laughs the star.

Thus, the series' first year had the agents smoking ("No!" said Hoover), drinking (No again!), putting their feet up on the desk (Not ever!), and romancing women (No way!). "The FBI was something else," chuckles series director Michael Caffey. "They were not your normal people. They were a little bit strange. They were in all their little suits. No one had a belly." And that's how they were portrayed on the series. Ed Kemper and Dick Douce were certainly not that way. Both men drank. Douce was something of a wine connoisseur. Kemper liked having a drink with the prop man in the prop man's trailer. There didn't seem to be one person who did the series who didn't enjoy working with the real agents, including die-hard liberal Jonathan Goldsmith. Goldsmith had the honor of appearing in the opening sequence of the series' premiere episode, "The Monster." He had some qualms over the agents' initial reception towards him. "I feared I'd be persona non grata," relates Goldsmith. "I was very much against the Vietnam War, so I had led some marches. But the agents were very happy to answer my questions. I've always gravitated towards technical advisers. I've always enjoyed cops. I find the work they do very interesting and intriguing." "The real agents were very easy to work with," agrees guest star Peter Mark Richman. "They were nice fellas. They took a lot of kidding."

Often from series director William Hale. "One time," laughs Hale, "I wore this Eugene McCarthy button to the set. That created a big stir. McCarthy wanted to do away with half of the FBI agents. Another time, the crew took this guy from skid row, this really dirty-looking bum, and put him behind 'Hoover's' desk. The FBI guys were just climbing the walls." Which wasn't surprising, for as the series continued, the FBI men seemed to grow more and more perfect and less and less human. For example, in episode #7, "How to Murder an Iron Horse," producer Charles Larson and writer Don Brinkley learned that "FBI agents do not get sick!" Sometime later Anthony Spinner found out "FBI agents do not drink coffee when on duty!" When Philip Saltzman did the fifth season's "Diamond Millstone," he discovered that "FBI agents do not kill women in shoot-outs!" which was a reasonable complaint, as was the bureau's objection to shows where FBI witnesses were threatened. "That was a good story area," feels Saltzman, "but Hoover didn't want to dramatize that. Witnesses were a major area of concern for the bureau." During the first season, however, Charles Larson had done such a show, "All the Streets Are Silent," guest-starring future *Dan August* star Burt Reynolds. Reynolds played a member of the Mafia.

According to the Hoover detractors, because of Hoover's connections to the Mafia, *The FBI* never did Mafia stories. "All the Streets Are Silent" proved them wrong, as did "The Gold Card," "Line of Fire," "Act of Violence" (again with Reynolds), "The Messenger," and "The Predators." All of those episodes aired in the series' third season. At

Jeffrey Hunter (as escaped federal prisoner Francis K. Jerome) and QM favorite Dina Merrill (as socialite Jean Davis) in the September 19, 1965, ABC-TV *FBI* premiere, "The Monster."

least one Mafia tale aired each season. *FBI* producer Anthony Spinner explains how he managed to do them. "We had this scene with Zimbalist and Phil Abbott, who was Zimbalist's boss [Assistant to the Director Arthur Ward], and behind Phil Abbott, there's this huge portrait of Hoover," says Spinner. "So Abbot and Zimbalist are talking about the case, and at one point Abbott says, 'Why don't I call the director?' and Zimbalist says, 'Well, I guess we're at that point where we need help.' So they call the director, and, guess what? Hoover's advice—off screen—solves the case! Well, the show aired on Sundays, and the first time I did this, I came in to work on Monday; the two FBI agents came up to me. They said, 'Oh. We wanted you to know that the director thought last night's episode was the finest episode ever made by *The FBI*.' I thought, Oh, I got this guy's number. Whenever you're in trouble, make him God. He's Nero. So, whenever we had trouble, we always had a little line—'Ah, the director's solved this,' or 'The director did that.' That way, Hoover stayed off my back."

Mixed in with the Mafia stories were tales of sexual deviancy—"Confessions of a Madman"—directed by Philip Abbott; religious cults—"The Forests of the Night"; student radicals—like Geoffrey Deuel, Wayne Maunder, and Diana Ewing in "Time Bomb"; extortionists—such as heart-attack prone Andrew Prine in "The

From the left: William Reynolds (as Special Agent Tom Colby), Philip Abbott (as Assistant to the Director Arthur Ward) and Efrem Zimbalist, Jr. (as Inspector Lewis Erskine), in a publicity shot for the September 19, 1965–September 8, 1974, ABC-TV series, *The FBI.*

Mechanized Accomplice"; bank robbers—including Pete Deuel in 1930s dress, and a Halloween mask in "Slow March Up a Steep Hill"; and murderers of all types and sexes—e.g. Wayne Rogers, Edward Asner, and Judee Morton in "The Tormentors." Despite one source's claim that it was not until the latter years that the show began doing Cold War shows, there was a good sampling of such stories throughout the series' run. Among the many first-year offerings were "The Problem of the Honorable Wife," "The Sacrifice" (Ed Begley as the main character) and "The Spy Master." The FBI also battled Neo-Nazis. Writer Barry Oringer's fourth-year contribution, "The Butcher," had Neo-Nazi Ralph Bellamy bringing Nazi war criminal Charles Korvin to the United States to spearhead a Nazi movement in the States. Korvin has avoided capture through the years by posing as a Jew. During his first few years in exile, he'd made an intensive study of Jewish customs and culture. Later in the story he takes refuge in a synagogue, run by Harold Gould, a survivor of Auschwitz. "I was permitted to stretch out on that occasion," recalls Oringer. "I had the opportunity to create this rabbi-type character. That was very unusual, very uncommon in television. You didn't get to do a lot of interesting Jewish characters on television." Nor was it common to see shows where Nazis had romances—as Korvin does with Anne Helm, who played Bellamy's pro–Nazi daughter—much less hide out in synagogues. That was rather distasteful, rather controversial. "The FBI had no problem with controversial shows," reveals Muffet Martin. "If those were done the right way, and the FBI was presented as the good guys, they had no objection at all."

The bureau had no objection to first season regular Lynn Loring either. Quinn Martin was excited about Loring's role as Inspector Erskine's college-aged daughter, Barbara. The daughter gave Erskine a home life, made him more interesting. Barbara Erskine's romance with the Inspector's partner Jim Rhodes added further drama. The Inspector was opposed to the couple's impending marriage. He worried that Barbara might lose Rhodes in an FBI shoot-out. The Inspector had lost his own wife that way. However, when Quinn discussed the idea with Efrem Zimbalist, Jr., the actor was none too excited. "I hated the whole idea," states Zimbalist, "partly from sheer vanity. At my screen age, I was not ready for a daughter. I had one in real life, but my screen persona was not ready for one. My other objection was the plot-line was so boring. It was so much like soap-opera. So I told Quinn how I felt. He said, 'Listen. If you don't like the idea, she's out! Period.' I said, 'Wait a minute. No no no. You're the producer. I'm just an actor. I could be wrong. Let's try it and see what happens.' So we did. Then one day, the phone rang on the set. It was Quinn. He said, 'You were right. She's no longer on the show.' It wasn't that I had anything against Lynn Loring. I bore her no ill will. I hope she bears me no ill will. She just didn't fit into that show." Nothing made that plainer than the series' fourth episode "Slow March Up a Steep Hill." Starting out with Barbara Erskine and Jim Rhodes just days away from their upcoming marriage, "Slow March" then quickly followed with a sequence in which a married FBI agent is killed in the line of duty. A short time later Erskine and Rhodes visit his grieving widow. At the end of the story, Barbara Erskine and Jim Rhodes decide to postpone their wedding.

Lewis Erskine's on-again, off-again romance with FBI technical assistant Joanna Laurens (Lee Meriwether) was examined in the same episode. Thanks to Lee Meriwether's light-hearted characterization, this subplot was much more interesting, much more believable. "That was a dream come true," enthuses Meriwether. "When I was twelve years old, I'd written to J. Edgar Hoover. I wanted to be an FBI agent. He sent back this lovely little letter telling me that while a woman could not apply for that position, there were many many jobs available to women in the Bureau, particularly in the fingerprint department." So I was real happy when I got to play an FBI technician on the show. I was, 'Yay. I got to work for the FBI.'"

Efrem Zimbalist, Jr., was no less enthusiastic about the series. A long-time admirer of the FBI, Zimbalist was excited about doing the show. Never having worked with Quinn Martin however, he still had reservations about doing the show. One phone call to *Fugitive* star David Janssen eliminated those. "Take the part!" Janssen urged Zimbalist. "You're crazy if you don't!" Since Zimbalist would be playing an FBI agent, he, and everybody else who played an FBI character, was subjected to a background search. Hoover didn't want anyone with any kind of record playing an FBI employee. According to the series' detractors, these background searches were very probing. This particular charge may not have been all that accurate. At least when it came to series regular Shelly Novack. Novack was doing drugs at the time he was starring on Quinn Martin's *Most Wanted*. From all accounts, he'd been doing drugs for years. "Which sort of tells you that the FBI's investigations weren't as thorough as they claimed," says William W. Spencer.

Never having done drugs, or committed any kind of legal infraction, Efrem Zimbalist, Jr., had no objections to his background search. Once he was cleared, the actor then traveled to FBI headquarters in Washington, D.C., for a "familiarization course with the bureau. It lasted a week," remembers Zimbalist. "I met all the heads of the divisions, went out to the [FBI] Academy at Quantico, then the last day I interviewed with J. Edgar Hoover. That lasted two hours, four minutes, as I recall. I was astounded by Hoover. He never stopped talking; talked about every subject on earth—Hollywood, society, the Hope Diamond, Shirley Temple, Truman, and Khruschev—any number of things. He just sort of flitted around with great facility. He was an athlete at conversation, so much so I had very little time to throw in the amenities—little 'Oh yesses,' whatever they were. He talked like a machine gun. He was fascinating, absolutely fascinating. I admired his whole career. He had his faults like anyone else, but as an American, I think he was monumental."

Thanks to his admiration of both Hoover and the FBI, Efrem Zimbalist, Jr., played his part of Inspector Lewis Erskine with much enthusiasm. Making the character interesting was none too easy. "The part was very challenging because there were strict limitations," explains Zimbalist. "It was like a military code. You could not smoke, drink, put your feet up on the desk, a lot of things like that, so to play this part, to make it interesting and appealing within these limitations was a challenge that I think we all enjoyed. I think that the success of the show was that all of us were able to meet that challenge." Whoever was playing the FBI agent in Joan Van

Ark's first series appearance, "The Maze," really had a challenge. "I had this scene with the FBI guy," remembers Van Ark. "We'd rehearsed the scene on the set, then I went to go get dressed while they were lighting the scene. So I go to my dressing room. I get completely naked, pretty much. Suddenly the door flies open. Standing right outside the door is the guy I've just rehearsed with. I bend over to cover myself, and there's a full-length mirror right behind me so he stands there transfixed. The more I bent over, the worse it got. I mean with a full-length mirror behind me, what he didn't see in front, he definitely got a rear view. So it was truly ... I couldn't stop giggling— once he got over the shock, and I got over the shock. Then we had to go out there, and do the scene. Talk about an actress! I had to act really more than they were paying me. I'll never ever forget that. Only my gynecologist knows more than that actor does."

In Van Ark's next *FBI*, "The Condemned," she played a manipulative crook who comes between none too bright bank-robber Tim McIntire and his brainy partner, Martin Sheen. McIntire and Sheen's performances in "The Condemned" received glowing reviews in *Variety*. Their performances overshadowed those of series star Efrem Zimbalist, Jr., and the other actors who were playing FBI agents in "The Condemned." Some of those actors might have been upset by that. Not Efrem Zimbalist. "The crime side was more interesting than the crime detection side," says the actor. "In the very first frames we always told who did it. That enabled Quinn to show the full side of the criminals. We were able to go into the motives and all of that in very great detail. That made it very easy for me. I only worked four days out of seven on that show. I was literally in only half of the show. I had some rather weird experiences when I was doing that show. I remember one day, we were shooting in Long Beach. I drove down there, arrived at the location, parked the car, started to get out ... I couldn't move. My back just went out. I had to be helped out of the car, and up on top of a roof where we were shooting a fight sequence that day. The stunt doubles did the master fight, then the director asked me if I could do some of the close-ups. I said, 'Well, Let's try it.' So they pulled me in there. The minute the cameras rolled, I felt absolutely nothing. I went through all of the motions perfectly. But the minute the director said, 'Cut,' this same thing came back on again. It was that way all day. It was absolutely weird. As long as the cameras were rolling, I felt nothing. But the minute they cut, I couldn't move. The next day, I was fine."

Possessing this sort of ability to act when needed was to guest Richard Anderson the sign of "a pure professional. Efrem did a crack-up job in that part," believes Anderson. "That show was on, what? Nine years? Well, a lot of that had to do with Efrem. Efrem is a great guy. He's one of the great, great guys in our business. He had a great presence in front of the camera." Quinn Martin definitely agreed. Nothing made that more obvious than the discussion he had with Zimbalist at the end of the fifth season. "My contract was for five years," explains Zimbalist, "and after five years, I wanted to get out. I'd been playing that one note long enough. Well, Quinn wanted me to sign for another five years. He said, 'Listen, this is everything in the world to me—this show. It's everything that I hope. All my future plans, everything, depend on just a few more years of this. Two or three years is all that I need—but that's what I'm asking you to give me.' I said, 'Well, okay, all right, you got it. But I hope it doesn't go five more years.' He said, 'Oh, it'll never go five years.' Well, it went four. But it made his fortune. It allowed him to build that magnificent house in Rancho Santa Fe, where he moved with his wife, Muffet. It made everything that he could ever want. The rest of the things that he did, he was able to do them the way that he wanted."

Zimbalist was also open to signing autographs, and appearing at charity benefits, while he was doing the series. Ditto filming promotions for the bureau, and asking *The FBI*'s audience to contact the bureau if they had any information concerning any current FBI Top Ten Fugitives. One such request led to the capture of Martin Luther King assassin James Earl Ray. The actor was just as willing to promote the series' regular sponsor—the Ford Motor Company. Every spring, Zimbalist flew to Washington, D.C., to film the closing credit shots for the upcoming season. The closing credits were great publicity for Ford. They always featured Zimbalist driving past such D.C. landmarks as the Capitol in the company's newest model. "It was just a shell of a car," remembers Zimbalist, "with an engine and a body of some kind, but no dash. I always got in it very gingerly because if you slammed the doors, the whole thing would fall apart. I never felt too safe driving it."

Nonetheless, Zimbalist continued to film the closing credits season after season. Had it not been for Ford, *The FBI* would have been canceled. "The first year we were going down the tubes," reveals John Elizalde. "We had a very bad time slot; the show was not well received." "We didn't have a big enough budget," adds Alston. "It couldn't be done for the amount of money ABC was willing to pay. It was just too big a show. We had too much night shooting, too much of everything. It was just a bigger show than anybody else had ever done." "We wouldn't have lasted past the first year if it hadn't been for Ford," declares Elizalde. "Ford was looking for a way to dispel the Tin Lizzie heritage that they had. They wanted something that was rock solid institutionally. When they saw the show, they said they'd pick it up for six years." "The first year we had two sponsors—Alcoa and Ford," adds Muffet Martin. "Alcoa wanted to sponsor the series again in the second year; Ford had the option of taking it all. They took it all."

"Ford really helped us out," Ralph Senensky says in praise of the company. "Their cars all had personalities. They added to the characters." "Quinn had this deal with Ford that they would give us X how many cars as long as we used only Ford cars," remembers Anthony Spinner. "If you ever watched the show when I was doing it, you'd think Ford was the only make in the world. Everybody drove Fords, including the bad guys. I thought that was pretty strange advertising, but, what the hell. As long as there's a Ford in the shot, I guess there's no such thing as bad publicity." Like the real FBI, Ford had its demands when it came to the series' presentation of their product. "You couldn't use any of the stock footage from the previous season when you were doing your next season," reveals editor Richard Brockway. "The past year's footage showed the wrong kind of vehicle." Fords didn't have faulty brakes.

Ralph Senensky learned that when he did "Ordeal." No character was to be killed in a Ford; the company didn't want the cars excessively damaged; they didn't want to see their cars rolling over. Though Ford had a wide variety of automobiles which came in handy for the equally wide variety of stories, sometimes it was necessary to use vehicles produced by other automobile companies. Case in point, Senensky's, "The Plunderers." "It started with an armored car robbery, but Ford didn't produce an armored car," laughs Senensky. "Tom De Palo [Ford's representative at the series' pre-production meetings] said, 'Can't you do it with a pickup truck?' We said 'No.' Eventually they let us use an armored car."

As much of *The FBI* was filmed on location, Ford never had a problem if the company filmed Chryslers and other auto-makers' vehicles while shooting an episode. With one exception. "Under no circumstances were we ever allowed to show a Volkswagen," says William Spencer. "Volkswagen was really hot then. They didn't want to give them any publicity." Ford had considerable clout, as was made clear on one occasion. "One time," recalls Paul Wurtzel, "they were planning this show about this Japanese prison guard in WWII. I think his nickname was 'The Meatball.' He was very cruel to the prisoners. After the war, he somehow wound up in this country as a citizen. Well, one of the prisoners who'd been in this prison camp in Japan spotted this guy walking down a street in San Francisco." The former prisoner told the authorities; the ex–prison guard was arrested and convicted of war crimes. "When they started interviewing Japanese actors for the part of the war criminal and the Japanese lawyer who defended him, one of the actors they interviewed was a lawyer," continues Wurtzel. "He told them, 'Don't make this picture.' If we did, he said, we'd be sued. So, Quinn told Hoover the problem. Hoover says, 'The hell with him. Go ahead and make it.' Well, when the lawyer heard that, he told us, 'If you release this, I will have all the Japanese-Americans in America boycott Ford cars.' That upset Ford. 'Don't air the show,' the company told QM. They didn't."

"There were always special interest groups who were getting upset," remembers Muffet Martin. "There were always people threatening to sue. When they did the civil rights show [the 1975 four-hour movie special, *Attack on Terror: The FBI Versus the Ku Klux Klan*], the sheriff who'd been convicted sued. He claimed the show had kept him from getting a job. The show was taken straight from the court case. They faced a lot of small suits over the years. They were always fighting to make what they wanted to make."

Often the fights were with the FBI. "The FBI was always butting in," continues Muffet Martin. "They butt in a lot. I think they were humored quite a bit. Quinn and the others usually got their way." Perhaps no one was better at humoring the FBI than the series' first producer, Charles Larson. "Charlie had a really difficult job," explains Howard Alston. "The first year he had to listen to all the FBI's input, to all of the people who felt they knew more about how to do the show than he did. Charlie never did anything he didn't want to do. He listened to people, then he did what he felt was right, but he did it in a way that made them feel good." "He was a good diplomat," agrees series writer Don Brinkley. "He handled things very well. He had a lot to do with the show's success. I don't think the show would have made it without him. He was able to keep the FBI at bay, and keep them happy. He kept the writers happy too."

Not Anthony Spinner. "Tony Spinner didn't like writing for the show," says Brinkley. "He didn't like writing for any show. He just was a sourpuss." Spinner couldn't be blamed. "They controlled everything," groans Spinner. "They had to approve every story, every script. You had to wait three weeks for somebody to get back to you; and when they did, they'd get back to you with such nonsense: 'Oh, it says in the story that he drove from Dover, Delaware, to Washington, D.C., in two hours, and, actually, in real time, it would be, if he was following the speed limit, two hours and eighteen minutes.' 'Well,' I used to say to Dick Douce. 'This guy's a bank robber. I don't think he was worried about the speed limit.'"

The FBI was very concerned about the scripts; they were just as concerned about the people who worked for the series, and with reason. Years ago there'd been an officially approved radio series, *This Is Your FBI*. Don Brinkley had written for the program. "Later it turned out that the producer of the show Jerry D. Lewis was married to a bomb-throwing Communist," chuckles Brinkley. "So they were pretty sensitive about anyone who did the TV series." "It was the first time the FBI had ever given anyone permission to do a TV show about them, so everybody was really nervous," elaborates series director Billy Graham. "They did a background check on me. I'd had them before." There were no problems with Billy Graham. Graham had served in the Navy during World War II. In the Intelligence Division. He'd had a hand in breaking the Japanese code. Series announcer Hank Simms' background was examined too. Ditto Howard Alston. Alston had applied for gun permits in the past. Naturally, his fingerprints were on file. The FBI had no objections to Howard Alston. They did, however, to guest star Carol Rossen. Years ago, the actress's father, screen director Robert Rossen, had been questioned before the House Un-American Activities Committee. "So because I was his daughter, I was on their damn list," snaps Rossen. "I never would have known that had it not been for Quinn. Quinn got me cleared so I could work on *The FBI*. Now that's quite extraordinary; he didn't have to do that. But he just wouldn't stand for it. That's the kind of person Quinn Martin was."

Peter Mark Richman's background check, by contrast, was rather amusing. "They came to me and said, 'We need a few strands of your hair,'" remembers Richman. "I said, 'What? What do you mean?' They said, 'We have to analyze your hair. All the people doing the show have to be investigated.' I said, 'You're kidding me.' They weren't. They took my hair, sent it to Washington, and analyzed it to see if I was one of their undesirables. And here I am shooting the show. They're gonna re-cut the picture if I was?" Adds series producer Anthony Spinner, "I'd have to tell [casting director] Dodie McLean, 'I want John Vernon or Leslie Nielsen. Then she'd have to call Washington or one of the agents and see if that person was acceptable. Whatever the FBI had in the computer, if it was something they didn't want, we didn't get the actor." One time however, for the ninth-season episode, "The Confession,"

Spinner got the performer he wanted: singer-actress Nancy Wilson. To do that, he had to threaten the FBI with "goin' public." As it turned out, the damaging information the FBI had on Nancy Wilson was completely untrue.

Far more absurd was the request the bureau made when the series first started. "The first year the bureau wanted approval of everybody, including the day players [one-day guests]," recalls Ralph Senensky. "Johnny Conwell said, 'That's just not possible.' Because usually with the day players, you'd be casting the roles at the last minute. So we compromised. We'd select the guests, then submit the names to Ed Kemper or Dick Douce. You had to get approval for the main guest stars. The supporting actors and day players did the show, then after they did the show the entire cast list went back to the FBI. Johnny always kept a file. If some of the supporting guests or day players did not pass muster, they were not called back for another *FBI*." Of course those who met the bureau's approval were.

FBI series fan Bette Davis never had the chance to do the series. She wanted to; she asked casting director John Conwell to keep an eye out for a show in which he could use her. "All of a sudden came this script in the first year with this wonderful cameo which was perfect for Bette," relates Senensky. "Johnny was so excited, he sent her the script and an offer, then he realized he hadn't checked her out with the bureau. He submitted her name. It came back rejected. So now Johnny was sweating blood. He's got this firm offer out, but he's not gonna be able to use Bette. Well fortunately she was not available, so that saved him. Now the next year I was handed this show ["The Courier"—one of the series' few shows in which there was a female villain] and the character was perfect for Bette. So Johnny and I got together with Ed Kemper. We said, 'Look, we want Bette Davis in this show. This is a wonderful role for her. This is the first lady of the American screen.' Ed agreed. He turned her name in. They said, 'No.' They never said why. Just 'No.'" According to an anonymous source, Davis was rejected because years earlier she'd been suspected of killing her husband. "There was a lot of investigation about it at the time," says the source. "Some of the people who'd worked at Warner Bros. at that time were the ones who told me. There was some other stuff too." The role went to Ruth Roman.

Adding to the difficulties created by the bureau's investigation of the guest casts, directors, writers, and so forth were the problems the producers and writers had in devising stories that made it possible for the FBI to enter a case. "There were only so many cases where the FBI had jurisdiction," points out assistant director David Whorf. "You were hamstrung by the FBI's ability to only enter certain cases. So you wound up doing variations on the same story. I started work on that series in 1969. That was about the time the Patty Hearst Symbionese Liberation Army stuff was going on. So you found yourself doing the Patty Hearst story over and over. You'd be 'Oh okay, this is Patty Hearst #4 we're doing.' There must have been more variations on that story than any other story that year." The show also did remakes of previous FBI shows, as well as some very poor stories. "'Deathwind' was the worst one I did," insists Senensky. "The script was just dumb. There was all this stuff about the 'tsunami.' We started calling it the salami."

Series regular Philip Abbott's directorial debut—the fifth season's "The Quest"—was none too remarkable for that matter. The conclusion in a fun-house hall of mirrors was worth waiting for though. "That show was a nightmare," recalls William Spencer. "At one point we had to cut in this one mirror an opening of about four by four inches, making it just about eye-height. We had to stick the lens through that opening in the mirror and shoot. We had other mirrors that were all at different angles. That was a very very difficult sequence. It was so hard to keep the camera and the people out of the scene because you picked up everything. We had a lot of problems with that. That was very time consuming. It was tough for Phil Abbott because he'd never had any directorial experience. So he relied on me, the a.d., and the script supervisor to get us through that show." The fourth season's "The Nightmare" was nothing special either. At least when it came to the characters portrayed by William Windom, Bruce Dern, and Lane Bradbury. None of those three criminal characters was as memorable as the one played by Lee Meriwether. "I did the whole show in an iron lung," reveals Meriwether. "[*Mission: Impossible* creator-producer] Bruce Geller saw that show. As a direct result of that show, he hired me for *Mission: Impossible*. That particular *FBI* was a challenge. I had to learn to breathe and to talk when I exhaled because the machine was supposedly breathing for me. Then to have Billy Windom and Efrem tickling me through the armholes! That made concentration very difficult."

One week after "Nightmare," *The FBI* presented one of the series' few comedies, "Breakthrough." "I loved that show," exclaims guest star Peter Mark Richman. "I played this ex-con who'd just been released from prison and rented this house from Dorothy Provine. We sort of fall in love, and Dorothy's character is kind of clumsy. There's a scene where she's changing this light-bulb and cracks it on my head. That was one of the best shows I've ever done." "Getting comedy past Quinn in that show was tough," remembers "Breakthrough" director Robert Day. "The FBI was on his back all the time."

Robert Day had started his career at QM in late 1967. Impressed with Day's direction in the popular British espionage series, *The Avengers*, Martin had brought the director over to the United States to direct one episode of *The FBI*—"The Daughter." "When I went back to England," says Day, "nothing was happening. Then I got this telegram from Quinn, offering me a contract. I came back to this country. I've never left." Having directed a few Peter Sellers comedies, and even more *Tarzan* features, Robert Day was amply qualified to handle the ambitious, and generally action-filled productions so common to *The FBI*. "We did more exteriors in that series than any other series," reveals William W. Spencer. "There was a tremendous amount of work. The hours were horrific. We put in sixty to eighty hours a week. There was so much night work, so many locations. The toughest one we ever did [the eighth season's "Canyon of No Return"] was up in Grant's Pass, Oregon, on the Rogue River. It was difficult going through the rapids. Some of the camera crew got dumped. One guy almost drowned. We were fairly near the shore so he was able to grab a tree root that was underwater and pull himself up on the bank."

Walter Grauman was one *FBI* series director who was able to adapt to such disastrous situations very quickly, as Grauman proved during the filming of the last season's "Selkirk's War." "We had this single-engine, high-wing plane, and two of the heavies were standing eight to ten feet in front of the camera while the propeller was idling," remembers Spencer. "The pilot of the plane was sitting in the doorway of the plane, and while the two actors were talking, Wally yelled to the pilot to speed up the idling of the engine. The pilot leaned in there, reached over toward the panel, and somehow he pumped it wide open. The plane started moving forward, the pilot fell out, and we all ran because the plane was coming straight at the camera. The propeller chewed up one of the arc lights, hit the camera, knocked that on the ground. The plane spun around. Then somebody ran in and shut it off. About thirty minutes later, Wally had all of us back shooting."

The 20th Century–Fox ranch was the location on this particular occasion. In the first season's hijack story, "Flight to Harbin," the location was Los Angeles International Airport. Though TWA was happy to give QM a plane, QM had to create a fictitious airline—TWA didn't want one of their planes being hijacked. "We made it TLA," laughs Paul Wurtzel. "We glued this fake insignia over the TWA plane. It took us some time to do that. Then TWA came and took the plane. They needed an airplane for their passengers because theirs wouldn't fly. They took ours. They didn't care about the fake sign. It took us hours to find a replacement. We finally found something that was broken down. By the time we did, the sun had come up."

Overtime expenses almost occurred in the William Hale directed, fourth-season opener, "Wind It Up and It Betrays You," thanks to a bad casting move of Hale's. "There was this guy," chuckles Hale, "whose name was Larry; he was an aspiring actor and a very good car painter. I said, 'Larry I've got a small part for you on *FBI* if you'll paint my car.' He said, 'Oh God. Yeah. Sure.' It was a very small part, a Washington cop, and when we did the scene on a Friday night it was getting very close to midnight. Now when midnight hits, everybody starts taking home the big checks, so I had to get this shot done before midnight. Well, we're shooting on the Warner back-lot, the rain machines are going, Larry comes out, he looks down at the body in the gutter, then says, in this Southern drawl, 'What's wrong with him?' I said, 'Larry, lose the drawl. You're playing a Washington cop.' We did it again; he did the same thing. We wound up doing about six takes; he never got it. Well, come Monday morning, the shit hit the fan. The FBI guy wanted to know who cast this person, how come they weren't in on the casting because the guy was awful. So, I'm sitting there in the office, not saying anything; I look out the window, here's my car pulling in the driveway—freshly painted—with Larry at the wheel. That's the closest I've ever come to a showdown with the FBI."

QM almost had a showdown with the Screen Extras Guild when the company made *The FBI* episode "How to Murder an Iron Horse." To save the train's passengers from extortionist-bomber David Macklin, the FBI arranges other transportation, replacing the passengers with cardboard cut-outs. The cut-outs were designed by art director Dick Haman. "We got in a lot of trouble with the Guild for using the cut-outs," laughs Wurtzel. "They wanted us to use their people." The series' budget had necessitated that change. The show simply couldn't afford the extras. Charles Larson's finding a way to work this change into the show was a perfect example of his talent. Charles Larson was always looking for ways to expand *The FBI*'s story base, as was evidenced in an inter-office memo Larson sent to Martin early in the development of the series' December 26, 1965, episode, "The Hijackers." Said Larson in the memo, "A famous #15 hijacking case (which we do not have on file here but which Kemper can send to Washington for) concerns a competent professional group of gangsters who laid great plans for the hijacking of a truck full of expensive furs, and ended up instead with a truck full of National Biscuit Company cookies. It was a terrible mish-mash and must have been a source of shame and embarrassment to these old pros for years. It seems to me that there may be a very funny Lavender Hill Mob type of story in a reverse on the above situation." (Larson was referring to the 1951 Alec Guinness comedy, *The Lavender Hill Mob*. In *Lavender*, Guinness played a meek bank clerk who devises the perfect plan for stealing a fortune in gold bullion from an armored truck.)

In Larson's first draft, "a group of suburban amateurs led by Alec Guinness [the character played in "Hijackers" by Arthur O'Connell] tortuously plan the heist of a truck of crackers [in the aired episode, cheese] possibly as revenge against the company for firing Guinness—and end up, through a series of mistakes, with $250,000 worth of furs." Following his one-page synopsis for the episode, Larson then pointed out to Quinn Martin the advantages in doing "The Hijackers." "Curiously enough we would be examining here one of the most serious and perplexing problems the FBI has to face—how to deal with the amateur criminal who brings off a big job and leaves no M.O. and frequently no trace. I think it might be wise to indicate now and then that the FBI is not all solemnity and sub-machine guns, and I feel that this notion might give us that with no sacrifice of action and suspense. It would, of course, not be played as slapstick, but, I would hope, as a warm, funny, perhaps touching reverse-English comment on the difficulties of amateur criminality—from the point of view of both sides." "Charles, I love it," replied Martin on the memo's first page. "Go ahead."

The following season Larson opened up all kinds of story areas with "Sky on Fire." "Sky on Fire" was one of the series' most ambitious productions. The story featured forest fires, airplanes, and helicopters. Almost all of Act IV was devoted to a helicopter-automobile chase featuring, respectively, Inspector Lewis Erskine and arsonist-murderer Bradford Dillman, "We had a couple days of pre-production on that," recalls helicopter pilot James Gavin. "We shot it up in the Lake Arrowhead area, at a place called the Rim of the World Highway [the highway that led up to Lake Arrowhead]. We had to pick highways where we could photograph the car." Co-written by Don Brinkley, and (mostly, says Brinkley), Charles Larson, "Sky on Fire" was a foreshadowing of Quinn Martin's second most successful series, *Barnaby Jones*. On *Barnaby Jones,* nearly all of the villains were ordinary people made criminal by accident. Bradford Dillman's George Bellamy was exactly this sort of criminal in "Sky on Fire." Bellamy hadn't intended to murder his blackmailer Charles Grodin, much less set off a raging forest fire. As the story progressed, Bellamy set off more fires. He'd learned that the authorities believed that a professional arsonist was at work. Setting off such fires was a way to throw the authorities off the track in regards to his own crime. Plot-lines like this were a commonplace on *Barnaby Jones*. Thus it was rather fitting that in that series' first episode, "Requiem for a Son," Bradford Dillman portray the villain.

"Sky on Fire" was further notable for another reason. This time, the villain wasn't the bizarre character. It was the young woman who'd unintentionally made him a criminal. Playing that young woman was Lynda Day George. "The story had me getting pregnant by Brad," chuckles George, "and somehow or other this resulted in his setting off all these forest fires. That was an interesting script. It was different, and, my character was different than most of the other [law-abiding] characters they had done on *The FBI* up to that time. That was about the time when television was starting to take chances on characters. They were really experimenting, doing a lot of really neat, unusual, and bizarre characters. I was very lucky. I had the opportunity to play a lot of those characters."

There was nothing bizarre, however, about the characters played by George and co-star Henry Silva in the actress' next *FBI*, "Line of Fire." "Line of Fire" was another departure for *The FBI*. This time the series' character-growth study focused on professional nurse George, not colorful, wise-cracking villain Silva. Had it not been for Henry Silva, Lynda Day George might very well have squandered the fine dramatic showcase QM Productions had given her. "I think we had just moved into a house in Beverly Hills when I started that show," recalls the actress, "so quite often my mind was divided about what I had to do there, and what I had to do on the set. Henry Silva was great. Hank helped keep my mind on the set." Henry Silva's attitude was admirable. Not only did "Line of Fire" allow Lynda Day George to do what she did best — character-growth studies — a good portion of the story took place in a "bloody hot" car mock-up. "We were always having trouble with the car," laughs the actress. "We did the car stuff over and over and over. I think the lights went out one time — we ran over a cord, pulled a cable loose or something, and poor Hank spent so much time down on the floor of the car. Well, when you turned off the car, the heat from the engine came right through the back of the thing there." Despite this intense heat, George wasn't sweating. The actress wasn't much one to perspire. In "Line of Fire," it was dramatically crucial that she do so. "So they sponge painted," reveals the actress. "They painted glycerine drops on my face."

George's third *FBI*, the fourth season's "The Widow," was a milestone in *FBI* history. It was the first time a young actress was cast as the title criminal. It was also one of the few times the show featured a female criminal. With the next season's new producer Philip Saltzman, this was soon to change. Without a doubt, Lynda Day George's parole-violator murderess Joyce Carr was the most anti–American criminal ever presented on *The FBI*. The all–American looking Joyce had been born on that most American of holidays, July 4th. Joyce killed a certain kind of man — the

American serviceman. She married these men, then murdered them. Joyce's first victim was World War II hero Arch Johnson. Her next target was Vietnam soldier Patrick Wayne. Actually, Joyce didn't want to commit any crimes. The only reason she did was because it was what her boyfriend Clifford Holm (Glenn Corbett) wanted. Unlike Joyce Carr, who knew what she was doing was wrong, and who wanted to be punished for her crimes, Clifford Holm had no guilt feelings about the murders. Nor did he show much consideration for Joyce. Seeing perennial nice-guy Glenn Corbett as such a cold-hearted, cold-blooded character was a real shock for those who were familiar with Corbett's work.

"It was the first time Glenn Corbett ever played a bad guy," reveals George. "He really enjoyed playing that character. He kept telling me, 'This is so wonderful, getting to play this hard, tough character.' I really miss Glenn Corbett. He was such a good performer, very underrated—sadly underrated, in my opinion." Quinn Martin agreed with the actress. Following his exceptional performance in "The Widow," Glenn Corbett would portray criminal characters on such QM series as *Cannon* and *Barnaby Jones*. None ever had the impact of "The Widow."

"That show was one of my favorites," says George, "because of the opportunity it gave Glenn, and because it showed that sometimes even the nicest of people can wind up doing things that are totally inappropriate. We don't often see that as a reality, but it is a reality. I don't think I took the show in a different direction by emphasizing that. Around that time on *The FBI*, there was this emphasis on making the bad guys even more sympathetic than they had been, or even more pathetic. As I recall, my character in that show was rather pathetic. That's part of what made *The FBI* such a good series. Very early on, they had chosen to go forward with this process of letting the audience get to know the bad guys, of explaining to them why they were doing what they were doing, of showing the audience that these people were human. And, whenever you portray a villain, you have to remember, they are human beings—I mean, even Hitler was loved and adored by someone."

The series' next producer, Philip Saltzman, definitely shared Lynda Day George's view when it came to the criminals. During Saltzman's four years on the series, the audience was to see more and more human and sympathetic criminals. "I always thought the villains were the most interesting characters," says Saltzman. "My villains weren't just black-and-white evil people. There was always some driving force that turned them into that. I tried to do stories with interesting villains. I used women killers too. I liked the idea of having women be the killers. It made the shows more interesting." Philip Saltzman came into *The FBI* at just the right time. After four years of producing the program, predecessor Charles Larson was eager to leave. "The show was taking a terrible toll on him," remembers Saltzman. "He was battling with the FBI on scripts and all kinds of things. He was developing scripts without their help. He'd send these finished scripts to the FBI in Washington. Then they'd jump all over them and say, 'This isn't right. This isn't how we do it. We didn't approve this,' and on and on and on. So, at the last minute, when they were getting ready to shoot, he wouldn't have a script. He'd have to do massive rewrites to get their approval."

"Well, when I came in, I changed things. I made Dick Douce kind of a story editor. I said, 'Dick, I'm not gonna send this stuff to the FBI and get it knocked down at the last minute. I want you to sit in on meetings between me and the writers. I want you to read the story ideas, or I'll tell you what the idea is.' So Dick would approve the scripts on his own and, when it came time for the scripts to go to Washington and the calls came back, Dick would field those. Because now he had a personal stake in the stories, he was the one fighting with Washington. That worked out to be a very good system. I never had any real problems during my whole four years on the show."

Of course it didn't hurt that one of the first shows Saltzman produced, "Nightmare Road," presented the FBI in a very good light. "We did the death of an FBI agent," remembers the producer. "That really worked. The Bureau wrote me a letter commending me for that show. Harvey Hart was the director on that one. He was shooting a very fluid camera. It kind of underlined the B side of the story. There's the A side, which is your criminal, the B side which is the Bureau [and in this episode] the agent's widow and children." "Harvey Hart did almost an eight-minute sequence when Efrem was in a hospital bed, all on one camera, one lens—hundred-millimeter lens—panning from person to person—to the nurse, to the doctor, to Efrem, and he did it in one take," marvels Howard Alston. "Quinn and Artie almost had a heart attack when they saw that because Harvey hadn't given them any coverage. Then they realized that the scene was brilliant, that it really worked." Harvey Hart would go on to direct a number of special shows for QM, among these the TV movies *Murder or Mercy* and *Panic on the 5:22.*

New story consultant Robert Heverly also proved quite an asset early in the fifth season. "I'd discovered Bob when I was working at Four-Star," recalls Saltzman. "When we were doing *The Goodyear Alcoa Playhouse*, I'd read some material that was very offbeat. It was Bob's. I had him come in. We chatted. He was a very original kind of character. Then I introduced him to Sam Peckinpah. Sam was at Four-Star doing *Rifleman*. I said, 'Sam, this guy is an original. He can write Westerns.' So Bob wrote for Sam on two or three shows. Then Sam used him on *The Westerner* [the short-lived, and very offbeat, Brian Keith series]." Being an "original," Robert Heverly was thus quite adept at making work on paper the bizarre villains who peopled *The FBI*. "He was crazy," laughs Paul Wurtzel. "He'd come to the office in combat boots and fatigues. He was a veteran or something. I guess he never got over the war. He was a great big guy, kinda off the wall." "He was a very private man," adds QM production coordinator Debbie Yates Marks, "but he'd have these screaming and hollering fits. People used to comment about how strange he was."

Thanks to "off the wall" talents like Heverly, *The FBI* continued to pull strong ratings throughout its fifth year. Considering the political climate at the time, this was extraordinary. "It was right after the riots," remembers Saltzman. "When I went to Washington [for orientation], they were still cleaning up. I was very surprised when the FBI agent said, 'Don't go out at night. We never go out at night.' I thought, My God! You're armed. You're FBI." It didn't take long for Saltzman to appreciate the agent's warning. "One time I sent the crew up north to Santa Rosa, where they encountered hecklers," recalls the producer. "So, they set up a false unit. They sent a second camera and a skeleton crew into one area of town to draw the hecklers away. Then they moved the real crew into the other section and shot the scene."

"I did a lot of experimenting that first year," continues Saltzman. "There was a lot of concern about the show's violence. We started doing less violent shows." Perhaps the least violent was the February 15, 1970, episode, "Return to Power"—Lynda Day George's final guest shot on the series. Starring Christopher George and Peter Mark Richman as two brothers struggling for the top spot in a Mafia family, "Return to Power" eventually brought the two men together for a showdown, which, because of the overwhelming number of Mafiosi and FBI agents who were present, looked to be the series' most explosive and most exciting conclusion ever. With Don Medford as the show's director, that was almost a certainty. Instead, what resulted was the most restrained and least exciting conclusion viewers ever saw on the program. "Don Medford liked that because it was so different," says Lynda Day George. "He enjoyed that. It was a challenge for him. That was really kind of fun for me knowing that this was something different for him. Don Medford was an extraordinary director. He'd been around for a long long time. He knew what he was doing all the time. That show was a real compromise between what we both wanted and what we both were willing to accept. It was quite an exciting show for me. I always enjoyed working with Don, and of course, I always enjoyed working with Chris."

Thanks to uncommon shows like "Return to Power" and Robert Heverly's terrific twist-laden "Boomerang," in which a fake kidnapping becomes a real kidnapping and then a double kidnapping, *The FBI* began to improve in the ratings. "We were directly opposite first-run movies on CBS," remembers Saltzman. "They knocked us off, and brought our ratings down a couple of times, but as the season wore on, we built a bigger audience spread and we knocked them off. I remember being very happy when our ratings began to climb. Sometimes we were second, maybe third, in the country." CBS head of programming Fred Silverman didn't forget that. Shortly after *The FBI*'s cancellation, Silverman proposed a series of *FBI* movie specials. Philip Saltzman was to produce all three.

Saltzman enjoyed making those movies. He liked doing *The FBI* too. There were plenty of unpleasant situations though. "I almost had a fist-fight with [guest star] Vic Morrow," remembers the producer. "He wanted to change the [FBI-approved] dialogue." Having directed a number of episodes of his own series, *Combat*, Vic Morrow often seemed to think he knew more than anyone else. Assistant editor Martin Fox recalls the problem this created on one occasion. "They were gonna go out in a car—with these two guys in the car—and shoot all these scenes for four different episodes," explains Fox. "They'd taped all the script pages on the dash, and they'd put the assistant cameraman in the back of the car, and they were getting ready to

Opposite page: An inter-office memo from producer Charles Larson to Quinn Martin concerning an idea that would result in the December 26, 1965, episode "The Hijackers."

QM productions

INTER-OFFICE MEMO

TO _QUINN MARTIN_ DATE 2 APRIL 1965

FROM_ CHARLES LARSON_ SUBJECT_ THE F B I

THE LAVENDER HILL MOB NOTION

A famous #15 hijacking case (which we do not have on file here, but which Kemper can send to Washington for) concerns a competent professional group of gangsters who laid great plans for the hijacking of a truck full of expensive furs, and ended up instead with a truck full of National Biscuit Company cookies. It was a terrible mish-mash and must have been a source of shame and embarrassment to these old pros for years.

It seems to me that there may be a very funny Lavender Hill Mob type of story in a reverse on the above situation.

*****

A group of suburban amateurs led by Alec Guiness tortuously plan the heist of a truck of crackers, possibly as revenge against the company for firing Guiness -- and end up, through a series of mistakes, with $250,000 worth of furs.

At first Erskine and Rhodes feel that this will be a reasonably routine affair despite the daring and skill of the crime because there are just so many gangs capable of a job this clever, and only so many fences capable of handling the stuff when the gang finally tries to unload it.

The problem is that the Guiness mob is 100% amateur. Though they try to be resourceful crooks, they create havoc in Erskine's investigation because they never do what he expects they should do. Erskine cannot even successfully stake out a fence because Guiness doesn't know how to contact a fence in the first place.

Meanwhile, the gang is going to pieces and fighting internally because of shame and fear and guilt. They feel the FBI must be closing in and that they are all trapped like rats in a pipe. Erskine, of course, could close in much faster except that he can barely bring himself to believe the things he is uncovering.

He does in time crack the case and haul Guiness and the mob off to justice.

COMMENT: Curiously enough we would be examining here one of the most serious and perplexing problems the FBI has to face -- how to deal with the amateur criminal who brings off a big job and leaves no M.O. and frequently no trace. I think it might be wise to indicate now and then that the FBI is not all solemnity and sub-machine guns and

----

LAVENDER HILL MOB NOTION
Pg 2.

I feel that this notion might give us that with no sacrifice of action and suspense. It would, of course, not be played as slapstick, but, I would hope, as a warm, funny, perhaps touching reverse-English comment on the difficulties of amateur criminality -- from the point of view of both sides.

CL:sg

cc: Ed Kemper

put in the guy with the clap-board who would mark each scene. Vic Morrow says, 'Ah we don't need him. We'll just do this ourselves. We'll just clap our hands to mark the scene. Okay, here's scene forty-two, scene such and such, clap clap clap.' So the film comes into the editing room. The editors have got these three cameras going, and they're saying, 'What the hell is this?' I mean here you've got these guys clapping their hands, but the scene's not been marked with the marker. So what scene is it? Well, they had all these assistants working all day long trying to figure out what scene is it, which scene goes with what? The editors were ready to go out and shoot those guys."

Philip Saltzman felt similarly one time towards Adrian Samish. "They always timed whatever they'd shot," reveals Saltzman, "and late one afternoon, they came to me and said, 'We're running two or three minutes short on this picture. Can you hurry up and write a scene that we can shoot on this set with these actors while they're still here?' Well, I was used to doing that at *Four-Star* when I worked there. So Mark Weingart (Saltzman's associate producer) and I wrote a scene very quickly which they could shoot. The next day I got this nasty call from Adrian, saying, 'Who approved that?' I said, 'Adrian, there wasn't time to send it over to you guys for approval. We were running short. We weren't sure they were gonna use it, but they needed time. This was the time.'" The two men continued to argue. Finally Saltzman "got so mad I threatened to go over to Adrian's office and beat him up. And I'm not a physical guy." But before Saltzman could make good his threat, "Quinn called. He says, 'Gee, I just walked into Adrian's office. He's white as a sheet. What happened?' So I told him. He says, 'Aw, you know. People get set in their ways.' Anyway, after that, I never had any trouble with Adrian."

Quinn Martin could grow just as angry as Samish. "He had some really weird ideas," remembers director Robert Day. "I did this one *FBI* where Simon Oakland was crying. He's just learned of the death of his daughter. Quinn didn't like that at all. I had to re-shoot the scene." Yet some of Martin's objections weren't "weird." "We did this big long scene with Dabney Coleman talking to a kid," recalls Paul Wurtzel. "Dabney had a matchstick or toothpick in his mouth. When Quinn saw that, he was furious. He didn't like seeing this guy talking to a kid with a matchstick in his mouth. He thought it was distracting."

J. Edgar Hoover was just as rigid when it came to the fictional FBI agents' physical appearance and image. That appearance and image changed in the series' last season. "The last year they could wear sideburns," reveals Wurtzel. "The last year, a whole new regime came in. Hoover had died. The whole thing kind of broke down." New FBI director Clarence Kelly's less rigid standards were not the reason longtime series regular William Reynolds was replaced by the more casual Shelly Novack. "That was ABC's idea," states Zimbalist. "They wanted to give the series a younger look."

Former football player Novack's casting didn't hurt *The FBI*'s ratings. In fact, the show was still going strong at the time it was canceled. According to the series' detractors, the program was canceled because of the problems the real FBI was facing.

Once again, the critics got it wrong. "We'd dropped down to Number Twenty in the ratings," remembers Zimbalist, "and we were doing fine—very very popular still, but ABC decided to replace us with 'Sonny Baby' [Sonny Bono]. They got 'Sonny Baby' to do a show [*The Sonny Comedy Revue*]. He replaced us, and he was canceled within a few weeks. It was a disaster. To this day, I don't know why they canceled it. Why networks do anything nobody could ever figure out anyway. There's no logic to it. There never was any logic. Networks are networks."

Not long after its cancellation, *The FBI* went into syndication. Unlike most syndicated series of the '60s and '70s, the show didn't enjoy a great success in syndication. "Nobody ever got any decent residuals out of that show," says Philip Saltzman. "I think part of that was because there was a big anti-violence movement in Washington at the time they set up the deal. I guess they thought we were too violent. I never thought the shows I did were that violent. I always thought we were doing a character study."

While *The FBI* may not have fared well in its country of origin, once it was released overseas, the reaction was quite different. "People in Europe loved the show," reveals Zimbalist. "Most of the mail that I get today concerning *The FBI* comes from Europe. The Germans are crazy about it. They always have been. I get letters from Germany about *The FBI* practically every day."

Quinn Martin's next television series also proved a hit in Europe, especially in France. Years later, this series was to be revived in America. During this run, the series built such a good audience, it was decided to remake the original show as a miniseries. The miniseries didn't match the quality of the original program. For that matter, few science-fiction series of the 1960s and the 1970s met the high standards of *The Invaders*.

Chapter 6

THE INVADERS

Nobody understood the show. It always amazed me that any of them were any good.
Invaders *associate producer Anthony Spinner*

When *The Invaders* premiered on ABC on January 10, 1967, opposite *The Red Skelton Hour* on CBS and the first half hour of *The NBC Tuesday Night Movie*, there wasn't much chance the show would succeed, though not just because of the competition. With the exception of *The Twilight Zone*, no science-fiction, horror, or fantasy series did very well in the 1960s. *Star Trek* certainly didn't. In the 1960s, *Star Trek*'s hand-held communicators seemed unbelievable. With the advent of cell phones, they didn't. As for *The Invaders*, its premise that there were people on the earth who'd kill others in order to establish their own world, that seemed pretty farfetched. Sadly, as the events of September 11, 2001, and beyond were to show, such an idea could be a reality. "When we made that show," reflects assistant director Paul Wurtzel, "we didn't realize we were ahead of the times." *The Invaders'* executive producer Quinn Martin never lived to see the truth of his series. Martin wasn't that enthusiastic about *The Invaders*. To him it was just a copy of *The Fugitive*. Series director William Hale knew that it wasn't.

"It was one of Quinn's better shows," says Hale. "You never knew who the enemy was. The stories were good. They had variety. They had talented people doing the show. Alan Armer was a very good producer; Roy Thinnes, a good lead. Roy Thinnes was an underrated actor. He was potentially star material. I would have liked to see that show last longer. It had a very good, very interesting premise."

That premise had series protagonist—architect David Vincent (Thinnes)—going about the country branding others enemies of the state. Similarity to Senator Joseph McCarthy's Communist witch-hunts of the 1950s was intentional. But in Vincent's case, his McCarthyish behavior was justified, as viewers had seen in the series' pilot "Beachhead" ("the best pilot" series producer Alan Armer's agent ever saw). In

"Beachhead," David Vincent learned that a race of alien beings had adopted human form in order to conquer the earth. As the aliens were infiltrating all manner of human institutions, as they possessed all kinds of menacing equipment, trying to defeat them was none too easy for David Vincent. Making his job even tougher was the difficulty in identifying an alien. True, many had an awkwardly extended little finger on one hand; however not all possessed that deformity. As for the other distinguishing marks of an alien—no pulse, no bleeding when

Title card for the January 10, 1967–September 17, 1968, ABC-TV series, *The Invaders*.

cut, no skeletal structure—these were, to put it mildly, none too easy to examine.

Not every human being who knew of the alien presence was eager to help David Vincent. Certainly not embittered war hero Jack Lord in the first-season's "Vikor." Alien leader Alfred Ryder had promised Lord an important position in the new world order. Thus Lord was more than happy to allow the aliens to house their regeneration chambers at his plant. (The regeneration chambers allowed the aliens to retain their human form.) If it was necessary to murder his wife Diana Hyland in order to keep these regeneration chambers a secret, so be it. General Andrew Duggan also assisted the aliens in "Doomsday Minus One." Former World War II hero Duggan was sickened by war. He worried of nuclear confrontation. By cooperating with the aliens he could eliminate that. So he thought.

Not all of the aliens David Vincent encountered in *The Invaders* were against him. The rather unemotional Suzanne Pleshette in "The Mutation" was on Vincent's side. So was the uncontrollably emotional Suzanne Pleshette in "The Pursued." In both cases, the Pleshette character sacrificed her life in trying to help Vincent. Diana Hyland's alien character in the two part "Summit Meeting" also helped Vincent, as did aliens Barry Morse and Diana Muldaur in "The Life-seekers." None of those three alien characters lost their lives when they helped Vincent, which made it pretty clear that although it may have seemed predictable, *The Invaders* was anything but.

"*The Invaders* was very dark. It had a lot of intensity and mystery," says series guest and series fan Lynda Day George. "It didn't have as much novelty as *Star Trek* to rely on, so it had to be a better show structurally. It had to be a really good show. It didn't have the option of going off the wall for character or something like that to hold people's interest. That was always available to *Star Trek* in a dim moment. When things looked pretty sparse on *Star Trek*, they could always spice up the character with something." Adds *Star Trek* director Robert Butler, who directed the *Star Trek* original pilot, "The Cage," "technically, *The Invaders* was better drama than *Star Trek*. *Star Trek* was quite verbal and ideological. It was kind of the weighing

QM favorite Suzanne Pleshette (as the alien go-go dancer Vikki) and Roy Thinnes (as architect David Vincent) in the January 24, 1967, first-season ABC-TV *Invaders* episode, "The Mutation."

of ideas. Although that's admirable, it doesn't make for very good drama." "I think the reason *The Invaders* succeeded was because it had a dark kind of Kafka-esque feeling," muses the series' associate producer Anthony Spinner. "It was kind of new and different. I think the reason it didn't last long was because it was too sophisticated for the audience. It was ten levels above the audience of that time."

Science-fiction writer Harlan Ellison (writer of the much ballyhooed first season *Star Trek* episode, "The City on the Edge of Forever") seemed to agree. Ellison talked friend John W. Bloch into writing for the series. Bloch wrote many of the series' best episodes. His first, "Genesis" showed the aliens creating alien life. Another, "Moonshot" (co-written with Rita Lakin—the series' one woman writer), had the Invaders infiltrating the United States' space program. The second season's "The Enemy" showed Vietnam battle-weary nurse Barbara Barrie exhibiting romantic interest in wounded alien Richard Anderson; in Bloch's "The Possessed," the aliens dabbled with human mind control. Harlan Ellison himself seemed eager to write for *The Invaders*. After a heated story conference with Quinn Martin's assistant, Adrian Samish, he could forget that. Ellison grew so angry during their discussion, he jumped over the table and socked Samish.

Offbeat to a considerable degree, Harlan Ellison would have been perfect for *The Invaders*. "It was so far out," states series writer Don Brinkley. "It was difficult to write, but it opened new doors. It went directions most dramatic shows didn't." (Brinkley's "The Ivy Curtain" was a perfect example. In "Curtain," David Vincent discovers an Ivy League school which is teaching its young aliens how to blend into human society. The solution—adopt human teenagers' lingo and their attitudes towards the Establishment.) "I enjoyed that series," says Brinkley. "It was a great show, an interesting show. It had a great concept—paranoia unlimited. I think people were a little wary of that. I mean that show was based on inherent paranoia. You could do wild things because of that. Making them believable was where the problems came in. I didn't care for that extended finger business. I tried to minimize that as a plot device. We all made jokes about that finger."

Series creator Larry Cohen had put in the extended finger deliberately. An extended finger was a mark of effeminacy, of homosexuality. In 1960s Hollywood, the homosexual community generally chose to keep their sexual inclinations a secret. Keeping their identity secret was the goal of the alien invaders. By giving the aliens an extended finger, Cohen was therefore making a commentary on the behavior of 1960s Hollywood homosexuals. Cohen thought this commentary subtle and clever. There wasn't one person involved with *The Invaders* who shared that opinion. To John Conwell's secretary, Lois Winslow, the extended finger was "ridiculous." "Larry Cohen was a very inventive, very smart guy," states Robert Butler, "but that business of the finger.... God almighty, there had to be other characteristics and tweaks that were better than that. That was just a dumb, stupid idea. That made the show a little hollow, a little thin. That silly little finger—anybody who could buy that in a television show isn't really thinking that clearly." "That was before Viagra," chuckles assistant director Paul Wurtzel. "We joked about that all the time." "They could have thought longer and harder about that one," agrees William Hale. "Quinn could make some really serious mistakes from time to time; that crooked pinky stuff was a little silly. It always got a laugh when somebody did it. That wasn't thought through very well."

Apparently nothing was thought through on *The Invaders*. Like other series of the 1960s and '70s, the show hadn't developed a story bible. *The Fugitive* hadn't developed one—the show had gotten along just fine despite that. In a show like *The Invaders*, however, a story bible was desperately needed. Recalls Anthony Spinner, "The writers would come in and say, 'Can they throw a fire truck across the street?' 'Can they? I don't know. Let me think about that for two days. I don't know what these guys do.' I wrote an opening, 'aliens from a dying planet, blah, blah, blah,' to give us and the viewers some idea of what the show was about, but we made it up as we went along. The story conferences went on for hours and hours; I'd literally get dizzy. I wished I were someplace else."

Being a fan of science-fiction, series producer Alan Armer was even more frustrated than Spinner. Believing that the potential existed to do the series "on a realistic level," Armer tried very hard to make the program work. "Alan was very methodical," says production manager Howard Alston. "Alan considered everything before he did anything. He would worry and worry and worry." "Alan was a chronic worrier," adds Don Brinkley. "But he worried for the right reasons." "He was so lost," laughs Wurtzel. "I felt so sorry for him. We'd go up to his office and ask him, 'How the hell are we supposed to do this?' He'd just stand there in a corner, in a kind of fetal position, and almost suck his thumb or something. He didn't know what to tell us."

Trying to talk series star Roy Thinnes into softening his rather cold-hearted character was an added challenge. "Roy had this concept that this is a guy whom the world thinks is a nut," remembers Armer; "so he played him as a guy with a chip on his shoulder, a guy who's at war with the world. Quinn and I would have these long discussions with Roy, where we'd tell him that the first thing you have to do as a leading man is to get the audience to care about you, to root for you. But no matter what we said, Roy continued to play David Vincent as a sullen, surly guy." Former *FBI* regular Lynn Loring's influence may have been the reason. At that time Thinnes was married to Loring. Loring's mother was Thinnes' agent. Bright and ambitious, Loring, who would go on to produce such big-screen hits as *Mr. Mom*, prevented her husband from "having a relationship with anybody on the show," reveals Lois Winslow. "As soon as Roy finished a scene, she'd whisk him away to his dressing room." "Lynn Loring and her mother were sort of a pain in the butt," adds Wurtzel. "They used to hang around and tell him, 'Do this. Do that.'"

Given this, one might have expected Loring to cause a number of problems when she guest-starred in *The Invaders* episode, "Panic." Robert Butler directed that episode. Butler had no problems with Loring. "Lynn Loring was one of the finest actresses I ever worked with," states Butler. "She was quite exceptional. She'd worked with Kazan. Lynn was intense, creative, very smart. In style, she was at the opposite end of the spectrum from Lynda Day George. Lynda's style was easier, and gentler. Lynn's was powerful and psychologically complex. Lynda was more in the wisdom end of things. Lynn was more in the intelligent."

Being "wise," Lynda Day George formed her own opinion of Loring. "She was a crazy person," laughs George, "so wonderfully crazy. She was very active, very animated, came to the set a lot, talked a lot. I really enjoyed working with her husband. Roy was very intense about his work and the show. Very well prepared. He knew what he wanted to do, had a very good eye. He was very interested in learning about camera angles." According to one of her most frequent directors, Robert Day, Lynda Day George exhibited similar interests. "That was one thing Roy and I both had in common," admits the actress. "We were very intensely interested in the work. We worked well together. Roy was very accommodating. He was very willing to rehearse. Not all actors are like that."

Possessing a similar intensity, *The Invaders'* most frequent director Paul Wendkos worked very well with both actors. When he and George teamed up for the 1969 film noir TV horror feature, *Fear No Evil,* the result was "one of the best things I've ever done," declares Wendkos. The director was equally proud of his work on *The Invaders*. "Quinn wanted me for *The Invaders*," reveals Wendkos. "He needed a team to sink themselves into the material and come up with a style for the show." The style that Wendkos and his hand-picked director of photography Andrew J. McIntyre chose was film noir. "That was built into the series premise," declares Wendkos. "It was basically a chase film [with] life and death situations. Andy McIntyre was extremely well-trained. When I first met him at Columbia Pictures (in the 1950s) he was working for Bernard Guffey. Bernie Guffey was one of the great cinematographers of Hollywood. Andy was his operator at the time. I thought Andy was ready to move up by the time we did *The Invaders*. He was. Naturally he brought all of the film noir cultish techniques of early film-noir innovators to *The Invaders*. Andy was decisive and quick. He had very daring, risk-taking ideas."

The mixture of this with Wendkos' cold, detached directorial style was an asset to such *Invaders* episodes as "The Storm" and "Nightmare." If these episodes were any indication of the kind of pilot Larry Cohen would have written for the series, it was probably a good thing Quinn Martin talked Cohen into letting Anthony Wilson write the series pilot. Both "The Storm" and "Nightmare" were based on

Roy Thinnes (as architect David Vincent) and Ahna Capri (as Believers' secretary Joan Serratt) in the January 9, 1968, second-season ABC-TV *Invaders* episode, "Counterattack."

story concepts Cohen had submitted when making his initial proposal for *The Invaders* to ABC. "It was comic-book stuff," relates Alan Armer. "In 'The Storm' the aliens had this electric thing on a boat that created hurricanes. In 'Nightmare,' they were breeding these carnivorous insects. It just seemed so stupid."

That was where Paul Wendkos proved invaluable. "The crazier stories challenged you creatively because you had to come up with innovations that would serve the script yet still be believable to the audience," explains Wendkos. "That was the major challenge—to make all of these stories believable and acceptable, while at the same time allowing the audience to lose themselves in the show so that they wouldn't be sitting back and constantly questioning everything. We had to cause a suspension of disbelief to borrow a Hitchcock term. We were constantly fighting to achieve that."

Depicting the gunplay between the aliens and David Vincent was no less challenging. "The aliens had this weapon that they used," continues Wendkos, "and if you hid behind a rock and they shot at you, there was no defense. Because the rock disappeared. [It burned up.] So the hero always had to be able to roll away from whatever he was hiding behind in order to survive. We always had to come up with some kind of choreography, stage the scene in some way so that his escape would seem believable."

Roy Thinnes' approach to his character added a lot of believability and realism to the series. "Roy Thinnes actually believed that there were aliens," exclaims Spinner. "He believed he and Lynn Loring had seen a spaceship. I said to myself, 'Now I'm really losing my mind. The actor believes this.'" So whenever director Wendkos made jokes about the aliens, Thinnes got upset. "It kind of undercut Roy's character," states Alan Armer. "Roy needed to believe that. He needed to believe that his character had validity in what he was doing. The minute I pointed that out to Paul, Paul stopped. We had no trouble after that." "By absorbing that belief in extraterrestrial life into his work," notes Wendkos, "Roy made the series work. When you looked at him, you knew that he believed he was seeing something that could happen and did happen. He wasn't manufacturing something. When I made those jokes, I wasn't trying to undercut Roy. I liked Roy. I was friends with both him and Lynn. But to get through the sheer hard work of that show, you had to have humor. You had to laugh; otherwise you would never get through it. I mean we worked twelve to fourteen hours a day. So we just laughed our way through it. Paul Wurtzel [Wendkos' assistant director] had a really sardonic sense of humor. That fed right into my feeling for the absurd." "I got along with Paul Wendkos pretty well," admits Wurtzel. "You could always kid him. He was a little off-center though. You couldn't say the word, 'Fart' in front of him, because he'd start laughing, and get hysterical—he couldn't work. For some reason, he thought that was funny. Quinn liked him because he was weird enough that he got something different when he directed."

Paul Wendkos always had definite ideas when he directed a show, including how it should be lit. Wurtzel remembers one occasion when the director and cinematographer Andrew J. McIntyre clashed over that very thing. "Andy McIntyre was an old timer," reveals Wurtzel. "He was a tough old bird who really knew what he was doing. Well, Wendkos always wanted a certain effect, and he had this habit of going in and using the scrims and other things to change the light. But you don't go in and touch a cameraman's equipment. Wendkos would. So, one morning they got in this big fight. We were lighting this set—some guys are in a projection room watching something, and it's the first shot of the day. Wendkos says, 'Don't make it too light.' Andy says, 'I won't.' Well, Wendkos wasn't satisfied. Andy says, 'I'm not gonna re-light it,' Wendkos says. 'Then I'm not gonna shoot it.' They both sat down. So I called Howard Alston at home. I said, 'Geezus neither one of these guys will give in. We're sitting here with a stage full of people. We've got all these actors and the crew. What are we gonna do?' So Howard, who lived way the hell out of town, jumped in his car and came to the studio. We had a big argument with them, wasted about two hours. Then we finally went ahead and did it."

"We were always having a problem of some sort," agrees Alston. "Everybody worked a little harder on *The Invaders* than on the other shows. My wife and I spent innumerable weekends looking for locations, trying to find something that looked unusual. Trying to find something to match what the writers devised was one of the more interesting problems." Props were just as difficult—one alien weapon looked like half of a hard-boiled egg; the alien uniforms looked like jumpsuits. They were. They came from former racing-car drivers. "That show was a nightmare," declares Wurtzel. "It was one of the toughest shows I ever worked on. We were trying to figure out what it would be like if aliens landed on the earth, trying not to look ridiculous, but nobody really knew what they were doing." "We were presenting alien technology, alien culture," adds Alston, "and there's nothing tougher than trying to envision that, and making it look realistic."

Art director George Chan was the one to devise the alien spaceship and the plexiglass regeneration chambers so frequently seen on the program. He created many other alien items as well. Alan Armer, Anthony Spinner, and all of the series' directors also assisted in the creation of the alien technology and culture. "The directors had a big say because they were gonna photograph it," explains Alston. "We made several drawings, several sketches. There was a lot of communication between Quinn, the producers, the art department."

As usual, Quinn Martin insisted on much location shooting. Location shooting always caused its share of problems on the QM shows. On *The Invaders*, these problems were horrendous. "We needed more hours per day to shoot the show," explains Alston. "That was always a problem with Roy. Roy didn't like working long hours or at night. We shot a lot at night because the visual effects were much better at night." "We went to the Fox Ranch in Malibu Canyon for the pilot," remembers Wurtzel. "We had to bring on all kinds of heavy lighting equipment just to light an empty field so we could shoot this background. That cost a fortune, but Quinn wanted it done the right way. We used Temecula for the town. Today Temecula has vineyards and resort hotels; when we shot there, there was nothing. We also shot near El Segundo, at the Hyperion Sewage Plant. It was a huge, tremendous, bizarre plant. You could smell it. We built a whole bunch of huge plexi-glass tubes which we used in the interiors."

Transporting the alien spaceship was a continuing headache. "That drove me crazy," says Wurtzel, "lugging that thing around on a truck. You were always running into rain, and mud, and people chasing you away." "It cost money to do the alien stuff," adds Alston. "We always needed more time so the construction crews could go out and set up the spaceship. They had to get permits every time they hauled it out to a location." Probably the worst spaceship location used in the series was when the company shot "The Innocents" at the futuristic-looking Rossmore Leisure World. "It had rained the night before," recalls Wurtzel, "and when we put up the spaceship, it sunk in the mire. All the old people who lived there were paying lots of money for these places. They wanted us to get the hell out of there. We were cluttering up the road."

The spaceship was just one of the special effects items which caused problems. For the climax of the Gene Hackman guest shot, "The Spores," the special effects people planned on blowing out a couple of panes of glass in a greenhouse. Instead they blew up the greenhouse. For some reason or other, filming of the sequence had been delayed. When it finally came time to shoot, the special effects people forgot that they'd filled the containers with gasoline. They added more gas. "The greenhouse was right near Interstate 5," reveals "Spores" director William Hale. "When they blew up that thing, it blew up like Hiroshima. Traffic on the freeway came to a screeching halt, cars bumped into each other, a major ambulance accident resulted. Because people were looking off the freeway! They saw Hiroshima happening. Hackman hadn't really acted that much in movies and television. He wasn't aware of the stuff that could go wrong. He sees this thing going off—he says, 'Holy shit!'"

The explosion that climaxed Paul Wendkos' "Doomsday Minus One" was far more spectacular. In charge of rigging that explosion was famous Hollywood special effects artist Ira Anderson. "He had all kinds of explosive powder and stuff he'd collected over the years," says Wurtzel. "He figured this would be a good time to get rid of it. He just couldn't wait. He planted it out in Placereda Canyon. Maybe it was Sand Canyon. Anyway the stuff went off. He almost blew up the whole country." When special effects expert Justus Gibbs set off an explosion on a boat in "The Storm," he was almost killed. The boat caught on fire. Gibbs couldn't swim. "We couldn't put out the fire because the boat was fifty or a hundred yards from the pier," explains Alston. "That's when we learned he couldn't swim. We had a little motor boat there just for an emergency in case something happened, so we were able to get him off the yacht in time." All that remained of the cabin cruiser were the two engines that later washed ashore.

Peter Mark Richman "just missed getting decapitated by inches" by the "wildly swinging blades" of the helicopter used in "The Leeches." "We'd just landed, I got out of the copter, and it was hilly terrain," remembers Richman. "I inadvertently walked out, walked towards the camera, and, as I did, the whole crew went 'Oh!' The blades brushed my hair. It scared the shit out of me. But sometimes in a moment of shooting, you lose yourself in the character. It took me quite a few minutes to recover."

R.G. Armstrong felt similarly in "Panic." Required to climb a ladder to the top of a fire-tower where his character would then be shot off by alien Robert Walker, Armstrong froze more than halfway up the ladder. "I came the closest to freezin' and panickin' I ever had in my whole life," laughs Armstrong. "I just hung there. I was afraid for my life. I wasn't gonna go down or up. I'm thinkin' I cannot let this happen to me. I cannot be a wimp. They needed me to go ten more feet to get to the top, so I did everything I could. I started puttin' one hand up on the next rung, and then the next. It was like crawlin' for your life. You talk about actin', I mean seriously being into it. I was almost into it—that feelin' was panic I'll never forget in my wildest nightmare. So to get up—to finally get up to the top of that thing. I can't tell you the feelin' of relief I had when I got to the top. I mean, I was saved."

Written by future QM producer Robert Sherman, "Panic" was one of the *Invaders'* best episodes. Robert Butler's approach to the series was why. "The thing I paid the most attention to was the validity of the performances because the whole idea was off the ground," states Butler. "I really saw to the sense of the performers and the way they behaved so the show didn't get totally off the ground and silly. I tried to make Roy as accessible and believable as possible. I liked Roy, but Roy could be a little particular, a little persnickety. That show had a slightly different slant from *The Fugitive*. In *The Fugitive*, David had to keep his secret. He was drawn from his secrecy to help others. That was his basic formula. In *The Invaders*, Roy was trying to keep his secret from the villains. He was trying to get more truth and evidence so he could help the country and humanity. He was trying to prove the truth as he knew it to be."

Which put *The Invaders* on a much grander scale, and made it the more challenging show. "We got more calls on *The Invaders* than any of the other QM shows," reveals "Quinn Martin Films" secretary Debi Lahr Lawlor. "People were always asking what had happened to it. It was a very popular series."

That the program gained such popularity was astonishing. Dramatically, the series was sorely lacking in continuity. Whereas *The Fugitive* maintained its audience by adding to, and evolving its character, *The Invaders* weakened its potentially powerful impact by jumping back and forth from stories on the personal level ("Wall of Crystal," "The Betrayed," "The Trial") to those on a grand scale ("The Experiment," "Doomsday Minus One," "Summit Meeting"). "Wall of Crystal" was one of *The Invaders'* most personal episodes. In "Wall," the aliens tortured David Vincent's brother (Linden Chiles) and Chiles' wife (Julie Sommars). "It was my idea to give Vincent a brother," states "Wall of Crystal's" author Don Brinkley. "So many of these TV protagonists had no ties to anybody. If you gave them those ties, that gave you an opportunity to give Vincent more background as a character." By giving David Vincent a brother, Don Brinkley helped *The Invaders*.

The involvement of the Howard A. Anderson company also helped the series. The Anderson company was the company that did all of the series' optical effects, including its two most frequent, the landing or departure of the alien spaceship and the "burning up" of the aliens. "The immolation effect was designed between me, Darrell Anderson, Quinn, and Arthur Fellows," reveals Howard Alston. "We needed a way to get rid of the bodies so that there was never any evidence that there were aliens. That was very important to Quinn, because if there were bodies lying around, then why didn't people believe Vincent?"

"Darrell Anderson actually supervised when they were shooting the immolations," discloses assistant editor Martin Fox. "They liked to shoot those first and get 'em out of the way so that the Anderson company could work on them. It took three shots to do the immolation sequence. They'd lock the camera down, shoot the alien dying, shoot a blank screen, then spread dust where the alien had been and shoot that." "The optical house blended all that together," continues editor Richard Brockway. "We'd give them notes on the kinds of effects we wanted. They worked very hard on that stuff. They didn't have much time, because it took us a couple of days to get the shots, and you never really knew until you got your effects back if it was what you wanted. Quinn was always involved in the effects. You had to show him all the special effects. If he didn't like them, you had to do it over. I'd say we worked probably twice as long with the optical people on that show as opposed to the other QM shows. They'd keep coming over, bringing material to you to see if it would work. If it didn't, they'd go back to work that night, and probably by the next afternoon they'd have something you could look at again, not the finished product, but a facsimile of what it was going to look like. Maybe the third time, it would be perfect. Quinn had known Howard and Darrell Anderson for many years. He kind of helped them get started. They were very loyal to Quinn. They worked on all of the QM shows."

Contributing composer Duane Tatro also guaranteed himself steady employment at QM after scoring *The Invaders* episode, "The Prophet." In "The Prophet," Pat Hingle portrayed an alien evangelist who by risking the loss of his human form is amassing quite a following. (When the aliens start to lose their human form, they begin to glow.) As a result, the earth people think Hingle is some kind of messiah. "They did that show, but they didn't think they were gonna air it," recalls Tatro. "They couldn't come up with the right music for it. So they gave me a shot at it. I saw something there [the trumpets blown by Hingle's disciples] that I could use to give it an ersatz religious tone. That kind of brought the show to life. It just gave it a dimension which they hadn't realized. That really cemented my relationship with Quinn Martin. That show was really different than anything I've ever written since." "The second I heard Duane's stuff, I knew we'd found a gold-mine," enthuses John Elizalde. "Duane's music is quite dissonant, even twelve-toned at times. There's nothing in it to which you could put any lyrics. Duane had done some ghosting before for other people. He did an awful lot for the show."

In addition to "The Prophet," Tatro's other scores included, "Valley of the Shadow" and "The Spores." "'The Spores' was very challenging," recalls Tatro. "You had to be a little careful with it musically. It was kind of an eerie show, kind of an icky show. You had these incomplete aliens." Brought to the earth by alien Gene Hackman in a briefcase made of alien material, "The Spores" continue to grow in the briefcase. Later they are planted in dirt boxes in a greenhouse. When the greenhouse later burns up, the spores make a weird sound as they die. John Elizalde created that sound by recording the cries of seagulls, then playing these cries backwards. "The special effects guys really did a good job on that show," says William Hale in praise of them. "They had this duplicate briefcase, and whenever Hackman put down the briefcase on the table, they had the other one rigged so they could work on it from underneath. So when Hackman put down the briefcase, you'd cut away to somebody's face or something, then come back to the other briefcase which was lit exactly the same way. You opened the cover, and there were the spores."

With "The Spores," the fourth of five back to back good *Invaders* shows, *The Invaders* finally seemed to have broken its dramatically treacherous pattern of alternating between the personal-level, small-town based shows, and the United States government-national catastrophe type dramas of the first season. In the next episode, "Dark Outpost," the aliens brainwash David Vincent and his newly found allies into thinking one of their group has been executed. *How* is the question? One of the group members has seen the person hung, another shot by a firing squad. Directing "Dark Outpost" was George McCowan. Quinn Martin liked George McCowan. Thanks to McCowan's excellent direction of the 1971 series pilot, *Cannon*, Martin acquired another hit series. Being a technical director more interested in "painting pictures" than in extracting performances from actors, George McCowan was therefore the perfect director for the many physical elements featured in "Dark Outpost."

"Valley of the Shadow" was even more ambitious. In "Valley of the Shadow" an entire town witnesses the immolation death of an alien. The aliens have no choice but to destroy the town. David Vincent suggests another approach—take the entire town back a day, and replay the incident to achieve a different outcome. By featuring this temporary cooperation between Vincent and the aliens to reach a common goal, "Valley of the Shadow" opened up a new dramatic door for the series. Future episodes, like "The Peace-maker" and "The Life-seekers" made use of that opportunity. "That was a very good script," states Alan Armer, "but the show was badly directed. I was very disappointed in that show. It should have been a marvelous show."

The following episode was also good, thanks to writer John W. Bloch, guest stars Richard Anderson and Barbara Barrie, and director Robert Butler. "When I did those shows," muses Butler, "I always felt I was doing two shows—one show with the regulars where I would try to present and flatter them as best I could, and one with the guest people. The guest people most took my attention because we were inventing something." (In the case of "The Enemy," this was the gradually developing romance between nurse Barrie and wounded alien Anderson.)

"Barbara Barrie was very naturalistic," says Butler. "She was a little kooky, a little oriented in the method. She didn't think in terms other than character. Her consumption and preoccupation was with behavior and character in the orientation of that character in that world. I don't think she got as far as where the character's house was located, or what car got the character to her driveway, but she was kind of a vague, relaxed gal. I wasn't always able to reach her. She pointed to a vehicle once and asked me, 'Is that my car?' So that was kind of amusing. I enjoyed that, and I teased her. But she didn't change at all. She wasn't interested in the immediate externals."

Richard Anderson being the more unbelievable character of the two, Butler spent more time with him. "I didn't want to remind people that he was an alien," states the director. "I wanted to dwell on the fact that he was closer to being one of us, that this was an individual who was this thing that he didn't want to be, that he was wanting to change, wanting to become something he couldn't become. That was interesting and kind of sad. I'm pretty sure that was on Richard's mind too. That's what he and I worked at, because to treat him humanistically, rather than as a villain, that's just better for the story, for the character, for everything. Then to have this lonely gal Barbara Barrie falling in love with him. When this guy comes into her life and pays her some attention, that moves her, that makes her sympathetic to him. She doesn't want to see him suffering. That's a good character thrust—not wanting to see anyone suffer. So when I think of that show, I remember Barbara Barrie and Richard Anderson quite vividly, and with a certain sadness because of their story."

Butler's preference for the more personal dramas made him the perfect director for the following week's "The Trial." "That was a show that we pulled together at the last minute," recalls Armer. "Selette Cole, who later married George Eckstein, was in that show. She played a waitress. That was an interesting show, having to do with whether aliens could procreate. It wasn't just action-adventure. That was a good show." According to a two part article by author Stephen Bowie in the 2000-2001 issues (Numbers 22 and 23) of the national magazine *Outre*, "The Trial" was the best show in the entire series.

Which was astonishing. The show was written at the last minute. Co-producers George Eckstein and David W. Rintels put it together when the writer they'd expected to deliver that week's script failed to produce. Thanks to Howard Alston's suggestion that the series do a courtroom show to save on costs, Eckstein and Rintels at least had the germ of an idea. "The budget determined the plot," explains Eckstein. "It was a 'bottle show.' A 'bottle show' is a show you can pretty much shoot on one set. It just took longer to shoot than we expected. When you're in a courtroom, you think it's gonna be easy. You think you're gonna get it done in six days. We did it in seven, just like all the other shows."

"The show was manageable and simple," says Butler. "It was thoughtful, and that was because of David Rintels. David Rintels was a socially conscious guy. It was a serious, slightly more responsible script, stark and to the point. I remember David's being there while we were shooting the show and being very pleased. That show was so easy for me. Everybody knew their words, knew their character. All I did was place the camera and get the job done. Don Gordon and Lynda Day George were the guest stars in that show, and they were fun to work with because we were partnering in the creation of character and story, and that's very rewarding. That show felt like a real collaboration, a real partnership. I remember that feeling particularly with Don, and certainly with Lynda."

Like Don Brinkley's "Wall of Crystal," Eckstein and Rintel's "The Trial" gave the David Vincent character some background. This time Vincent has a personal reason for taking on the aliens — his old Korean War buddy (Gordon) has been arrested for the murder of a man he claims was an alien. There is no body of course. The aliens always burned up when they died. Eckstein and Rintels' placing the alien's death near the scene of a blast furnace was very clever. For all the viewers knew, Gordon might well have killed the man. It would have been easy to get rid of the body in the furnace. Further weakening Gordon's claim that he's killed an alien instead of a man is the fact that his ex-girlfriend, George, was married to the dead man. Moreover, she'd borne him a child. This being the case, if the dead man was an alien, then perhaps George is alien too. She certainly does keep twisting her little finger.

"That was Lynda's idea," reveals Butler. "She thought it would be good to throw that in there. Lynda was a soft, creative gal, very creative, very sensitive, academically smart. She worked behaviorally and psychologically on her characters. She was very good at arousing people's curiosity. Because she did that, she kept us guessing as to whether she was alien or not. That's a provocative question mark in that character, a great twist at that turn in the story." The remainder of the story, in which George must disclose her sexual relations with the dead man in open court, eventually admitting in the end that Gordon is the true father of her child, made for powerful drama. Controversial drama too.

Says *Invaders* director Robert Day, those were the kinds of shows producer David Rintels wanted to do. "David Rintels was a good writer," declares Day. "A hell of a good writer! He wanted to do controversial themes. He was really into that." Few shows were as controversial as "The Vise." "That was a very good script," says Alan Armer, "a very good show in which David Vincent realizes that this black civil-rights hero is an alien because his palms are black, not pale and pink like that of black people. That was a good point. That was a show I liked a lot. It made some good points in terms of the brotherhood of man."

Like "Valley of the Shadow," "The Vise" began another series of good *Invaders* stories. Unfortunately, by that time *The Invaders* was dying. The introduction of "The Believers" (a small group dedicated to the defeat of the aliens) had really hurt the show. "I thought "The Believers" was a good idea," states "Believers" director Paul Wendkos. "It widened the scope, widened the opportunity to tell more varied stories." "'The Believers' added value to the show," agrees Lynda Day George. "I thought it was great when they added those characters. After a while, ideas and story plots wear thin. There're only so many ways you can go with a series."

"The Believers" was a good idea, but, like so many other things on *The Invaders*, it wasn't thought through very well. Why the show had even bothered to introduce "The Believers" was puzzling. Nobody seemed to know what to do with them except kill them. By the time the series aired its final episode, "Inquisition," there was just one "Believer" left. Depressed by the failure of the series, Alan A. Armer was not sorry to see *The Invaders* end. The final broadcast was on September 17, 1968. As for Quinn Martin, he was too busy with *The FBI* and his other projects, including his one big-screen feature, *The Mephisto Waltz*.

Quinn Martin Presents: The Mephisto Waltz

It required a fairly sophisticated, educated audience. It wasn't easy material for the general mass audience to absorb. It wasn't the ordinary horror picture of today where somebody's head is decapitated. It was a very very difficult and sophisticated idea, a piece of material that required the audience to think, and to know about soul transference and soul transmogrification. All those exotic qualities and things that are the language of paranormal behavior.

Mephisto Waltz *director Paul Wendkos*

Having seen the 1969 TV horror movie classic, *Fear No Evil*, it was only natural that when Quinn Martin began making his own horror movie, the 1971 20th Century–

Fox feature, *The Mephisto Waltz*, he hire *Fear No Evil* director Paul Wendkos as his director. Wendkos had done a superb job in *Fear No Evil*. Martin was hoping for the same in *Mephisto Waltz*. "Paul was a classy guy, very positive about what he wanted," says QM production manager Howard Alston. "When it came time to find somebody to do *The Mephisto Waltz*, Quinn turned to Paul—he thought he'd give him a quality show. He did. Paul did a wonderful job of directing, but there were some wonderful scenes in that picture that didn't get in. When it got to the editing room, they had to cut it. That's because Paul got out of hand in that picture. They had four hours of film when they got through."

Wendkos couldn't be blamed for getting out of hand. Not only was *The Mephisto Waltz* script too long, bringing the Fred Mustard Stewart novel to the screen was difficult. Besides its primary focus on soul transference and soul transmogrification (changing oneself into another shape or form), *Mephisto* included: a Black Mass held by Jacqueline Bisset, a funeral attended by devil worshippers, an extensive dream sequence, a dog trying to fornicate with Bisset, a bathtub overflowing with Bisset's blood. "*Mephisto Waltz* entered into very difficult territory," explains Wendkos. "When you're looking to tell a story about the transmogrification of souls, and soul transference, it's very difficult to depict such extrasensory material. There really was no accurate way to understand it. That's why we used stylistic devices to [help the audience] enter into the realm of understanding the paranormal."

"When it first started, it was gonna be a bigger production than it was," recalls Muffet Martin, "but [20th Century–Fox studio head] Darryl Zanuck was on the edge of being kicked out. They'd already signed Alan Alda [who played the journalist turned pianist] and Jacqueline Bisset [Alda's wife]." Cast as the devil-worshipping, dying musician who later takes possession of Alda was German actor Curt Jurgens. "Curt Jurgens was a buffoon," declares Wendkos. "He had the typical German arrogance which came across in that character, but then that was part of the character he was playing. He was playing a conductor of orchestras, and arrogance is a quality that is quite common in conductors. Just through the sheer force of their personalities, conductors can control a hundred musicians—all of whom have fierce egos of their own. So the conductors have to have super egos in order to command over a hundred and twenty other artists. Curt Jurgens brought that to the role, and he added to it his own unique robustness and feeling of superiority. That always resulted in good acting, I must say."

"A lot of that story depended on Jacqueline Bisset," continues Wendkos. "Jackie was never involved in anything as complicated as *Mephisto Waltz*, or anything that required the acting technique that was going to be required to do a non-realistic piece of work. She was limited in training, and she was just moving into the acting field, but she did a very nice job. I liked her work. And of course, she was extraordinarily beautiful. Alan Alda was from the theater; so he had a totally different background from Jackie's. Working on the piano demanded a lot of concentration and commitment. The technical assistants taught him to just play sections of the piece his character was performing. You didn't see him playing the piano in every shot, but there were two or three shots where he was. He had to memorize the sections they gave him. He did that very skillfully. The reason we chose those shots of him playing the piano was to create the illusion that he was playing the whole piece. I thought his piano work was extraordinary."

Wendkos was not pleased with every member of the cast however. Despite his increasing loss of power at 20th Century–Fox, studio head Darryl Zanuck still had some clout when it came to that casting. "Some of the casting was out of control because the studio was involved, and they wanted certain names for distribution purposes," recalls Wendkos. "Certain actors were friends of Darryl Zanuck's; so we were sort of forced to use actors I didn't particularly like. One actor in particular was not my favorite. It was one of the main players." Wendkos did some casting of his own too. Having directed Khigh Dhiegh in the TV movie pilot for the long-running hit series, *Hawaii Five-O*, he found a part for the actor in *Mephisto*.

Wendkos also found the perfect house for the picture—the same house he'd used in *Fear No Evil*—the Al Capone mansion in Pasadena. "People first saw it in *Fear No Evil*," says Wendkos, "and after that, it became a very popular shooting site. It had a Gothic quality that I liked—very Gothic, dark, heavy wood trim inside, high ceilings. It had a mystery to it. It wasn't a particularly warm or gracious house. But it was Gothic. That's what appealed to me. It was a nice big house, with huge grounds, great for shooting, and the neighbors didn't bother you. It was too big for the people who lived there. They'd rent it out for shoots, rent it out to make money."

Other locations included the Hollywood Hills, a business section in L.A. ("where we manufactured the Christmas season," chuckles Wendkos), and the main lot at Fox studios. Most of the picture was shot at Fox, which was practically an inevitability, given the story's many bizarre sequences. "We had one sequence in a den that had red flocked paper on the walls, canvas with a lot of glass, bric-a-brac. It was a very difficult sequence," remembers the film's Academy Award nominated director of photography William W. Spencer. "We had another where Jackie Bisset is hallucinating. It was distorted, very strange. We used a lot of Vaseline on the camera lens, and put it around the edges to make it look out of focus, the middle of the lens was sharp though." "The Vaseline on the lens gave the picture a very foggy, misty, mysterious look," adds Wendkos. "In another sequence, I had the camera spinning. That created the illusion of psychological turmoil. For our dream sequence we used special distortion lenses, nine millimeter, very extremely wide angle lenses. The cobwebs in that sequence were created with rubber cement. When you spun those out of a special machine, they looked like cobwebs. (Art director) Dick Haman viewed that movie as a challenge. It's not everyday you get to do something as imaginative as that and he was thrilled, absolutely thrilled." Equally pleased were composer Jerry Goldsmith and cinematographer Spencer. Spencer was less than pleased, however, with director Wendkos.

"I was always having troubles with Paul Wendkos," says Spencer. "He'd interfere with my work, walk around, turning on and turning off lamps. He was very antagonistic. He gave one of my cameramen a bad time about lighting. Jackie Bisset was always angry at Wendkos. She felt he was mistreating different people in the crew. She got very upset about that. I remember one time she was reading this Bible, my camera operator told her, 'Move it a half inch that way.' Wendkos got mad at him for telling her how to hold the Bible. He was just a nasty guy. The last week on the picture I finally quit. I'd had enough of him by then."

Paul Wendkos' view of the two men's working relationship was entirely different. "I was very happy with Billy Spencer," says the director. He'd never been involved with the kind of challenges that *Mephisto Waltz* presented. I think he loved that challenge. I think it exposed a side of him that he never knew he possessed. He had a lot of fun doing it. So did I." Especially when shooting the New Year's Eve masquerade party sequence. During this sequence, the audience is treated to incest, homosexuality, nudity, etc. "It was an attempt to illustrate the total decadence of the group," explains Wendkos. "I didn't have any trouble with the censors when I did such scenes. I may have had to snip here and there when we edited the picture, but when we made the movie we anticipated some problems. If we thought that something may not go, we'd shoot it both ways. That way we protected ourselves. I really liked the masquerade party sequence. The other scene I really enjoyed was when Alan Alda first went under the influence of the drug (which allows for Jurgens to possess him). It started up in his bedroom. He came down the stairs into the living room, and wound up in this mirror, this strange distorting mirror. I thought that was a terrific shot. It captured the ambiguity of his grip on reality. He didn't know where he was. His consciousness was swimming before his eyes. I used some trick lenses for that sequence. Again it was an enormous challenge to Billy Spencer, and he did it, and he did it beautifully. He was absolutely thrilled with the way the shot came out."

Less than thrilled with the sequence in which her character performs a Black Mass was Jacqueline Bisset. "When Jackie Bisset had to summon the devil, she was frightened, really frightened," states Wendkos. "Those actors who have Catholic backgrounds, when you do a Black Mass, that really frightens them, and Jackie was very frightened. It affected her dreams and her sleep when she was sleeping at home. It got into her unconscious life, which is why it made for an interesting movie. It developed its own reality. The actor has to believe that stuff so that the audience will believe it." Bisset was equally unnerved by the film's dog attack sequence. "The implication of that scene was that the dog was trying to fornicate with her," explains Wendkos. "If you studied the position you'll see that the dog was in a fornicating position. So was she. That was sort of subtly handled. But since the dog was really an extension of the devil—the devil was the one who really wanted to possess Jackie Bisset, and fornicate with her, and have a child with her—it was very weird stuff."

According to Muffet Martin, Quinn Martin was disappointed with the final product. "Paul did not do a very good job of directing that movie," says the producer's widow. "It was so slow, it was very difficult to cut, and it had no pace. But because it was a movie, Paul got such grand ideas. He spent so much time on things that didn't matter. He went overboard on some of the acting." All of Muffet Martin's points were valid. Yet so were those of Paul Wendkos.

Indeed, that the director was able to create any sense out of a production backed by a studio at that time plagued by infighting, and undergoing a change in personnel, was a tribute to both his talent and sense of command. In fact, reveals a proud Wendkos, "there's a group that considers it the greatest movie they've ever seen." One year earlier, director Robert Day had tackled his own challenging QM feature, the flashback laden, rather gory, *House on Greenapple Road.*

Chapter 7

DAN AUGUST

Get Burt! Burt would be perfect for you. Burt can do anything!
Christopher George recommending friend Burt Reynolds
for Dan August—the role George originated in
the series' pilot, The House on Greenapple Road

Given Quinn Martin's track record of series hits by 1970, any actor would have jumped at the offer of his own QM series. Christopher George was not any actor. George proved that during the 1969-70 season. During that season, Christopher George made, and sold, three television series pilots: *Escape (*a.k.a. *The Magician*), *The Immortal*, and *The House on Greenapple Road*. In the latter, George portrayed Santa Luisa police detective Dan August. "It was the first time any actor in television had sold every one of his pilots," reveals George's proud widow, Lynda Day George. "That was really unusual. You don't find that opportunity very often to choose a series you really want to do. Well, Bill Bixby wanted to do *The Magician*, so that left *The Immortal* and *Dan August* (September 23, 1970–August 25, 1971, ABC). Chris wanted to do *The Immortal*. I of course was looking for the long run."

So was Quinn Martin. Martin wanted Christopher George to portray Dan August. "That's why he cast Chris in the role in the first place," affirms Lynda Day George. "When you do a pilot, you cast the people that you want in the show. Quinn wanted Chris in that show." Nothing made that clearer than the one conversation Quinn Martin and Lynda Day George had some time after the broadcast of *The House on Greenapple Road*. "I hear Chris is planning to do *The Immortal,*" said Martin to the actress. "Yeah," George replied. "It doesn't seem like you like that particularly," mused Martin. "Not really," answered George. "I liked *The House on Greenapple Road* better. I liked the character he played in that better." "Good," said Martin. "I did too!"

Christopher George certainly liked the character of Dan August. The actor enjoyed playing detectives and policemen. Having been a private investigator in real life (for two weeks), he had some background for portraying a police lieutenant.

Carol Lynley (as Sylvia Cartwright) and Christopher George (as race-car driver Ben Richards) in the September 30, 1969, ABC-TV series pilot, *The Immortal*. (Christopher George portrayed Detective Lieutenant Dan August in the January 11, 1970, ABC-TV *Dan August* pilot, *The House on Greenapple Road*. Both Quinn Martin and George's wife Lynda Day George wanted the actor to play August in the subsequent series. George opted to do *The Immortal* instead.)

Moreover, like so much of his previous work, e.g. the 1966 art piece *The Gentle Rain*, *The House on Greenapple Road* was extremely offbeat. Though not just in its flash-back-laden story of a murder without a corpse; in its initial broadcast, January 11, 1970, *The House on Greenapple Road* aired an unprecedented two and a quarter hours (including commercials). "That didn't go over too well with the network," remembers *House* director Robert Day. "They wanted to cut the movie. Quinn told me he wasn't going to do that. He was so insistent on that running time. The story warranted that running time he said. He just didn't want to forfeit it." Martin got his way.

Quinn Martin pulled out all the stops in producing his first TV movie. Surrounding his leading man Christopher George with an impressive cast of major motion-picture stars (Janet Leigh, Walter Pidgeon, Barry Sullivan), stage greats (Julie Harris), and QM players (William Windom, Joanne Linville, Tim O'Connor, Peter Mark Richman, Lynda Day George), the producer opened the movie with a shocking musical score by QM composer Duane Tatro. "The music set the tone for the whole thing," states Tatro. "Quinn was very concerned about the main title. The music I did for the main title was what really caught Quinn's attention. I remember him jumping up in the dubbing room and saying, 'Boy, we really picked the right guy for this show.'" Martin wanted to grab the audience's attention immediately. With Duane Tatro's opening score, he did. "The main title was twelve-toned," reveals Tatro. "It was very strange, but the bizarre quality of the opening sequence allowed for that." That opening sequence featured the goriest scene ever seen on television up to that time. Coming home after her day at school, little Margaret Ord (Eve Plumb) enters her house in search of her mother Marian (Leigh). Finding the woman in neither the living or dining room, the little girl then enters the kitchen. Blood is spattered everywhere in the kitchen—on the walls, on the refrigerator, on the floors. More than likely Marian Ord has been murdered. Her corpse is nowhere to be found.

Originally entitled *The Red Kitchen Murder*—the title of the Harold Daniels novel on which the film was based—*The House on Greenapple Road* underwent a lot of changes in its transfer to the screen. Writer George Eckstein's alterations included police detective "Dan Nalon" becoming "Dan August," frequent wisecracks from detective August and his partner, Det. Sgt. Charles Wilentz (Keenan Wynn), and a complete character overhaul for secretary Lillian Crane (Lynda Day George). Although a minor character in both the book and the movie, Lillian Crane had a very important function in the story. She was the only person who could provide chief murder suspect George Ord (Tim O'Connor) with an alibi. In the book, Lillian couldn't do that because she died in a house fire. In the movie, she couldn't because she was always smoking pot.

"I liked playing that character," says George. "She was really neat. Playing her was fun because she was a weird little druggie. She was cool, kinda fun. It was something different for me." Getting the chance to work with her husband was one reason Lynda Day George turned down another producer's offer so she could do *The House on Greenapple Road*. Playing Lillian Crane was the other reason. The character only taking one day and having no more than two or three scenes, George was shocked at the salary Martin paid her for the bit part. "He paid me incredibly, ridiculously well," exclaims the actress. "Especially for then. It was exorbitant."

No less overwhelming were the production requirements for the picture. Featuring a dizzying array of suspects, and other characters, as well as countless flashback sequences (a necessity because of the plot), *The House on Greenapple Road* was a challenge for its director, Robert Day. "It was the first movie I ever made in this country," reveals Day. "[Executive editor] Arthur Fellows didn't like me. He wanted his own way all the time. I had to fight him to get my way. I had my own ideas on how to cut the picture."

According to Lynda Day George, who often visited the set during the five or six week shoot, Day "always kept his cool. He had immense things going on in that movie," states the actress. "There were so many flashback sequences. Flashbacks weren't too popular at that time. Plus there were so many location moves, huge location moves. That whole production was tough. But Bob Day could handle that. Bob Day could handle almost anything."

Including a not always calm Janet Leigh. As the sexually promiscuous Marian Ord, whose numerous affairs, from married men to New Age ministers, seemed more than enough motive for her husband George Ord to kill her, Leigh delivered the majority of her performance in flashback. That plus the blood-spattered kitchen and stabbing scene were reminiscent of her role in *Psycho*. At times, Leigh found the movie hard to do. There were parts of it that unnerved her. Apparently Leigh had no problems in performing her first scene with Peter Mark Richman. "Janet and I are good friends now," says Richman, "but I'd never met her until then. The first scene that we shot was after Janet and I have just had sex and I'm asking her how I was. That's the way it is in this business. You meet one another for the first time, then the first scene you do is a scene where you've just had a very intimate experience. That's where the acting comes in."

That was apparently the case with Christopher George and Keenan Wynn. When not acting, the two were drinking. While George could handle his excessive daily intake, Wynn was another matter. "We always had to make sure where he was at lunch," laughs Eckstein. "One time we were getting ready to do this shot; then somebody says, 'Where's Keenan?' We found him having a few in the bar." "I had problems with him more than once," adds Robert Day. "When I worked with him in *The Streets of San Francisco*, I had to stand him up a couple of times."

Day had absolutely no problems with Janet Leigh. "She was wonderful!" raves the director, nor with Peter Mark Richman. Over the years, the director became friends with Richman, as well as George Eckstein. As for leading man Christopher George's wife, Lynda Day George, "I really liked Lynda," enthuses Day. "She's a nice lady, a good woman. Philosophically, she has good things to say and to think about. She's a very bright woman; she's a thinking actress. That was the first time I worked with Lynda. John Conwell introduced me to her. He thought very highly of Lynda. He recommended her as a good actress. Lynda was always interested in what I was doing. She'd ask me questions, she was very observant, she seemed very interested in movie-making."

If Robert Day had a challenge in filming *House on Greenapple Road*, Duane Tatro had as much of a challenge in coming up with background music and themes for the picture. "I had a jazz score for part of the show," recalls Tatro, "a working theme for the Chris George and Keenan Wynn characters, a musical device to get into the flashbacks. I liked the scenes I did for Janet Leigh. That was a nice contrast to the main title. I played music backwards in other scenes. Every once in a while, I'm asked to lecture at USC about film music. Whenever I do, I take pieces from *The House on Greenapple Road* and *The Manhunter*. I use those in my lectures."

George Eckstein had a special reason to like *House* too. "My wife [Selette Cole] was in the first shot," laughs Eckstein. "Somebody drives up to the [Ord] house to let the little girl out. That's my wife in the car. I enjoyed writing that script. I helped in some of the casting. I was very happy with that cast." Especially Janet Leigh. "The

Janet Leigh character was an interesting character," states Eckstein. "She was an appealing and universally recognized character—a woman who thought she only existed for her physical attributes."

Despite his excellent and often witty script, not to mention that unexpected conclusion, George Eckstein had nothing to do with the *Dan August* series that grew out of *The House on Greenapple Road*. "That was the strange part," says Eckstein. "It went to series after I left the company [to begin producing *Banacek* among other things]. Quinn had had me under contract for another year after *The Invaders*. During that time I wrote *The House on Greenapple Road*. I never received any residuals from that show or from the series. Evidently I had signed a contract that bought out all my rights."

Like George Eckstein, Christopher George had nothing to do with *Dan August* when it went to series. Quinn Martin and Lynda Day George had tried their very best to change that, particularly when the actress's husband was trying to decide whether to play Ben Richards (*The Immortal*) or *Dan August*. "Quinn really wanted Chris in the part," says George. "He really wanted him to do it. He said, 'He would be so much better in this. This would be so much better for him.' I said, 'I agree.' So we talked about it, and I think it was during one of our conversations when Quinn said, 'You know what I think? I think he's gonna do *The Immortal*.' I said, 'Oh, I hope you're not right. I hope you're wrong.' Because I did not like Ben Richards. I did not like that show. I felt that Dan August would have been a much more attractive character for Chris to play because he was all of the stuff that folks were crazy about at the time. Ben Richards was not. I think that Chris would have been much better off doing *Dan August*. *Dan August* was the kind of character Chris could really play with. He could have fun with that character, do some interesting things with that character. That character had more empathy than Ben Richards."

In the planned QM series, Dan August was to have an unpleasant task. Whenever his life-long friends and neighbors broke the law in his small home-town of Santa Luisa, California, it would be August's duty to arrest them. Christopher George had played a similar character in his first TV series, *The Rat Patrol*. So, "the part of *Dan August* would have suited Chris to a tee," declares his widow. "Chris was very well versed at playing those kinds of characters. Those were the kinds of characters he was really good at. He did some wonderful work on those kinds of characters. He liked that kind of work."

Knowing that the part was perfect for George, Quinn Martin kept after the actor for a long time. "At one point," says Lynda Day George, "Quinn was even willing to work out something with Paramount [the studio that produced *The Immortal*], so that Chris could shoot both series on the same lot consecutively." Neither that, nor his unusual guest appearance in *The FBI*, nor the guarantee of enjoying a percentage of the *Dan August* series profits were enough to sway Christopher George into accepting the role of August, though.

"Chris wanted to do *The Immortal*, and so he did," states his widow. "He was very stubborn. When he made up his mind, that was it. You couldn't talk him out of it. He was tough. It was hard to get through to Chris sometimes. He had his own ideas, and sometimes trying to change his mind only made him more steadfast in his choice. There was a point where there was a diminishing return at trying to get him to do something else. He was like a kid sometimes."

Fortunately for Lynda Day George, her husband's obstinacy did not damage her own employment at QM Productions, or her friendship with Quinn Martin. "Quinn didn't hold any of that against me," laughs George, "but he was plenty mad at Chris."

To his credit, Christopher George frequently mentioned the same actor as being perfect for the *Dan August* character whenever Christopher George and Quinn Martin discussed the series. "At the time," says Lynda Day George, "Chris and Burt Reynolds were good friends, and Chris kept saying to Quinn, 'Look! You've gotta get Burt. You've gotta get Burt.'" Christopher George went much further than just recommending Reynolds. "Chris had some of Burt's shows like *Hawk* on three-quarter inch tape," reveals the actress. "He got those together, took them over to Quinn, showed them to Quinn, Adrian Samish, John Conwell [Howard Alston]. They finally said, 'All right. We'll call the guy. We'll see what he has to offer.'"

As soon became clear, Reynolds had a lot to offer. "Burt tried very hard to make the show go because he had just had a series, *Hawk*, that had not done well," explains *Dan August* script supervisor Kenneth Gilbert. "He was very interested in becoming a major player in Hollywood. He really put himself into the character. He tried to make it as believable and entertaining as possible." "It was very important to Burt that *Dan August* succeed," adds series director Ralph Senensky. "This was his fourth series [*Riverboat* and *Gunsmoke* were the other two; the latter had launched Dennis Weaver]. If Burt didn't make it this time, where did he go next? He was absolutely tireless in his work and in his attitude toward the show. If an actor had a twelve-hour turnaround, Burt without hesitation, rather than making the company wait two hours, would revoke his own turnaround and agree to come in early without penalty. He was tireless in wanting to promote the show. He flew out to Minneapolis to participate in some big festival one Friday night just to be there so he could plug the show."

One of the first things Reynolds did was to establish a good rapport with his co-stars. "When the show was bought, I got a lovely telegram from him saying how glad he was that we were going to be working together," recalls series regular Richard Anderson. "I didn't realize he was part Native American until one morning when I was in make-up. Burt comes in. He says, 'Hey, I just saw your *Gunsmoke*—the one where you played an Indian. You were wonderful.' Burt and I had a great respect for one another. He was a lot of fun to work with. He was a very good-hearted fellow. He always made fun of [his frequently changing] toupee. He'd say stuff like, 'I gotta find a rug that works.' He played with that kind of stuff throughout his career. That was part of his charm. He was so self-deprecating. I remember one time he said, 'If Richard were to go to Palm Beach,' where Burt's father was sheriff, 'if Richard were to walk into a hotel or a casino in Palm Beach, they'd greet him at the front door, and at the front desk, and give him anything he wanted. If I walked in, they'd send me around back.'"

Being of what Anderson calls "a humorous tilt," Reynolds could never resist the opportunity to play pranks on co-star Norman Fell. "The jokes were always on Norman," chuckles Anderson. "Norman was always complaining about his health. He was very straight-faced. So, Burt was always setting up these pranks. One time he put a toilet in Norman's dressing room; that kind of stuff went on all the time. Norman came up to me. He says, 'I can't handle this any more. I gotta put a stop to this.' That made Norman the perfect foil for Burt. Norman was a funny, funny guy." "Norman was a nervous wreck all the time," agrees series producer Anthony Spinner. "He was always calling my office every three days to see how we were doing in the ratings. A rating to him was life and death. I said, 'Norman, I have no control over the ratings. We're on a weak network. We can't change that. You guys are doing good work. The scripts are good; the reviews are good,' but he was like having an ulcer about it, and then of course he went on to have a terrific career. So all of that worry, and all of that strain was for nuthin.' But I have a hunch that even after he became a star, Norman probably stayed as neurotic and as frightened till the day he died. That was his personality—he was never gonna work again. I said, 'Norman, you've been working all your life. You'll work again.'"

As a result of the pranks Burt Reynolds could not resist playing on the jumpy Fell, and Reynolds' own take-charge attitude when it came to eliminating any tensions on the set, the *Dan August* set was a happy set—not that Reynolds himself didn't create some tension. Director Gerald Mayer, whose one *Dan August,* "The Worst Crime," special guest–starred Reynolds' good friend Fernando Lamas (as Tony Storm) found the shooting of the episode "a pain in the ass. Reynolds kinda ran the set like it was his show," says Mayer. "I mean when you asked the actor to do something, the actor looked at Reynolds to see if it was okay. I don't know why Reynolds wanted all that control; it seemed to me that was just creating grief for himself. But he was surrounded by his buddies. The buddies were there to do what he wanted. That's why I only did one of those."

Pleased with Burt Reynolds' enthusiasm for the series after butting heads with the ultra-stubborn Christopher George, Quinn Martin gave his series lead some extraordinary concessions. "As part of the deal," reveals Richard Anderson, "Quinn gave Burt his own office, and his own assistant. Burt and Quinn always seemed to be in communication on how to make things better. I remember that at the end of the series, at the end of the year, Burt told me that he was spending a lot of time with Quinn, that the two of them were talking about the future of the show."

Though Martin had anxieties about a series lead performing his own stunts, he agreed to let Reynolds perform his. The actor insisted on that. That was no stunt-man sliding down the church aisle on his belly in the series' opening credits, that was Burt Reynolds. "Burt was a stunt-man at heart," explains Howard Alston. "He wanted to do his own stunts, and that resulted in a good action show. We came up with some good ideas for the stunts. For example, Burt was interested in stock-car racing. We worked that into the show. We had this car—a Ford Mustang—made up of parts from the guy who designed the Ford Roadster. It was a fast car. Burt drove that as his personal car." Reynolds also rode motorcycles, fenced, hurled his body through windows. That resulted in injuries from time to time. "One time," remembers series producer Anthony Spinner, "we had a boat blow up. What was left of Burt's toupee caught on fire, he got smoke inhalation too." Sometimes Reynolds injured himself even when not performing a stunt. "One day," remembers Anderson, "he came in and you could tell that something was on his mind. Well he was doing this confrontation scene, and in the scene, he came down hard on the table with his fist. A lot harder than he needed to. He was in a cast for about a week after that."

Trying to work Reynolds' cast into the next show, "Bullet for a Hero," brought about a massive alteration in that episode's conclusion. Originally, the conclusion was to feature a motorboat chase between August and bad-guy Peter White. Once August caught up with White, the two men would then fight it out on the water. "Well, there was no way Burt could do that scene," explains "Bullet" director Ralph Senensky. "So we had to figure out something else for the conclusion. Now, in Oxnard [the series fictional Santa Luisa] they had these huge huge scaffoldings with the stairway going up to the top of the tower. So we had Peter's character jumping out of his car, and running up the stairs, because he's gonna jump off the tower and kill himself. August catches up with him. He lunges and grabs him and pulls him off the railing toward the ground. Burt says to Peter "Don't worry about any of this stuff. I'll take care of it." He did. It worked out fine. Well, that was Peter's last day of shooting. He left, stopped someplace for a few days; then his back started to bother him. So he got in a swimming pool, and his back locked. It turned out he'd broken it. He spent the next year in a cast."

Burt Reynolds wasn't the only actor to perform stunt-work in the series, as Lee Meriwether learned when she guest-starred in Senensky's "The Law." "I had to kill Walter Pidgeon," laughs Meriwether. "I hung him over a stairwell. So I was a real baddie, and because of that I had to do a certain amount of stunt-work, which I'd never done. I had to fall over and over again a couple of times. Later they threw me down in a woodshed—some kind of gardener's woodshed."

If having a guest actress do her own stunts was innovative, the series' theme was just as innovative. "The music alone was very arresting," states post-production supervisor John Elizalde. "Dave Grusin did the music. Dave was the one who came up with playing that buzz kalimba for our opening credits. It's an African instrument. It's a hollow sound board, with usually four or five flattened-out nails on the board. When you strike it, you get a very distinctive, twangy sound. You get a varying pitch depending on how you tweak it."

Quinn Martin had no problems with Grusin's unusual score. He did however have problems with what he termed the "relevant dramas" which Anthony Spinner seemed to be favoring. Among the series' controversial topics were racism, labor strikes, and homosexuality. "Quinn said to me, 'Are we doing propaganda here?,'" remembers Spinner. "I said, 'Yeah, because I'm tired of diamond heists and kidnapped girls and all that stuff. I mean, Geezus! How many times can you do that?'" "Getting a homosexual-themed show on in those days was tough," reveals Richard

Anderson. "So that episode we did ["Dead Witness to a Killing"], that was ground-breaking." "You had to really fight to get on that kind of material," adds Senensky. "By doing those kinds of shows, Tony was trying to break the boundaries of the formula cop show. There was nothing overt in that show, but the homosexuality was talked about. There's a scene where Burt and Norman come into a gay bar. A scene where someone talks about [guest stars] Martin Sheen and Laurence Luckinbill being lovers."

Another topically-themed episode that annoyed Martin was the series' second-aired episode, "The Murder of a Small Town." In "Murder," guest star Ricardo Montalban portrayed a Cesar Chavez–like labor leader. "He was as smooth as silk," recalls script supervisor Kenneth Gilbert. "He was wonderful to all the extras who played the field hands. They almost looked up to him as if he was Cesar Chavez." For producer Spinner, getting Montalban required some doing. "Ricardo didn't do television," chuckles Spinner, "so he was sitting there in my office, debating and debating, and finally he says, 'Listen. I'll do it if you give me an aria.' I said, 'An aria? What do you mean by an aria?' He says, 'A big speech, where I denounce the grape growers for two pages. Where I'm on camera alone.' I said, 'You got it. I'll write it tonight. Then I'll send it to your home.' So he read it. 'Oh, I like this,' he says. 'Okay. Now I'll do the show.'"

Very distasteful to Adrian Samish was the beginning of the aforementioned "Bullet for a Hero." "There was a shooting right at the very beginning of the show," reveals Ralph Senensky, "a naval officer is killed, and at his funeral, this one-legged amputee steps right in front of the casket and beats on the casket with his crutch. Adrian just had conniptions at that scene. He thought the guy was beating on the flag. But the whole thing was we wanted to establish this disgruntled, unhappy veteran as our potential killer."

Despite such powerful scenes, despite producer Spinner's tackling of controversial subjects, and despite Burt Reynolds' exceptional efforts in making the series work, *Dan August* simply could not make a dent in the ratings opposite its fierce CBS competition, *Hawaii Five*-O. Still, says Howard Alston, "it could have been a long-lasting series. The ratings weren't all that bad. There was something going on—I don't know what—between Quinn and the network. [The lawsuit that ABC had filed against Martin]. There was more behind the scenes between Quinn and the network that had nothing to do with the show. There was one show they canceled right in the middle of production. We were told to cease and desist from making that show. I mean the show just stopped. There was this guy carrying lumber up the street. He just had to put it down."

"Burt did everything he could to get us a pick-up," remembers Richard Anderson. "When the show went down, Burt went into seclusion. I tried to go in and see him, but his assistant or secretary, whoever it was, they said, 'Burt just cannot talk. He doesn't want to see anyone.'"

In the end, Burt Reynolds realized his dream. His fourth TV series finally won him the stardom he craved. Yet it wasn't the character or the series that did it. "Off

Burt Reynolds (right, as Detective Lieutenant Dan August) and guest-star Ricardo Montalban (as labor leader Manuel Acava) in the September 30, 1970, ABC-TV *Dan August* episode, "The Murder of a Small Town."

set," says Howard Alston, "Burt was a lot of fun, a lot of laughs. But when you put him in front of the camera, he became a stick. Well, we made this gag reel [put together by assistant editor James Newcom]—a reel of out-takes and funny incidents that happened when we were doing the series—and when the show was canceled, Burt took that gag reel, he went on these talk shows, and he changed his whole career around because he would go on these shows and make comments about the gag reel. He had this whole personality change in front of the camera as a result. He became a motion-picture actor on the basis of that gag reel. From then on, he was very loose on the set."

It was a good thing for post-production supervisor John Elizalde that the censors of the time were much stricter when it came to bad language. "I used to do voice-overs from time to time," laughs Elizalde, "and in one of the *Dan August* shows, I played the part of a tower operator. His name was McCracken. We had a page of stuff that was involved, but there were so many malapropisms in there that I had to correct them. Well, rather than retyping the whole thing, I just put little arrows and notes in the margin which I could follow. So, I'd made it maybe halfway through this thing and then I lost my place. I started getting mad, I got madder and madder, profanity followed profanity, and all of this was going on while Burt was driving the car in this scene. Norman was next to him. They looked at one another from time to time in total disbelief. So, Burt had a copy of this, and when they played it on the air, they bleeped out all the profanities. I never saw the show where Burt played this tape, but my son did. He said, 'Boy, Pop you sure were funny on the show last night.' John Elizalde later got to see, and hear the gag reel. The gag reels were always shown at the wrap parties Quinn Martin always threw at the end of a series season. "It was kind of embarrassing," chuckles Elizalde. "I'm a pretty staid and proper type person. I always had a coat and tie and everything. All of a sudden I'm revealed as this ogre."

Thanks to Burt Reynolds' superstardom, *Dan August* was to enjoy better ratings a few seasons later when Quinn Martin's new network home, CBS, reran the series as a midseason replacement in 1973 and 1975. Wanting to get out as much of the old ABC series as they could, the network asked Martin to combine a number of the series' one-hour episodes into two-hour movies. Recalls editor Richard Brockway, "Quinn told me, 'You're gonna have to come up with something which will allow us to combine these shows.' I said, 'Oh, that's neat.' Well, we were gonna do six two-hour movies, so I went back and read the scripts we were gonna do. I wrote something up where they'd fade out at the end of the show into a new scene where maybe Dan August was in the hospital or something, where he's on the telephone. You'd take that scene where he's on the telephone, then find a scene where Richard Anderson is talking to him on the phone, where he might be saying something like, 'Dan, we've got a murder, or suicide or rape. I need you on this.' Then August says, 'Sure, I'll be right there.' That's the way we put together those shows."

Not, apparently, Ralph Senensky's shows. "They had to pay me a fairly nice lump sum for restructuring the shows," remembers Senensky. "They put a title at the beginning which was a new title. When they got to the epilog, they didn't do the epilog. They just started the next show. Just hooked 'em together. They didn't even try to tie them together."

Astonished by his friend Burt Reynolds' success, Christopher George later admitted to his wife, "The biggest mistake I ever made was turning down *Dan August*." Whether George would have enjoyed the great success his friend Reynolds eventually achieved because of *Dan August* is of course open to speculation. Fortunately for Quinn Martin, the next actor who was offered a QM series didn't hem and haw to the degree that Christopher George did. In fact, that actor was excited at the prospect of headlining his own television series. Thanks to that, and to the series' dramatic view that you can only be as good as you can be bad, Quinn Martin soon had another hit series on his hands.

Chapter 8

CANNON

There never was a man who was as wedded to anything as Bill Conrad was to that show. I think he wanted that show to go on forever. That show was his whole life.
Cannon producer Anthony Spinner

With *Cannon* (September 14, 1971–September 19, 1976, CBS), Quinn Martin did the impossible. He brought television stardom to William Conrad. Like most heavy-set actors, William Conrad had spent the majority of his on-screen career as a character actor, often as a villain. *Cannon* changed all that. In *Cannon*, Conrad was the good guy.

Former Los Angeles police lieutenant turned private detective Frank Cannon was quite a change from the typical TV detective. Whereas these individuals were slim and trim, Cannon was overweight. He liked food, lots of food—from gourmet dishes to tacos and hot dogs. He liked wine too, not to mention expensive brands of Scotch. As a result of such tastes, Frank Cannon had put on, and continued to put on, considerable weight over the years. Starting the series at some two-hundred-and-twenty five pounds, the five-foot, nine-and-a-half inch William Conrad was close to three hundred when the series ended five years later.

Being overweight, Frank Cannon couldn't move too fast. That could be a problem in catching bad guys, but Cannon didn't catch criminals like most TV detectives. He kicked bad guys in the stomach, or rear-end, stomped on their feet, slammed doors in their face, hurled them against walls. Cannon had no qualms in using his car as a weapon. It came in handy when a bad guy came around to the driver's side to order Cannon out of his car. "Sure," the sleuth would reply as he opened the door and then rammed it against the man's legs. Running down bad guys in his car was fun too. Especially if they were on foot. Needless to say, Cannon's methods were rather brutal, but that was okay. In *Cannon*, the bad guys, and girls, deserved brutal treatment. They were truly horrible people.

Caricature of William Conrad in his role as private detective Frank Cannon on the September 14, 1971–September 19, 1976, CBS-TV series, *Cannon*.

Take for example "Lady in Red's" Steve Forrest, who shot girlfriend Claudia Jennings in the face. Or "Death of a Hunter's" Edward Mulhare who dispatched his victim in a tiger cage. In "A Deadly Quiet Town," cult leader John Rubinstein and his disciples forced a drunk to dig his own grave. One week later they killed him. In the first season's "The Island Caper," neatnik James Olson sent his goons over to ex-con Keenan Wynn's restaurant to terrorize Wynn's wife Jacqueline Scott. While at the restaurant, the goons smashed up the kitchen, just for fun. A short time later Frank Cannon paid a visit to Olson and his boys. Within minutes, he started smashing up Olson's furniture, just for fun.

When it came to bad girls, "A Touch of Venom's" Catherine Burns was certainly in the running. In "Venom," revolutionary Burns and her associates forced Cannon to find their disenchanted former member Sondra Locke by shooting the detective full of snake venom. Once he did, they planned on killing both him and Locke. Kathleen Cody's days of being typecast as a nice girl were definitely over after the fourth season's "Perfect Fit for a Frame." In "Pefect Fit," Cody threw husband Ralph Meeker to the sharks. When Meeker somehow miraculously survived, Cody tricked her bodyguard Frank Cannon into killing her husband. Then she framed Cannon for the crime.

Good as Cody and Burns' bad women were, neither one matched the brutality of Christie Redfield (Lynda Day George) in the March 26, 1971, series pilot. Former schoolteacher Christie was not a nice girl. Thanks to her marriage to town deputy Kelly Redfield (J.D. Cannon) on whom she regularly cheated, Christie had the perfect cover for the many crimes she had committed and would commit. Starting her criminal career a few years earlier by electrocuting her first husband in their bathtub, Christie then used the money from his life insurance to finance her long-time lover's security warning systems business. That enabled the two to pull off a number of robberies. One resulted in the murder of a security guard, then the murder of Frank Cannon's friend Kenneth Langston who dropped by the Redfield home when Christie and her accomplices were divvying up the loot. Disposing of Langston's weighted-down body in a nearby lake, Christie then framed his wife Diana for the crime. Once Frank Cannon got Diana freed, Christie willingly went along with her cousin Virgil Holley's (Murray Hamilton) numerous attempts on Cannon's life. She herself staged a phony rape scene in the hopes of driving her husband Kelly Redfield to the point of killing Cannon. It almost worked. Had it not been for the unexpected arrival of Diana Langston when Christie got the drop on Cannon and Virgil in the story's finale, the girl would definitely have gotten away.

Loaded with excessive violence, an outrageous amount of criminal activities for its two-hour running time, and a truly cold-blooded murderess, the *Cannon* pilot achieved exactly the thing Quinn Martin wanted. "At some point," recalls Lynda Day George, "Quinn and I had talked in our discussions about those characters who are just plain bad. Well, not long after that the networks started asking for bad guys who could really be bad guys. I mean, the times had changed. So now when you did bad guys on TV, they could be really awful. Which was why Quinn so loved doing *Cannon*. It allowed him to express that thought."

Having seen George's critically well-received performance in her first TV movie-pilot, 1968's *The Sound of Anger*, in which "I was a real, royal nasty," Quinn Martin knew the actress would have no problem portraying the cold-blooded Christie Redfield, nor in hiding the girl's villainy from the audience. George's low-key, subtle performance style, her all–American, girl next door quality was the perfect contrast to William Conrad's less than nice private detective Frank Cannon.

So when Quinn Martin and his people began working on the *Cannon* feature, they called Lynda Day George in to discuss her character. "We discussed the character in our original meeting," recalls George, "then Quinn and I talked about her after that. Quinn thought it would be a really fun role for me, because the character didn't have any redeeming qualities. She wasn't one of those people whom you could make really likable. I loved playing that character. I mean this girl was a royal witch. She was just rotten."

But viewers didn't know that in the beginning. They hadn't seen Lynda Day George's Christie Redfield dumping Kenneth Langston's body in the lake and framing his wife for murder. All they'd seen was the figure of a running woman; all they'd heard were the click of her heels. Since these scenes provided Lynda Day George no on-screen face time, there was no need for the actress to travel to the distant locations in Arizona where the sequences were to be shot, not when any extra or stand-in could do them. George disagreed. "I like to do those things myself," states the actress. "They add some kind of reality to the overall character. Those things should be done by the person who's playing the character. Some other person who goes in to do that, no that's not okay, not with me."

Despite George's dedication, and importance to the story, Vera Miles had far more screen time than Lynda Day George. "That's the way the script was written," explains George. "The script was written not to allow me much screen time because my character was doing a lot of those things behind the scenes. Plus, I was just a guest star in the show. Vera Miles was going to be a regular. That was the original plan." That plan changed, which didn't keep Miles from guest-starring on *Cannon*, first as a scientist, then as a businesswoman. Both characters were more interesting than Diana Langston. Diana Langston was a very dull character, which may have explained why Vera Miles had absolutely nothing to do with Lynda Day George throughout the shooting of the pilot. "I was on the set with her only a couple of times," remembers George. "She was very distant, not terribly friendly to me. I'm not sure whether that was her or whether that was because of the role."

Great as the *Cannon* pilot was, according to *Cannon* producer Anthony Spinner, it almost never made it to the air. Remembers Spinner, "Quinn had called Fred Silverman, who ran CBS, and told him, 'I want to do a show with Bill Conrad.' 'Oh, great, great, great,' says Silverman. 'Put him in.' So I go in to the first day's dailies. Silverman's driven over from CBS to go in and see the dailies, and I hear this asthmatic breathing next to me, like somebody's gonna have a heart attack and it's Silverman. I said, 'What's the matter with him?' Because he's panting heavily. Finally the dailies are over. Silverman turns to Quinn. He says, 'Who the hell is that big fat guy in the striped shirt?' Quinn says, 'That's Bill Conrad.' Silverman says, 'Bill Conrad! I thought we were hiring Bob Conrad!' He stormed out of the projection room saying, 'This show will never air!' Well, he was wrong because Bill Paley [Silverman's boss at CBS] loved Bill Conrad from the days of *Gunsmoke* when Bill was playing Matt Dillon on the radio. So Paley said, 'We're gonna do the show.' Then Bill Conrad is a big hit, and suddenly there's a big article in *Variety* from Fred Silverman on 'How he picked Bill Conrad because he's changing the face of television.' I called Quinn. He said, 'Leave him alone. The man's got an ego. I've got the money. You've got the talent. He's got the ego.'"

William Paley wasn't the only fan of William Conrad. "Bill was an incredible guy," says *Cannon* producer Alan Armer. "He had great charm. Great power as an actor. Great authority as an actor. He was one of the great voices in the industry. For a man who was overweight, he was incredibly charming. Women because of his voice, and because of his charm, liked him. He had some successful relationships with women." Conrad certainly had a successful friendship with Lynda Day George. "Bill Conrad was probably the most gentlemanly person, the most kindly person that I ever worked with as an actor, and he was my hero from then on,' insists the actress. "He and Burl Ives were my all-time heroes. They were the only serious competition Chris ever faced. I was pleased to be in Bill's company. I tried to spend as much time with him as I possibly could. We liked each other very much. Bill and Chris spent a good bit of time together too. They had a good time. They both hit the bottle. They were weaned on it. I remember Bill's wife [former New York high fashion model Susan Randall] calling me one time. She says, 'You know Lynda, the two of us need to keep our husbands apart.'"

William Conrad definitely drank. "He was a fun guy," remembers Anthony Spinner. "I used to worry about the amount of food that he consumed, the amount of drinks that he consumed, the amount of cigars that he smoked. He had a dressing room that he lived in, next to my office. This trailer was all set up for him with hi-fis and a bar, and I liked Bill a lot, but I was married, and had two young children, and when Bill saw me leaving, I would be dragged into his office and I'd have to drink with him, and he'd call my wife and say, 'Hey, Tony and I are going out to dinner. Got any objections? Too bad,' and hang up with a laugh. So we'd go out to dinner and I never saw a man consume that much food in my life. We went one time to this restaurant, Emilio's, with one of our directors, George McCowan, whom Bill liked a lot. Before we went, Bill would pour these huge drinks. Everything about the man was massive. He had these Scotch glasses that were huge. He'd fill them to the top, and he'd be kind of put out if you didn't drink with

QM favorite Lynne Marta (Nicole Alexandre, a.k.a. rock singer "Judy Lorelei," a.k.a. rock singer "Nikki Kent") and William Conrad (as private detective Frank Cannon) in the October 26, 1971, first-season CBS-TV *Cannon* episode, "Girl in the Electric Coffin."

him; so we'd drink with him. We smoked Cuban cigars with him, and then when we were kinda loaded, we'd drive to this restaurant, and to get Bill into a car, the director had a small, I think it was a Ferrari, and Bill wanted to go in the Ferrari. So we had to cram him in like a sardine, pushing and shoving, and we got to the restaurant, and Bill ordered more to drink. Then—and I'll never forget this—he ordered two complete Italian dinners for himself—from start to finish, and he had his own wine that they kept in the wine cellar downstairs so he had a bottle of that brought up. Then, after I'm about ready to collapse just from watching him eat, he says, 'Now, what are we having for dessert?' I said, 'Bill, I'm not gonna be able to work tomorrow, and you have a six o'clock call. Why don't you say we call it a night?' 'Nah, we're gonna have some dessert.' So, we had dessert. I was so sick when I went home, I thought I was gonna die. I thought, he'll never be there on the set in the morning. I purposely got in very early at six, and there he is, sitting in my office, I remember, in a striped shirt, his stomach sticking out four feet, eating a Jelly doughnut and drinking coffee, and he looked fine. I looked like a wreck."

Like everything else about William Conrad, the actor's voracious appetite was worked into his television character, Frank Cannon. Frank Cannon was larger than life. So it only made sense that the criminals he battle be larger than life too. Gerald S. O'Loughlin certainly was in the first season's "A Flight of Hawks." In "Flight," O'Loughlin portrayed a mercenary plotting to overthrow an African government. The story opened with O'Loughlin chasing a car in his plane, strafing the car with machine-gun fire until the car finally crashed and blew up. "We always did excessively violent teasers," says series producer Harold Gast. "That way we could grab the audience. On that show, we filmed at a landing strip in the [Mojave] desert above Los Angeles [near Antelope Valley]. Conrad had to take apart and reassemble an aircraft machine gun in that one. At the climax he had to walk while holding the machine gun and fire it. It was very very heavy, but he managed to do it. We had a very bad accident on that show I remember. The script called for an open jeep [a Ford Bronco] to be buzzed at a very low level by a twin-engine plane. Jim Gavin was flying the plane. He got down so low the propellers cut about six inches into the windshield."

Camera operator Frank Beaschoea was in the passenger side of the jeep at the time. "Frank was supposed to pan up, and as the plane went by, then pan down through the windshield as the plane flew away," remembers sound mixer Dick Church. "The prop cut the window frame right above Frank's head. We all heard it. I was about two hundred yards away. It cut like a three-inch hunk out of the top of the door frame." "The jeep was driving towards me," adds Gavin. "I was flying towards it, and I was flying into the sun. I was supposed to veer off, but instead got too close, and of course it was the last shot of the day. Whenever you have an accident in this business, it's always the last shot of the day. They didn't want to come back out to the desert the next day just to get that shot. I could have said, 'It's too late. I don't want to do this,' but I didn't." William Conrad later had the pieces of the Bronco's window frame gilded, and mounted and gave it to Beaschoea as a present. Beaschoea appreciated the gift.

As did the entire crew when Conrad presented them with the "Cannon" belt buckles he'd had made to commemorate the great Goldwyn Studios fire. "They had this big fire—it kind of ran along Santa Monica Blvd., and we were on the bottom floor," remembers the series' production coordinator Karen Shaw. "They took the big *Barnaby Jones* semi and ran the fence down, so they could get the cars out. They lined up the cars according to their value. The fire was caused by *Sigmund and the Sea Monsters* [which also shot at Goldwyn]. They had these stryro-foam caves which ignited from the heat of the lights. The stage just imploded and the walls came down, and the next thing you know here comes Rip Taylor, dressed in a sea-monster outfit, waving his hands and running up and down the hall, and Johnnie Whittaker's behind him. They're all trying to get off the lot, and people are jumping out the windows, because it was a pretty devastating fire. We were all kind of amused. There was a lot of humor to it."

Humorous was the right description for what happened next. "We were herded outside by the firemen, who were coming in, pouring water," recalls Spinner. "We get out of there, and then my story editor [Stephen Kandel] and I say, 'My God! The scripts! The scripts are gonna burn up! All that work!' We rushed back in there, fighting the firemen, breaking through like we were rescuing a child. We piled the scripts under our arms, ran back out through the fire. We all made the news. I said, 'At last, I'm a hero. I saved the scripts.' But we lost an entire stage—everything. We had to go shoot other places for the rest of the season."

Given how he'd started out on *Cannon*, Anthony Spinner had justification for behaving so foolishly. "I'd just finished *The FBI* when Quinn called me," remembers Spinner. "He says, 'I'd like you to do either *The Manhunter* or *Cannon*. I'm not sure that *Hunter* is gonna last that long, so you'd probably be safer with *Cannon*.' I said, 'I don't know....' He says, 'You don't have time to think about it, because Friday is the last day for you on *The FBI*. I don't think it's gonna be renewed, and I need you over on *Cannon* on Monday.' I said, 'Why do you need me on Monday?' He said, 'Because there's a writer's strike coming and we're gonna continue shooting, and we don't have a single script.' I said, 'How can you not have a single script? You've been on the air a few years.' He said, 'We don't have a single script. You've gotta write the first show while getting other shows.' So, I wrote the first show of that season, and I didn't have time to do another draft because I was so busy getting other shows. I had writers going in and out of my office like a subway turnstile. I mean, there were writers there every twenty minutes, and I was giving them these stories. I'd call Quinn, 'By the way, did you do this kind of story?' 'No.' 'Okay. Bye,' and slam down the phone. So the first month was madness, because I was getting scripts in three, four, five days from the writers, and then either I, or one of my story editors would go home and rewrite it that night. So that first month was madness, and the reward of course was that Quinn gave me *Caribe* to do at the same time, as well as the movie [*Panic on the 5:22*]."

Adding to Spinner's troubles was an often cantankerous William Conrad. Conrad's choosing to read his lines from off-set cue cards, frequently frustrated many series guests. "The first season," reveals assistant director David Whorf, "Bill was a dream-boat. He was a consummate artist. The first season he memorized his lines. The second season, he posted his lines on other actors' foreheads and chests, he put them on the camera, he used cue cards. With his heavy, fleshy face, you really didn't see a lot of his eyes, so you couldn't see that he was looking someplace other than directly at the other actor." "To Bill," adds series director William Hale, "this was filmed radio. He was used to reading his lines, and I remember we had this bald-headed assistant cameraman on the show. So with a marker pen they would write Conrad's dialogue on this guy's bald head, so when it came time, the guy would tip his head toward Conrad and Conrad would read his lines right off the guy's bald head." When Philip Pine guest-starred on the show, Conrad's dialogue was on a blackboard. "We started to shoot this scene going into the police station," recalls Pine, "and there's this guy with a big blackboard with Conrad's lines on it. We're doing this dolly shot, going along walking and talking and here he is—every shot that he did, he has the guy holding this big blackboard with his name on it, with his lines on it. God Almighty! That's very distracting for the other actor, but apparently Conrad just didn't want to bother."

Besides his refusal to learn dialogue, Conrad was a problem in other ways. "He was a hard-nosed tough individual who'd been head of Warner's television, so he knew everything," says *Cannon* director Michael Caffey. "He knew exactly what he was doing, why he was doing it. He didn't want to be on camera for anybody, didn't care, wasn't gonna do it. He had a temper. He'd bite at you, and then it was gone. There was no rancor. There was no carrying on or anything."

Conrad also "swore like a seaman," laughs script supervisor Kenneth Gilbert, "which never made any sense. The guy had such command of the language, but the words would come out. The women on the set never took offense. It was just the way he expressed himself. He was rough and hard, and because he had such an over-powering presence, you'd shake in your boots sometimes. But he really was a pussy-cat." William Conrad definitely treated Kenneth Gilbert very well. "One time," recalls Gilbert, "I was doing something that required a narrator, so I asked Bill if he'd do it. He said, 'Oh, sure.' So we went into his trailer and did it. He says, 'I'm not happy with that. Let me take it home. I've got some equipment there.' He went home, recorded the dialogue again. Now this is a guy who probably gets $6,000 a minute for his voice. Next day he hands it to me, says, 'Here you go.'" It was also Conrad who got Gilbert his first directing job on *Cannon*, "House of Cards." After Quinn Martin saw the show, he called Kenneth Gilbert into his office. "It's a very good show," Martin told Gilbert, "but you didn't let yourself be seen in any of this. This could have been a Walter Grauman show, or a Jesse Hibbs show. Bring your own creativity to the next one you do."

Assistant director David Whorf made his directorial debut the same season as Gilbert. Whorf's show was the fifth season's "Blood Lines." David Whorf was the perfect assistant director for *Cannon*. He and the series' most frequent director, George McCowan (a native Canadian and former Shakespearean actor) had worked together quite often on the 1966–69 Walter Grauman–Philip Saltzman series, *The Felony Squad*. "George was the only director who wasn't there when I started everything rolling," laughs Whorf. "He didn't say, 'Action!' He was a very quiet, unassuming guy. He was a dear man, loved by everybody, and he was perfect for Bill Conrad. George understated so much. He didn't over-manipulate people. He'd learned very early on that you choose certain places in the script to spend time. The rest, you just go in and out like a son of a bitch. He was totally prepared. There wasn't a mark or a note in his script about the camera angles. He had all that in his head."

Earning actor-director William Conrad's respect for both his acting and direct-ing credentials, George McCowan had another thing in common with the star. They could both drink heavily. Each also had a great sense of humor. Chuckles Whorf, "I will never forget this one time when we were shooting. We were up in Durango, Colorado, and it so happened it was my birthday. George McCowan comes into my room in the hotel. He says, 'You better get down to the bar. [Director of photography]

William Conrad (as private-detective Frank Cannon) plays off his character's name in an amusing publicity shot for the September 14, 1971–September 19, 1976, CBS-TV series, *Cannon*.

Jack Swain and Bill are fighting. I said, 'Oh shit, I'll be slaughtered in that. I'll be dead in the crossfire.' He says, 'You better do something.' He had me eating it all the way down to the bar, and there were Jack and Bill. Then they turned around, they started singing, 'Happy Birthday.' I said to George, 'You son of a bitch. You scared the shit out of me.'"

Says Michael Caffey, "Bill Conrad loved to put people on," too. "He'd do it with a straight face. He and Dick Church would get into these arguments. They'd start yelling back and forth, and one time it went too far. They got into the language. I thought they were gonna come to blows. They didn't, of course. It was all a joke." "Conrad was always acting up," agrees supervising editor Richard Brockway. "He was always giving people problems. Some of it was funny; some of it wasn't. Well he had this friend James Newcom who was an assistant editor who was in charge of the stock footage. So every time there was something strange or funny that we saw during the dailies, Newcom would pull that material and keep it for the gag reel. At the end of the year, he'd put this gag reel together with Conrad's help. They'd bring out the gag reel and play it every year at the Christmas party." "We had a lot of parties," recalls Karen Shaw. "The *Cannon* Christmas party just about put me away. I'd been working there only about three weeks. There was a lot of partying. The Christmas parties which were on the stage were pretty serious. They were for everybody. We drank pretty heavily."

If not partying on the stage, the crew was then down in Huntington Harbor, at the invitation of Jack Swain, to watch the big Christmas boat parade, after which the crew partied all night long on Swain's house-boat. "Jack Swain was kind of a gruff guy," remembers David Whorf. "Everybody said, 'Oh, watch out for him. He'll bite your head off.' That never happened to me. I somehow got on his good side. Jack was very businesslike, particularly with his own crew. He expected them to pay attention to him and do what he said." The father of seven sons whose license plate said, "Seven Sons" (William Conrad's said, "Darnoc," which was "Conrad" spelled backwards), Swain, who had served in John Ford's combat photography unit in the Navy in World War II, and later worked for the O.S.S., was perfect for the Western-type locations so frequently seen on *Cannon*. Swain's previous TV credits included *Daniel Boone*, and *Rawhide*. "I had nothing but the greatest respect for Jack," states Kenneth Gilbert. "He had this leather bound stool on which he'd sit right behind the camera, and he never left the set. I don't think he ever went to the bathroom in four years. He was there all the time. That's very unusual—it's such a high, stressful job."

Swain's dedication was a good thing. Like its star William Conrad, *Cannon* was a big, big show. "Quinn would propose expensive things," remembers series producer Harold Gast. "Once he suggested to me that we go and shoot a couple of *Cannon*s in Colorado, on location in the mountains. He said it would work out economically if we did two shows back to back. So we developed a couple of scripts that could be shot there." "Sky Above, Death Below" featured Indian ruins, the helicopter work of James Gavin, and a sequence on a ski-lift; the stunt-man had to jump from one moving ski-lift-car to the other. Harold Gast enjoyed being on location in Colorado. Gast always enjoyed being on location. In "Death of a Stone Seahorse," he was down at the waterfront. "Death" featured his daughter Nancy Gast, who wanted to be an actress at the time. She had a small part. Harold Gast was none too enthusiastic though about "To Kill a Guinea Pig," which was filmed on location at the Terminal Island prison. "It was a very chilling atmosphere," remembers the producer. "We had to be very careful where we went, what we did. Sometimes the inmates would howl and make noise when we were filming."

Although James Olson's performance as a neatnik villain in "The Island Caper" made for a great character, "that was not one of our best shows," says Gast. "We went over to Catalina that time. The script wasn't the most logical. Conrad brought me that idea." "Catalina wasn't the greatest town for a film company," adds assistant director/unit production manager Bob Jeffords. "We had people housed in bed and breakfast places all around town. We had to dig [guest star] Keenan Wynn out of the bar to get him to the set." Some rather unusual casting went on for the animal-based "Death of a Hunter." Recalls Karen Shaw, "I was in this little script closet, rooting around for my scripts, and the door of the office opened, and there's Gentle Ben standing in the doorway. There was a trainer on the other end of the rope, but I couldn't see· him. [Seamstress] Magda Hefty was up on a desk, just panic-stricken. We just kept on feeding that bear tootsie rolls."

By the time of "Death of a Hunter," the series had gone through two producers. Alan Armer had been the first. "That was kind of the end of my television career," states Armer. "I had a tough time with that series. I'd gone over to Universal, and I wasn't happy there. Then Quinn asked me if I wanted to do *Cannon*. I said, 'Sure.' But the network was looking for violence, and I was having trouble giving them that. It was

Cannon star William Conrad presented this dartboard to each member of the *Cannon* crew at the close of one season. (Photograph courtesy the late Bob Jeffords.)

not the kind of show that I had a good feel for. I'd never done a private-eye show before. So, about halfway through the year, I told Quinn I was not comfortable with the series. He says, 'Okay. I know another guy who can take over.'"

That "guy" was former *Judd, for the Defense* producer Harold Gast. Gast set about making the best show that he could. "The show hadn't been doing well," states Gast, "and after I got on it, it began doing very well. Then someone published an article to that effect, and when William Conrad saw that, he was furious. He didn't like the idea that he'd been doing a show that hadn't been doing well until I'd gotten on it."

Another thing Conrad didn't like was the tuba music series composer John Parker had written for his character. "He went to Quinn," remembers John Elizalde, "and told him, 'It's a caricature. It's too cartoony.' Quinn comes to me. He says, 'What about that?' I said, 'Well, yeah, it is a caricature. It's perfect for Conrad.' Eventually both Bill Conrad and Quinn wound up liking it. That was very unusual—giving Bill a theme like that. Very rarely did we assign musical themes to characters. Usually you just wrote the music for the scenes."

While William Conrad may have disliked the tuba music at the beginning, he could certainly laugh at his being overweight. He did that quite often through the series' five-year run. Conrad could also laugh at his often cranky disposition. "He had a great sense of humor," praises Bob Jeffords. "His Christmas present to us one year was a dart-board with his picture on it. Around the circle of his picture, it said, 'For all you bastards who've wanted to all year long. Have a ball.' As the *Cannon* gag reel proved, Conrad had no problems laughing about the difference between him and his stunt-man, Jimmy Casino." "Jimmy had to look like Bill in profile," explains Jeffords. "But the minute Bill started running, Bill would bend over from the waist, the top of his body would be almost parallel with the ground. Well, the minute Jimmy started running, he'd straighten up more. So you could immediately tell whether it was Bill or Jimmy doing the stunt."

"The *Cannon* series was always a really close series," continues Jeffords. "It was one of the few shows I'd been on where the crew was almost the same from beginning to end. That doesn't happen a lot. But for the most part, we were all together that whole five years. It was amazing how well we were all still getting along at the end."

Unfortunately, such was not the case with QM Productions' next television series. Its producer Ed Adamson didn't care to work with Quinn Martin or anyone from QM Productions. One couldn't blame Adamson. *Banyon* was not originally a Quinn Martin Production.

Chapter 9

BANYON

It was Ed Adamson's vision. It was Ed's show.
                    Banyon *casting director Meryl S. O'Loughlin*

Had Quinn Martin known of the problems he was going to have with *Banyon* producer Ed Adamson during the series' short run from September 15, 1972, to January 12, 1973, he might never have accepted the series when NBC-TV dropped it into his lap. Then again he might have. Quinn Martin loved *Banyon*. He loved that time period of the 1930s, so much so, he and his wife Muffet once attended a *Banyon* party in period dress. If Quinn Martin hadn't loved *Banyon*, he certainly wouldn't have cast such QM favorites as Marlyn Mason, Jessica Walter, Tim O'Connor, Fritz Weaver, and Jack Klugman in the series. He wouldn't have assigned one of his favorite directors, Ralph Senensky, to direct multiple episodes. He wouldn't have spent all the money that he would have needed to spend in order to make a good period piece. Nor would he have been trying to work out a deal with Lynda Day George so that she could guest star on *Banyon* at the same time she was starring in her own series, *Mission: Impossible*.

Banyon creator-producer Ed Adamson had developed *Banyon* as a showcase for his pal Robert Forster. In 1969, Adamson had seen a Gregory Peck Western called *The Stalking Moon*. In it, Forster played an Indian. Reveals Forster, "Ed saw a scene in that movie with me and a young Indian lad. He wrote my name down when the credits came up and said to himself, 'I'm gonna hire that guy someday,'" which Adamson did for the March 15, 1971, movie-pilot, *Banyon*.

Directed by Robert Day, the well-produced 1971 Warner Bros. pilot had former cop turned private detective Miles C. Banyon trying to clear himself of a murder charge after his young female client is found dead in his office, killed by his own gun. Banyon's office was located in the Bradbury Building, which Robert Forster calls "one of the great interiors of L.A. Outside it doesn't look like much, but when you walk inside, suddenly you're back a hundred and twenty years [because of the ornate cast iron architecture]." "The Bradbury Building was always a good location," says production manager Howard Alston. "It was all iron staircases and open grille elevators; it was unique. There were real offices in the building. The tenants got tired of having motion-picture companies running up and down the stairs, creating all that fuss and having that equipment in the place all the time. So when the building's owners changed hands, they didn't allow companies to shoot there for a long while. At the time we made the series however, we were the only company shooting in that building." "We never really had anything good to shoot there," states series director Ralph Senensky. "The building wasn't utilized as much as it should have been. They didn't write sequences for those great staircases, those banisters. Instead we shot up in the Hollywood Hills, or on the [Warner Bros.] back-lot, on the New York street. When we did that series, what we were really shooting was film noir."

Film noir made sense in a show whose title character was a detective in the Sam Spade–Philip Marlowe tradition. In other words, a down-on-his-luck private detective who'd take almost any kind of case, and was often beaten up by thugs. As evidenced by the series' pilot, "Ed Adamson was very much into all of that," says pilot director Robert Day. "He really was into the *Maltese Falcon* and all those 1930s and '40s shows. He was into that very much, and he wanted to keep it almost verbatim. I really liked his original script. He was a clever writer." As was the pilot's co-writer, Richard Alan Simmons. He and Ed Adamson had their own ideas on how to do the *Banyon* pilot. Those ideas weren't the same. The two men did not get along.

So, when NBC decided to do the *Banyon* series one year later, with Quinn Martin as their producer, Ed Adamson was not happy. "Ed felt ownership of the idea at the very least," says Robert Forster. "He created the show. He was the primary source and the link. "Ed Adamson really resented any interference from the QM organization," remembers Ralph Senensky. "There was an air of hostility between him and the QM people. I didn't have any actual out and out problems with it, but Quinn did make it a point to come to me and thank me after I'd finished one of the shows. He very seldom did that. Ed Adamson was a real problem. He was caught up in the fact that this was his baby, and that he was now doing it under Quinn's umbrella. Ed didn't want to be told what to do. Especially since he was ill at the time. So he figured he was gonna do it his way, which he did."

Robert Forster recalls, "Ed said to me once in his kind of gravelly voice, 'You know, Bob, you got your own patois there. Go right ahead and use it.' That gave me a little bit of flexibility in how to do the dialogue because part of this was set-up stuff. There were a lot of wisecracks, a lot of period dialogue. To make that work, you gotta work hard so that it doesn't sound artificial or stilted, you want it to sound believable." As far as casting director Meryl O'Loughlin was concerned, Forster was. "Bobby was perfect in the role," says O'Loughlin. "He had a twinkle in his eye, looked great in the clothes. Bobby was a very earthy guy. He came from a construction background, from Albany, New York. He wasn't part of the movie town. He didn't take the acting profession all that seriously." "Robert Forster was a terrific guy," agrees Alston. "He wanted to make the series work. He worked hard. He had a bad football knee that kept dislocating itself whenever he ran. We tried not to make him run too often."

Never having done a television show as a regular, and never having done much television period, Robert Forster learned very quickly "that there's nothing harder in the actor's spectrum than doing a one-hour drama show. It was the toughest thing I ever did in show business," says Forster. "It was a challenge, and challenges are great. I had so much to do in that show, learning scene after scene, changing them when they didn't work. Trying to put that together and working with new actors and new directors every week, that's a real, real job. Our first day's work was over twenty-one hours. They picked me up in the early morning. I was living out at the beach. They picked me up pre-dawn, and it was a long drive to a little airport somewhere. We started working at dawn or so. We didn't get home till two or three in the morning. It was over a twenty hour day. So after two or three weeks, I got sick. I had either the flu or a cold."

"I remember I was out doing a movie in South Dakota—*Journey through Rosebud*—when I learned that the pilot had gone to series. I got a call from my agent. He said, 'Quinn Martin wants to talk to you.' So when I finished the movie, I drove to L.A. and had this meeting with Quinn Martin where he told me he was going to take over the production of *Banyon*. Apparently Quinn decided he liked the show and wanted to put it under his banner. So after a season in which the show had not been picked up, he picked it up, and brought it to [prime-time television] on Friday nights."

Banyon premiered on September 15, 1972. One week and one day later, Quinn Martin launched his other crime-drama series of the 1972-73 season, *The Streets of San Francisco*. Walter Grauman directed that series' pilot, and many of its first-season episodes. "Walter was the lucky one," laughs Ralph Senensky. "He got *Streets*. I got *Banyon*. I was signed to do episodes one, three and five. Senensky's first *Banyon* was the premiere episode, "The Decent Thing to Do." "Decent Thing" provided its top guest Marlyn Mason with what she considered "a nice, dramatic character role," and an even odder role for Mason's fellow guest star, Peter White. "We made him the 'Man from Glad,'" chuckles Senensky. "We put Peter in a white suit and bleached his hair white."

The following week, Shelly Novack, one season away from joining *The FBI* in the role of Special Agent Chris Daniels, guest-starred in "The Old College Try." One week later, the series aired Senensky's "The Graveyard Vote." "Graveyard" reunited long-time Warner Bros. contract players Pat O'Brien (guest-starring in the episode) and *Banyon* series regular Joan Blondell. Blondell played Peggy Revere, owner of the Revere Secretarial School, which always provided Miles Banyon with a temporary secretary free of charge. "They hired Pat O'Brien for just one day," remembers Senensky. "He had all these scenes to do, but the publicity department was all over him because he and Joan Blondell were reunited on the Warner lot. So they wanted to do stories and interviews, and they were crowding all of this into one day. Pat was perturbed and rightfully so. He was trying to do the shoot." "That was one of the great days on the set," adds Robert Forster. "Suddenly everybody from all kinds of stages came over to visit and say hello to Pat. One after another, grips and executives, all day long, all kinds of people. That was a nice thing to see."

Robert Forster thoroughly enjoyed the *Banyon* episode, "Meal Ticket." Guest-starring in the episode was former *Bowery Boys–Dead End Kid* regular Gabriel Dell. "Gabe Dell gave me a great piece of acting advice," recalls Forster. "He told me that one of the things that used to go on in the Dead End Kids movies was that before the take, one of the guys would say to the other guy, 'Wait'll you see what I do to him.' Then another guy would be saying, 'Wait'll you see what I do to him.' So everything they did, it was spontaneous, and unexpected. The unexpected makes a scene interesting. Being spontaneous livens up the scene."

Forster also liked the episode in which the murder victim's name was Gene Parota. "I had a pal whose name was Gene Parota, and right in the beginning of the picture, he gets killed," explains Forster. "Then for the whole episode, every once in a while, somebody says something or other about Gene Parota. That was my idea. I put Gene's name in there, and got a great big kick out of it, and so did he, and so did all of the guys in Rochester who knew him. It must have been said eight or ten times." Guest star Elaine Giftos had a sense of humor too. "I said, 'How do you pronounce your name?'" chuckles Forster. "She said, 'Just remember, Never look a Giftos in the mouth.'"

Elaine Giftos was one of the better known actresses to play one of Miles C. Banyon's temporary secretaries. Others included Pamela McMyler, future 20th Century–Fox studio head Sherry Lansing, and *McCloud* semi-regular Teri Garr. "That was a great idea," says Meryl O'Loughlin, "giving him a different secretary every week. *Murphy Brown* picked up on that same idea years later. Teri Garr was wonderful. She was funny, ditzy, all the wonderful things you could think of. Sherry Lansing was a cute, sweet girl. At that time she was seriously pursuing acting." Banyon's secretary wasn't always female however. "The secretarial school was right next to my office," says Forster, "and each week if I didn't have much dough, I would get a trainee to be my secretary. That's why we had a new secretary every week. Well, one week there was this big guy, this wrestler, who didn't want to be a wrestler anymore. He wanted to have a better job, something he could really fall back on; so he became a secretary. Now my first meeting with this guy, I walk in my office. The guy doesn't know who I am. He doesn't want to let me in. The next thing you know, I come flying out of my office." Playing the part of the wrestler turned secretary was Lenny Montana. Montana had a very good part in *The Godfather*.

While the ever-changing secretary, Banyon's wisecracks, and the period costumes made for a fun series, producing it was anything but fun. "The cars were all antique cars," says Senensky. "They were a major problem. When you had a scene with a car, you knew it was gonna take time. To get them to start, it took forever." "We had to get special mechanics for the cars," remembers Alston. "Sometimes the cars broke down." "Driving those cars was like driving a refrigerator," adds Forster. "They were real heavy mechanical automobiles, not like what we're used to driving today. They had to really heft those things around back then. That's why the steering wheels were so big. You had to get some leverage on them."

Costumes, provided by Western Costume Company, were generally not a problem, "but you were always fighting the guy who'd come in with long hair, who didn't want to cut his hair," says Alston. "Plus you were always trying to doctor up locations to make it look like it was the 1930s. We didn't build a lot of sets. We just looked for exteriors and locations that didn't look modern. You couldn't have a huge amount of exteriors. When you were shooting on the street, you couldn't put all those people in costume. So we did a lot of night shooting. You can cover up a multitude of sins at night that you can't cover up in the daytime. I mean everything in front of the camera had to be period, so when we were shooting in the daytime, we'd put camouflage netting over things to hide them. Period pictures are always very difficult to do. Usually if we told people we were doing a shoot, and told them why we'd like to have them wait to cross the street until we finished, they were cooperative, but every once in a while, you'd get the guy who says, 'I'm crossing the street! I don't give a goddamn about your shot! I'm gonna cross the street!' And here you are in the middle of a shot, where you're shooting all these period cars, and this guy's dressed in a baseball hat. You want to kill him."

Yet it wasn't really the expense of doing *Banyon* that killed the show. It was the sudden loss of its creator, Ed Adamson. "Ed died during the shooting of the show," recalls Meryl O'Loughlin. "It was such a shock to everybody. One day he was there, the next day, he was dead." "We had an order of fifteen episodes," adds Forster, "and on the thirteenth episode, Ed died. He died at home. He was at my house Saturday night. Sunday I got a call from his wife, Helene. She told me Ed had just passed away. We talked about keeping the show going with Dick Donner running and producing the show, but we were sort of on the edge with the ratings."

Given the loss of its creator-producer Ed Adamson, its weak ratings, and its powerful competition (the last hour of the *CBS Friday Night Movie*, ABC's popular hour-long sitcom, *Love American Style*), NBC opted to cancel *Banyon*. The series' final episode, "Time Lapse," guest-starring Donna Mills, aired on January 12, 1973. On January 28 of that same year, Quinn Martin's second most successful series, *Barnaby Jones*, began its seven and a half year run. Quinn Martin liked *Barnaby Jones*, but not as much as the series that had preceded it five months earlier: *The Streets of San Francisco*.

Chapter 10

THE STREETS
OF SAN FRANCISCO

Quinn took such a proprietary interest in *Streets*. I was going in to see the dailies on *Barnaby Jones*, and I met Quinn coming out of the screening room with his entourage. He says, "Phil, I gotta tell ya. I've just seen a wonderful episode of *Streets*," and *Barnaby* and *Streets* were on the same night at the same time, on opposite networks—*Barnaby* on CBS, *Streets* on ABC. Quinn says, "We're gonna cream you with this show!" I said, "Quinn! They're both your shows!"
Barnaby Jones *producer/executive producer Philip Saltzman*

That Quinn Martin loved *The Streets of San Francisco* (September 16, 1972–June 23, 1977) was evident from the very beginning. Unlike all the other QM series, *The Streets of San Francisco* began its prime-time run one week after it had aired its pilot. Usually a series didn't begin its prime-time run until after its pilot had attracted an audience, or, at least, network interest. Obviously Quinn Martin and ABC had a lot of faith that *The Streets of San Francisco* would attract a sizable audience. It did.

"Quinn liked *Streets* very much," states Muffet Martin. "He loved San Francisco. It photographed beautifully. They had interesting guest stars on that show, interesting stories, and of course that's where his friendship with [series producer] John Wilder began. I liked that series myself. It was my second favorite." "I felt that *Streets* had much more depth than the other shows," says the series' unit production manager Bob Jeffords. "It didn't have their two-dimensional qualities. The characters in *Streets* made choices, faced dilemmas. You saw Mike Stone [Karl Malden] and Steve Keller [Michael Douglas] making mistakes. You saw the characters played by the guest casts start as basically good people, and watch them go bad." Of course, such human drama was the sum and substance of both *The FBI* and especially *Barnaby Jones*, but one thing that *Streets* had going for it, which those other two series didn't, was a demanding and perfectionist leading man like Karl Malden.

What with a resume that included such classic motion-pictures as *On the Waterfront, Baby Doll,* and *Patton,* and a no-less impressive roster of stage plays, Karl Malden had the highest of standards when it came to his work as a performer. *The Streets of San Francisco* reflected those standards. Especially when it came to its guest casts. First-year guests included Edmond O'Brien and Lew Ayres. Future seasons included Richard Basehart, Maurice Evans, Signe Hasso, and Dorothy Malone.

Title card for the September 16, 1972–June 23, 1977, ABC-TV series, *The Streets of San Francisco*.

"Karl was a perfection-ist," states production manager Howard Alston. "He knew what the story was about, knew why he was doing every scene. If he didn't have a script fourteen days before the next shoot, he wouldn't do it. We always had a script ahead of time on that show. Karl made that a rule with Quinn, and by extension the writers." "You practically had a shooting script the first day you went in for prep," elaborates series director Michael Caffey. "That's the way it should be. As far as Karl Malden was concerned, that was how it would be. He had that in his contract. Karl was a hard-nosed son of a bitch. He had to have the next script before he would start the one he was shoot-ing. He insisted on that. That way he could study it with his dialogue coach. So [when the time came to do the show] he knew it cold." "Working with Karl Malden was a real pleasure," says series director Kenneth Gilbert. "He was there to do the very best. I remember when I did my one show [the fifth season's "One Last Trick"], we were doing a line-up type of thing, and I was telling the cameraman, Michel Hugo, what I wanted. Karl says to Michel, 'Are you going to say something or am I going to say something?' Michel says, 'You go ahead.' Karl turns to me. He says, 'We did this exact same setup last week with Bill Hale directing. It looks like you're copy-ing. I know you didn't know he did it.' Karl didn't want to copy. He was always inter-ested in getting the best possible show. He wanted the show to have variety."

Like Kenneth Gilbert, William Hale was another director who got along with Malden. "I kept asking him about [*On the Waterfront* director] Elia Kazan," says Hale, "asking him, 'What would Kazan do.' But when Dick Donner directed, well, there was this scene that called for a clandestine meeting between Karl and somebody down at the wharf. Dick moved it to the porch of a hospital, where you saw the whole San Francisco skyline in the background. When Karl saw where it was being shot, he said to Dick, 'I know what you're doing. You're just filling in time until you get a feature to direct. I bet you don't even know what this scene is about.' Dick says, 'Oh yes, I do. It's a scene about two people walking and talking.'" That was the worst thing to say to Karl Malden. "To Karl," explains Alston, "there were no scenes that were just walk and talk. Karl never forgave Dick for that." Richard Donner only did a couple of *Streets of San Francisco*s. "Dick was more interested in the production values," continues Alston. "I liked Dick, but he was kind of ... he drove around in a Mercedes four-door convertible with a police dog in the back. It was a command car. Dick liked to be in command."

That guaranteed conflict. On *The Streets of San Francisco*, Karl Malden was in command. "Karl just ran over everybody," states Michael Caffey. "If you got in a scene with Karl, you better be on your toes. He was strong physically, had a strong voice, a strong presence." "He didn't take anything from anybody," adds Alston. "If he was wrong, he'd be the first one to admit it, but you had to convince him first. If you could convince him that black was white, he'd accept it, but you had to convince him."

Being a tough man himself, Walter Grauman was therefore the perfect director to work with Malden in *The Streets of San Francisco* pilot. "That was a big production," recalls Grauman, "it was like a theatrical film. At the very beginning of the shoot, I set up this shot in which I wanted the police car—the brown Ford that Karl and Michael always drove—to start down from Nob Hill. Now both Karl and Michael were in the car, and Michael was driving. I said, 'Michael, are you a good driver?' He says, 'Oh, yeah! I'm a great driver.' I said, 'Karl, do you want a stunt double?' He says, 'No. I'll do this.' So, they get in the car. I said, 'Okay. Now here's what I want you to do. I want you to, as fast as you safely can, come down the street, turn left in front of the Fairmont Hotel, go through several stunt cars who will have narrow misses with you; then you'll get to,' I think it was California Street. 'You just go right on over the edge,' and here's the whole bay, with Alcatraz and all this great scenery. I said, 'You just speed right on over that steep incline and go down the hill until I say, 'Cut!' Michael says, 'Yeah. I can do that.' They get in the car. He starts driving. They whip around the corner, and I'm on a huge crane with the camera. I'm watching. They turn a sharp left, go past the Fairmont, then go right off the edge, down the street, down this steep incline, and the car takes off. It's in the air. All four wheels are off the ground. They're going so fast, and all of a sudden, I can't see it, it's below the frame, and I hear this sound. I'm thinking, Oh my God! This is the end of the series. They're both dead. And then I hear a car vrrooomm, and brakes squealing. I jump off the crane. I asked the cameraman [William W. Spencer], 'Did you get it?' He says, 'Up to the time he went off the hill. After that, I couldn't see him.' I said, 'Don't say anything.'

"I go running down the hill after them. Karl gets out of the car, white as a sheet. He says, 'What the hell's going on here?' I said, 'Karl. I know it was scary. But we've got the greatest shot you can imagine. I mean a great opening main title. You racing here, and the city behind you, blah, blah, blah.' He says, 'Well, okay.' I said,

'I promise you. You don't have to do anything like that again.' He says, 'Oh, okay.' Michael gets out. He says, 'Geezus, Walter. That's quite a drop.' I said, 'Yeah, it is.' So they never knew I hadn't gotten the whole shot. Well, after the whole production was over, I took a stunt driver and a double brown Ford back up to San Francisco, and shot that same sequence, so I could get the second half of the shot. To this day, as far as I know, Karl and Michael think that that was the shot that they did."

Based on the Carolyn Weston novel, *Poor, Poor Ophelia*, *The Streets of San Francisco*'s two-hour pilot had Malden's Lieutenant Mike Stone, and Douglas' Inspector Steve Keller investigating the drowning of a young woman found in the San Francisco Bay, near the Golden Gate Bridge. An extra played the floating body of the dead girl. "We shot the pilot in March," recalls Grauman, "and the water was really, terribly cold. When Karl and Michael went running down the embankment, and into the bay to retrieve the body, the water was up to their thighs. They ran out. Karl yells, 'Geezus, Walter. How can you abuse that poor girl like that? That water is fucking freezing!'" Fortunately for the extra, she was in a wet-suit.

A far more unpleasant sequence in the water occurred in the first-season's Sausalito-based "Forty-five Minutes from Home." "We filmed that on a houseboat, and the year before they had passed a law that all the houseboats had to have holding tanks, because they were trying to get the Bay cleaned up," recalls Bob Jeffords. "But they didn't pass a law that the houseboats had to empty the holding tanks into a service vehicle; when the houseboats emptied their holding tanks, they were dumping it in the water. So when we went to do the stunt-work, which required that the stunt-men jump in the water, there were just chunks of this stuff floating in there. We had to get the stunt-men's eyes, ears, and mouths attended to because of that polluted water." Written by *Streets* story consultant John Wilder, "Forty-Five Minutes from Home" was an early indication of just how talented Wilder was. "It took forty-five minutes to fly from Los Angeles to San Francisco," states Wilder. "That was my inspiration for that story." By the end of the first season John Wilder had replaced his friend Cliff Gould as *The Streets of San Francisco*'s new producer.

"I'd had five producerships offered to me that year," remembers Wilder. "I opted to go work with Cliff as story consultant on *Streets* because I liked the concept, and Karl and Michael, and because of the fact that Quinn Martin was doing the best work on television." A fan of *The Fugitive, 12 O'clock High*, and *The Invaders*, John Wilder had started out in the business as a child actor, appearing (briefly) in the MGM hit musical, *Singin' in the Rain*, and on a "couple thousand radio shows," before going on to a more active career in such rock-and-roll musicals as *Rock, Pretty Baby; Summer Love*; and the MGM Glenn Ford comedy, *Imitation General.* On television, Wilder guest-starred on numerous shows, including *Wagon Train, Wanted: Dead or Alive,* and *The Alfred Hitchcock Hour.* He also played one of Rick Nelson's friends on his real-life friend Rick Nelson's popular sitcom, *The Adventures of Ozzie and Harriet.* More interested in writing for movies and television than in acting in them, Wilder started out writing episodes of *Branded*, before moving on to *Peyton Place*, and later to another prime-time soap opera, Harold Robbins' *The Survivors.* During the acting phase of his career, he became acquainted with casting director Cliff Gould. After Gould was appointed story consultant on the Glenn Ford series, *Cade's County*— produced by former *FBI* producer Charles Larson—Gould hired Wilder to write a show for the series. Obviously Gould was pleased with what Wilder did there, for when he started work on *The Streets of San Francisco*, he asked him to come and work for him.

"When Cliff and I came in," recalls Wilder, "we made the series a little more real. The pilot was somewhat melodramatic. Cliff got sick the first year. He was living in San Diego at the time, and the grind of doing the series just got to him. He wasn't there for the last five shows. I finished the rest of that season." As the series' new producer, John Wilder really got *The Streets of San Francisco* on track. "When I took over," remembers Wilder, "I went to San Francisco and spent a few days looking at the city from above. I got up in the high places, and realized the dramatic power we had in this show, because we had all these hills, all these elevations, and in legitimate stage, and legitimate theater, you use elevations for power. So my instructions to the series' directors were, 'Look for elevations. Go to the rooftops for chases.' So instead of having guys running through alleyways, I would have them running up fire escapes, and onto rooftops. That way we opened up the show so that you saw the city. We told the writers to write the city into their stories. We told them to treat it as if it were one of the regular characters."

Adds unit production manager Bob Jeffords, "When we first went up there, our crew complained all the time about getting to these apartments on hills, parking on the hills, carrying things up three flights of stairs. Then the first episode aired, and their whole attitude changed. They realized how much the city was one of the stars of the show. They started taking pride in all that extra work. There were forty hills in San Francisco, and I took this topographical map of the city, and circled all of the hills on the map. That was a great help in finding our locations. We shot on the Embarcadero a lot, Fisherman's Wharf, shot in Sausalito and Tiburon. After the first year we went out of town, went down to Santa Rosa, the Peninsula."

Very good at picking new locations—and in satisfying John Wilder's dramatic wants—was series director William Hale. "I had to approve all the locations," reveals Hale, "and when I was doing *Streets*, I had an apartment on Telegraph Hill, so I just rolled out of bed every morning and picked the locations." One of Hale's favorite *Streets* was the second season's "Before I Die." In "Before," Leslie Nielsen portrayed a dying cop, who before he dies plans on murdering syndicate boss Ray Danton. "Before" opened with an exciting car-chase sequence. "Quinn liked that chase so much he expanded the shooting schedule to eight days just so we could work on that chase," chuckles Hale. "It was a very successful project all-around. Now I wanted Leslie to live in a place that was up a flight of stairs, so I could play some stuff back and forth on the stairs. It's much more interesting when you get some elevation going for you. I also wanted him to live on a hillside with a sign that said 'Hill.' The location people found that. Right in front of his house. It was almost pop art."

That was just the sort of thing producer Wilder liked. "I got Bill Hale on that show as much as I could," says Wilder. "He was always in motion. He used the dolly better than anybody. He and Virgil Vogel always got the best-looking film." "Virgil did lots of coverage," adds Jeffords, "the classic master two-shot, lots of angles. He was the only director I know who could take a bad script, and make it look good. But when he had a good script, there was no difference." "When Virgil directed a scene," laughs series producer William Robert Yates, "he directed it as if he knew how he was already gonna cut it, and often when he said, 'Cut,' the actor would say, 'I'm not finished yet.' Virgil would tell him, 'Yes, you are.'" "He had no patience with any of that kind of stuff," elaborates Howard Alston. "If an actor asked him, 'What's my motivation in this scene? Why am I doing this?,' Virgil would reply, 'Damned if I know,' and walk away and laugh."

Having started out as an assistant director, and himself done some acting, William Hale worked better with actors than did Vogel. Hale also brought striking visuals to his work, which often took some time. "We always used to call him 'Drifting and Dreaming,'" laughs QM assistant director Paul Wurtzel, "because he was always walking around and trying to figure out how he was gonna shoot the scene. We were all like, 'Come on, come on. Make up your mind.'" "One time," adds Jeffords, "we were working at the Golden Gate Park, overlooking the bridge. Bill Hale set up a dolly shot that took two and a half or three hours." The length of time it took to film the sequence was not so much because of Hale's perfectionist streak. Rather it was the constantly changing San Francisco climate. "You'd start a scene in the sun," remembers the series script supervisor Michael Preece, "twenty minutes later it was foggy; so you just got part of the scene."

The city's frequent rains were the series' biggest weather problem. "The rain slowed you down," recalls Jeffords. "People couldn't communicate; you couldn't see as clearly, couldn't move as readily. You had to be careful about electricity, about doing car chases. But, because we had a lot of rain, we learned how to shoot in the rain. You'd put an umbrella over the camera, a big silk or something over the people for cover. You got a great production value from the rain, a lot of atmosphere, and the first year we had the worst rains, and because we were doing our interiors in L.A. [the police station set for example], we didn't have cover sets. We had nothing to cut away to. So one of the things we learned that first year was that we could put up with a lot of changes in the weather if we had something to cut away to when the weather changed." The company's frustrating experience on the first season's "Deathwatch" brought about this policy. "We had about seven boats, and this hover-craft," continues Jeffords, "and while we were working on these boats, it was constantly going from sun to shadow to rain. That's when we came up with the idea of switching to interiors when you started having problems shooting your exteriors."

Thanks to the company's excellent relationship with the San Francisco public, they were able to change locations rapidly. "We tried to create a good working relationship with the people who lived and worked there," explains Jeffords. "We had problems the second year, because there were two features that were shot there where the production teams had been very abusive and inconsiderate to the people of San

Francisco. So we told our crews, 'Look, this isn't our city. We don't live here. We come in for one day, and we're gone. The people that live and work here, they're here every day. This is their turf, not ours. They know that, and when you deal with them, keep that in mind." As a result of such consideration, the company was able to shoot most anywhere they wanted, especially since they could shoot their scenes very quickly.

To series director Michael Caffey, the system that Quinn Martin, Howard Alston, and their associates devised was nothing short of brilliant. "That whole show was shot with the streets in mind," reveals Caffey. "The system that they came up with eliminated the delays that you always had with every other company whenever you moved your production from one location to another. Whenever you move from one location to the other, you load the crap up, you break the camera down, you put it all away, you get in, you drive to the next location, you unload the crap, and that's what you do each and every time. Well, they didn't do any of that on *Streets*. What they had was one vehicle—a combination truck, and two very simple trailers for Karl and Michael and a honey-wagon [rest room/dressing room] for the rest of the actors— possibly another truck for wardrobe, but that was it. The camera, which was a hand-held Panaflex, hung on this special strap inside [driver] Fouad Said's truck, and the camera operator sat right alongside of it. Then we'd drive to the location, and if [director of photography] Jack Marquette wasn't there, you didn't wait for him. The camera operator got out, put the camera on his shoulder, you walked in, you shot the scene. That took you a maximum of twenty minutes. So there you were going into the biggest set in the world, the city of San Francisco, and you just shot it. Now other places, it took you two to three hours rigging time, maybe half a day, maybe longer. But, because of that system Quinn and the others invented, we could move five six seven times a day and go all over the place in San Francisco. Wherever you went, you had all of these elevations because of all the hills. That's why that was such an exciting show to do."

Making shooting run even more smoothly, not to mention more quickly, was *The Streets of San Francisco*'s regular director of photography—Jacques R. "One-Light" Marquette. "The guy was a genius in working without lights!" raves San Francisco–born Caffey. "Can you imagine San Francisco fog, no lights, getting the most beautiful stuff you'd ever seen? Night for night! No light! How do you do that? Well, if you're on a street that's lit a little bit, Jack would say, 'Now look Mike, if you move him over here just a little bit, he's lit.' See that streetlight way on top of there? He's lit.'" "Jack was a very unique d.p.," elaborates Bob Jeffords. "He often pushed the film to get a candlelit shot before the film really allowed it. At that time film speeds were much slower. One of his great joys was filming at the lowest light level that he could. So he was faster than other d.p's because he didn't use a lot of light. That gave it a very interesting look." Adds William Hale, "You'd give Jack a setup, go back to your chair; the thing was lit and ready to go by the time you got back to your chair." "Jack Marquette was one of my favorite cameramen," praises series director Robert Day. "When I did [the QM TV movie] *A Home of Our Own*, I took him down to Mexico with me. Anything that I wanted to do he would always accommodate me in terms of low-light situations. He was always taking photographic risks." "Jack was a down and dirty, documentary-like, feature quality cameraman," agrees Howard Alston. "One time Walter Grauman wanted to shoot in a hotel room that was maybe 12 by 12, or 12 by 16 feet. He wanted to shoot 360 degrees in it. Jack says, 'Where do the lights go? Where do I put my equipment?' Walter says, 'Oh, you can figure it out, Jack.' Jack finally put a light bulb in the ceiling. He lit the whole scene with that."

The San Francisco Police were no less adaptable, no less cooperative. "The police were superb," enthuses Jeffords. "San Francisco had the best system that I've ever worked with. That doesn't exist anywhere else. They had two officers who worked with you all the time. One of them was very bright, he anticipated everything, and he became as production-wise as many of our production people. The other officer was salt of the earth. If you gave him an instruction, he'd follow it till he died. Both of them were tremendously helpful."

As was Karl Malden to his co-star Michael Douglas. "Karl was responsible for Michael becoming an actor," states Howard Alston. "He'd watched Michael grow up. He made him tow the line." "Michael wanted to learn, and Karl was a great teacher," adds Hale. "He'd make suggestions, and Michael was always grateful for those suggestions. He was smart enough to swallow his pride and let Karl give him tips." "The two of them had a great relationship," agrees Caffey. "They got along very well, though Michael did have it in his contract that he could leave anytime. That's very rare."

Michael Douglas was planning to be more than just an actor. *Streets of San Francisco* guest star Philip Pine was among the first to learn of his other plans. "I had just made this picture," recalls Pine, "produced this picture, and I was talking about it to Art Batanides, who was also in this show. Michael heard us. He comes over. He says, 'What? What did you do? You produced a picture? Well, who's in it?' You know he started asking me all these questions, so I guess at that time he was beginning to think about doing that himself." "Michael was always asking me questions," remembers William Hale. "I taught Michael Douglas everything he knows. Michael and I were kind of buddies in San Francisco. I remember this one time these two whores came up to us. They told Michael, 'You're cute.' Then they looked at me, they said, 'You're cute too.'"

Michael Douglas definitely sowed some wild oats while working on the series. Laughs Caffey, "Karl would be on the set ready to go, but Michael would be in his dressing room still pulling on his pants. Karl would say, 'Well, you know, these young guys, they have to do their thing.' Nonetheless Douglas had a steady girlfriend during the series' original run—actress Brenda Vaccaro. "She gave Michael one of those London Fog double-breasted raincoats," remembers Michael Preece. "He wore that a lot in the show. He said, 'Oh boy, wait till Quinn sees this. He's gonna die.'"

Hired by production manager Howard Alston at the same time as his hair-stylist wife Evelyn ("Howard figured he could get two for the price of one," laughs Preece) Michael Preece and his wife enjoyed a good friendship with Michael Douglas. "Evelyn was Michael's best friend," states Preece. "She and Brenda liked to play pranks on him. They were always stealing his underwear." Being much older, and much more serious about acting, Karl Malden frowned on such things. "He was so straight-arrow it wasn't a whole lot of fun," reflects Preece. "I remember one time we were sitting in a coffee shop in downtown San Francisco waiting for it to get dark or something. We were all having wine. Karl was pacing back and forth in his raincoat. He saw us. He was like a policeman. You know, you can't drink when you're on duty."

Like his friend Michael Douglas, script supervisor Preece had directing ambitions, as he made clear to Quinn Martin. "When Quinn and John Conwell came up to San Francisco, they arrived in this big limousine" remembers Preece. "I went over. I said, 'Mr. Martin, there's something I want to ask you.' He says, 'Don't ask. I know what you want.' Well, within a week, my name was on a list to direct an episode. The show he gave me was a built-in winner. Later he told me why he gave me that show. He says, 'Look, directors are a dime a dozen. Good script supervisors are hand to find.'" Preece made his directorial debut in the series' third season.

The following season, Michael Douglas made his with the episode, "Spooks for Sale." "It was simply a run of the mill story in my mind," says series producer William Robert Yates, "but he liked it. He said, 'I'd like to direct this show. Can you hold it till the end of the season? That way, I'll have time to prepare it, and we can write it so that I'm not in it that much.'" Douglas was eager to get some experience as a director. He would soon leave the series to produce and direct the Jack Nicholson feature, *One Flew over the Cuckoo's Nest*, a film in which he'd originally hoped to cast his own father, Kirk Douglas. "When we did the show, "Asylum," Michael was very interested in that," recalls Yates. "The story-line was very similar to what he was thinking about doing in *Cuckoo's Nest*."

Disappointed about Douglas' departure from the series, Quinn Martin considered a number of different actors as Malden's new co-star. Including Carol Rossen. In the third season episode, "Ten Dollar Murder," Rossen had portrayed a police woman who was sickened to learn that her teenage son had committed murder. Giving her emotional support as she struggled through this crisis was Malden's Lt. Mike Stone. Martin wanted Rossen to come back in the same role and become more emotionally involved with Stone. Rossen didn't want to; she was going to have a baby.

Other actors considered as Douglas' replacement were Don Johnson and Tom Selleck In the end, Richard Hatch got the part. Almost immediately, Malden and Hatch clashed. "Karl liked to run the show," explains Hale, "and he felt he'd helped Michael Douglas become a good actor. So he tried to do the same thing with Richard Hatch, tried to give him some advice. Hatch didn't want it." Producer Yates saw the situation differently. "Richard was glad to have a dramatic series" says Yates. "He loved Karl—getting an opportunity to work with Karl Malden. That's a good job. He was very cooperative." Richard Hatch was no stranger to QM Productions. He'd worked for the company before as a guest star in episodes of *Barnaby Jones* and *Cannon*.

Semi-regular Darleen Carr had worked for QM even more. Carr's QM guest credits included: *The FBI, Barnaby Jones, The Manhunter,* and *Caribe.* "Darleen Carr was really terrific," enthuses John Wilder. "She was really pretty. You wouldn't call

From the left: **Michael Douglas (as Inspector Steve Keller), QM favorite Andrew Duggan (as Chief of Detectives A.E. Malone) and Karl Malden (as Det. Lt. Mike Stone) in the September 16, 1972, TV movie-pilot for the September 16, 1972–June 23, 1977, ABC TV-series,** *The Streets of San Francisco.*

Karl pretty, but Darleen had those same penetrating blue eyes that Karl had. They matched up as father and daughter so beautifully." "Darleen was a doll," adds Yates. "She wanted to work all the time, but we didn't want to have a family thing on this cop show. Quinn wanted to keep the anthological approach that we had on the show. I did also. We tried to use Darleen once or twice every season. Whenever we used her, we wanted to have a good meaty part for her. She's a very capable actress." In contrast to Lynn Loring's Barbara Erskine on *The FBI,* Darleen Carr's Jean Stone had a lot more to do when she appeared on *The Streets of San Francisco.* One of Carr's best *Streets* was the fourth season's "Deadly Silence." In "Deadly Silence," guest Meredith Baxter pulled out all the stops in her portrayal of a robber who, after losing her husband and brother to Mike Stone's bullet, lures Stone to a place where she can kill him. The bait for her trap: a kidnapped Jean Stone.

The same season featured "The Glass Dart Board" in which, for unexplained reasons, a sniper is taking pot-shots at various San Francisco high-rise buildings. Remembers Yates, "I thought, what if there's a sniper just randomly shooting out windows in these huge, forty-floor skyscrapers, from various angles? What a terrific idea for a crime, because it's random. But when we got to the script, I began to have doubts about the morality of our doing this. I thought, what if we get some crazy out there, who, because of our episode, starts doing this? I almost pulled that show out of production because of that, but I didn't; it was a good story. I just prayed that the show wouldn't be seen by some crazy. I guess we were lucky."

Crazy was the perfect description for the character John Davidson played in what most everyone associated with *The Streets of San Francisco* regards as the series' classic, "Mask of Death." Originally, John Wilder had considered casting his friend Dean Jones in the role of a schizophrenic female impersonator. Jones didn't want to do it. John Davidson did. "Davidson loved it," laughs Yates. "He didn't do a whole lot of television, and when he came in to read for us, he came in in all this make-up. I thought, he really wants to do it. He loved it. He did a wonderful job, and it was really his desire to do it that sold us on casting him." "It was an excellent show," adds the series' editor Richard Brockway, "kind of different from what we usually did."

Marlyn Mason played a similar character in the fifth season's "Who Killed Helen French?" "Oh, I was so glad to do that show," raves Mason. "I wish I could have worked with Michael Douglas, but I loved it, because I got to play a dual character— a woman who's a schizophrenic. That was lots of fun, hard work, but a nice meaty role." Another good fifth season entry was director Michael Preece's "Dead Lift." "That was with Arnold Schwarzenegger," remembers Preece. "I wanted Arnold to do the show. Quinn wanted Bill Smith. I said, 'The audience will love Arnold.' I managed to talk Quinn into using Arnold."

Thanks to production manager Howard Alston's decision to convert a warehouse in San Francisco into a police headquarters set at the beginning of the second season, the company was able to spend more time during that and subsequent seasons looking for locations. The second season's "Going Home," guest-starring Tom Bosley as a former Alcatraz inmate, was shot in the interiors of that prison. "The first time we filmed there," recalls Jeffords, "was not long after the American Indian Movement occupation. [Art director] George Chan took some spray cans with him because there was all this graffiti about Nixon on the doors of the cell. He sprayed over that. We came back a week later, the graffiti was back. The scenes with Tom we shot primarily in the cell-block. There were four cell-blocks that were part of the Federal Penitentiary. The cell we put Tom in was actually in the military section which the character would never have been in." "It was difficult working there," adds "Going Home" director Robert Day. "There was all of this security, and we had to get certain sections of the cell-blocks working again. We worked in the cell of the Birdman of Alcatraz. I remember I found a little anvil in the metal workshop there that I brought home with me. Now I use it as a doorstop. I always wondered if Al Capone used that."

Quinn Martin seemed to be wondering how he could keep series producer John Wilder from leaving at the end of the third season. Though the two men continued to remain friends, playing tennis and so forth, Wilder was growing more interested in doing movies, and setting up his own production company. One try at directing a *Streets of San Francisco* ("Rampage") was enough to tell Wilder he shouldn't be doing that. "He said he'd never do it again,' laughs Michael Preece. "At the end of the day, John looked like he'd been thrown into the ocean. He was sweating, his hair was all askew."

If Quinn Martin was worrying that John Wilder's departure would hurt *Streets*, he didn't worry long. Wilder's story consultant, William Robert Yates, was a more than adequate producer. Brought into the show during the second season by Wilder, who'd worked with Yates on *The Survivors*, former district attorney Yates was more like Alan Armer and William Gordon in his work as a producer. "Wilder was kind of an all-around producer," states William Hale. "He was into the production, the look of it, the places you shot. He was more of a David O. Selznick–type producer. Yates' total interest was the story and the characters." "John Wilder was a very good producer, very affable, very easygoing," adds Bob Jeffords. "Bill Yates was more nose to the grindstone. With Yates, his work was his love." "Bill Yates was one of the best guys Quinn had," feels Paul Wurtzel. "But he'd get so wound up, and sometimes drink so much, that when he called you, you didn't know what the hell he was talking about."

Similarly, viewers didn't know what San Francisco city scenes they were going to see in the opening credits in each week's episode. Since the number of guest stars changed from week to week, so too did the city scenes. "We had several versions of the credits," reveals post-production supervisor John Elizalde. "I thought that was the best title that we had. I thought it was a work of art. The network didn't want us to use it though. They thought it was too much advertising of the San Francisco restaurants. Pat Williams did a magnificent piece of music for those opening titles." "Most of the scenes in the opening credits came from the pilot," states Richard Brockway, "but every now and then when we saw a scene that we liked during the series, we'd yank it out and replace a scene we didn't like. Those credits really showed off San Francisco. Quinn liked that. He liked a good, snappy main title."

As any *Streets of San Francisco* viewer knew, some of the scenes in the opening credits were aerial shots. "We went up in the helicopter and shot scenes which they could use for the opening credits," recalls second-unit director James W. Gavin. "We did a lot of establishing shots of the city, shot some car chase sequences too. Dooley Webber was the cameraman most of the time."

Despite the turnaround in producers during its five seasons, *The Streets of San Francisco*'s crew was always a close-knit group. Incredibly, years later, the same people who had worked on *Streets* (John Wilder, William Robert Yates, Bob Jeffords, Dick Gallegly, George Chan, David Whorf) all found themselves working together again on the popular Robert Urich series, *Spenser: For Hire*. "We all got a kick out of that," laughs Jeffords, "and because the entire series was shot on location in Boston, Massachusetts, we called it *The Streets of Boston*."

While *The Streets of San Francisco*'s team was a close-knit group, there was no QM series' cast and crew who were quite as close, no QM set that was as warm and friendly as that of the producer's next series, *Barnaby Jones*. *Barnaby Jones* was proof positive that a crime drama didn't need excessive violence and sex to hold an audience. During its seven-and-a-half year run, CBS-TV frequently moved the show to a number of different time-slots, and a number of different days. If CBS was trying to kill the show in favor of adding more youthful programming, they didn't succeed. No matter where it was placed, *Barnaby Jones* always found an audience.

Chapter 11

BARNABY JONES

There was this rumor that *Barnaby Jones* was Richard Nixon's favorite TV show, and a lot of people seemed to think that that was an insult. I don't see how that was an insult. To have the president of the United States say you're his favorite TV show ... why, I think that's the greatest compliment you could receive.

Barnaby Jones *guest star (and series fan) Lynda Day George*

If the rumor was indeed true, then *Barnaby Jones* producer Philip Saltzman, who considered his series "the *Playhouse 90* of the Mississippi," had even more reason to be proud. As even his most die-hard enemies would admit, Richard Nixon was a brilliant man. *Barnaby Jones* (January 28, 1973–September 4, 1980, CBS) was a brilliant show. Described as a "countrified *Columbo*" by its creator, Quinn Martin, *Barnaby Jones* really had very little in common with *Columbo*. On *Columbo*, the crime was always murder. The crimes varied on *Barnaby Jones*. Sometimes one like extortion might result in murder. Sometimes there were a number of murders. There was usually just one killing on *Columbo*.

Both series differed in their kinds of criminals as well. The killers on *Columbo* were always the high-and-mighty—famous politicians, well-known scientists, hot-shot actors. On *Barnaby Jones*, the killer was the guy who pumped gas at the filling station, the middle-aged man who was trying to pay off the mortgage on his house, the kid who was hoping for an "A" on his college exams. Almost always, none of these people planned on murder. It generally happened by accident. As a result, the viewer felt pity for these characters. He could easily imagine himself in such a situation.

That wasn't the case on *Columbo*. Not being in the same social or economic strata as the *Columbo* villains, TV viewers couldn't be sympathetic towards them because they couldn't identify with them. The show wasn't structured that way anyway. Its first half depicted the villain's commission of the crime. The second half illustrated Lt. Columbo's solution of that crime. On *Barnaby Jones*, the depiction of the crime

147

only took a few minutes. The rest of the show revealed why the person had committed the crime, how what he'd done was now affecting him, and how, through both the gathering of evidence and his gentle manipulation of the criminal, private detective Barnaby Jones solved the case. In terms of drama, that made *Barnaby Jones* a very dramatic show. The reason why the series attracted such a loyal audience was very simple. The show was about ordinary people. Its protagonist was ordinary too.

When Quinn Martin created elderly private detective Barnaby Jones, he saw the character as a "foxy grandpa" who would use his cunning, along with the evidence he assembled, to trap the guilty parties. Barnaby did mix cunning with the clues he collected to solve his cases, but because Buddy Ebsen saw, and played, his character as a man with a job to do, the series' villains rarely saw Barnaby as a threat. As a result, Barnaby always got his man, quite often woman. There were a lot of female criminals on *Barnaby Jones*. The first season, there were three; the second season, ten or more; the third season, even more. While Barnaby's advanced age, which kept the action stuff to a minimum, allowed for a greater use of women killers, it was really producer Philip Saltzman who made the female criminal such a constant.

Thanks to Saltzman's heavy emphasis on female criminals, a lot of actresses received some very good parts on the series. Jessica Walter had an excellent role in the second season's "Venus as in Fly Trap." In "Venus," Walter played a man-hating feminist magazine publisher whose affair with a chauvinist author (Ed Nelson) results in the murder of his crippled wife. Unlike her accomplice Nelson, Walter was a hard-hearted sort. Being captured by an old-fashioned, sexist pig like Barnaby, really infuriated her. Claudette Nevins played a similarly cold-blooded character in the eighth and final season's "Run to Death." During the course of that story, Nevins committed more than one murder, including that of her accomplice, Michael Lerner. On this occasion, it was Barnaby's secretary, and daughter-in-law, Betty Jones (Lee Meriwether) who solved the case.

Betty Jones had gone to work for her father-in-law in the series' second episode, "To Catch a Dead Man." She'd lost her husband, Hal Jones (Robert Patten) in the preceding episode, "Requiem for a Son." Like his father, Hal Jones ran a private detective business. Having been trained by Barnaby, one of the best in the business, Hal was a good detective himself. In "Requiem" however, Hal encountered a case that was too difficult for him to handle on his own. So he called in his old friend, Frank Cannon (William Conrad). William Conrad was a little bit put out about guest-starring in "Requiem for a Son," understandably.

"The original plan was to do the *Barnaby Jones* pilot as an episode of *Cannon*," explains Lee Meriwether. "*Barnaby* was to be a spin-off from *Cannon*. I remember when I was called in to discuss the series with Quinn. I was rehearsing a musical. When I got this call to go see Quinn Martin, I thought, they mean the casting people at Quinn Martin, not Quinn Martin himself. I had met Quinn once before when I was doing *The FBI;* the only time I actually talked to him was when he wanted to see me about doing *Barnaby Jones*. He says, 'I'm thinking about doing this show, and I wonder if you'd be interested in doing it. If it sells, it'll be a series.' I thought, I don't wanna do another series." (Meriwether's last TV series, the 1971 CBS sitcom, *The New Andy Griffith Show*, had lasted half a season. Her previous series, Irwin Allen's *The Time Tunnel*, had made it a whole season.) "But this was Quinn Martin," continues Meriwether. "The quality of his work was legend. So I said, 'I'd be proud to do it.'"

The more involved Lee Meriwether became in *Barnaby Jones*, the more she realized she'd made the right decision. "Quinn stressed the fact that the amount of violence would be kept to a minimum," explains the actress. "He said, 'Let's not go with major fads. Let's keep our wardrobe conservative. Let's solve these mysteries with cleverness and

Clockwise from upper left: **Mark Shera (as Jedediah Romano "J.R." Jones), John Carter (as Lt. John Biddle), Lee Meriwether (as Betty Jones) and Buddy Ebsen (as private detective Barnaby Jones) in a rare group publicity shot for QM Productions' second biggest hit: the January 28, 1973–September 4, 1980, CBS-TV series,** *Barnaby Jones.*

cunning, not with strong hit 'em over the head stuff.' He wanted the kinds of stories that the audience would get right along with Buddy. He and the producers wanted very few stories where the audience would have pre-knowledge of the murderer and how Buddy was going to find them. It was more difficult to write the show that way, but that was a prerequisite on which Quinn insisted."

As for the show's tongue-in-cheek humor, says Meriwether, that was all Buddy Ebsen. "Buddy wanted that in the show," states the actress. "He wanted it light, wanted it easy. He wished they could write more humor into his character because he handled comedy so well. He himself was witty." *Barnaby Jones'* frequent spoofing of the private-detective genre made the series just as witty. During its seven and a half year run, the show poked fun at such private-detective clichés as the hard-drinking P.I. (Barnaby's drink of choice was milk), the detective's on-going romance with his gorgeous secretary (Barnaby's gorgeous secretary was his daughter-in-law), and the knock-down drag out fist-fights through which the private detective always subdued his enemy. Barnaby caught his villains with a garden hose ("Trial Run for Death"), or with a whole town ("Murder-Go-Round"), or by whistling to his horse ("Sunday: Doomsday").

The program also sent up numerous, over-used private detective story-lines such as the really old one about the bad beautiful blonde and her handsome, but impecunious lover bumping off her wealthy, older husband (Lynda Day George, former *FBI* regular Stephen Brooks, and Carl Betz in the second season's "Stand-In for Death"). There was also the equally tiresome story-line of the bad beautiful blonde setting up victims for her accomplice (George and Betz in the same show). In neither scenario was George a criminal. Betz was, because of immature, weak-willed George. Loaded with very human characters and numerous twists and turns (an inevitability when the writer was Robert W. Lenski), "Stand-In for Death" was something of a tribute to Carl Betz's Emmy-winning, twist-laden dramatic series, *Judd, for the Defense*. The episode also poked fun at Betz's previous series, the long-running sitcom, *The Donna Reed Show*. On that series, Carl Betz and wife Donna Reed shared the same bedroom; however they slept in separate beds. In "Stand-In for Death," husband Betz and wife George had the same arrangement.

The Donna Reed Show was not the only television series at which *Barnaby Jones* poked fun. During the detective drama's first season, James Luisi was among the guests to receive top billing in the episode, "Murder-Go-Round." Unlike the other guests to receive such billing, Luisi had very little to do in the episode. He was killed off moments after his introduction. That was something that regularly happened to the top-billed guest stars in Peter Falk's *Columbo*. The following year, in Luisi's second *Barnaby*, "The Deadly Prize," the series worked a twist on the actor's first guest appearance. Like "Murder-Go-Round," Luisi was killed off very early in the proceedings. Only this time, his death was phony. This time, it was he who was doing the killings. When former *Laugh-In* announcer Gary Owens played Gary Michaels in the first season *Barnaby Jones* episode, "Twenty Million Alibis," any *Laugh-In* devotee would have recognized his character. It was exactly the kind of character Owens played on *Laugh-In*. The character even used such *Laugh-In* catch phrases as "Here come de Judge. Here come de Judge."

In addition to making fun of other television series, *Barnaby Jones* made fun of Hollywood. On *Barnaby Jones*, actors killed actresses, and no-talent, big-name celebrities did away with their money-grubbing agents. In the second season's "Image in a Cracked Mirror," Teri Garr practically stole the show in her brief bit as an actress who'd never heard of English novelist Charles Dickens. ("Is he a screenwriter?" she asked Barnaby). Semi-regular Val Avery's telling Barnaby to "include me out" on another episode was pretty good too. That saying was one of MGM producer Samuel Goldwyn's best-known malapropisms.

Such humorous little bits and pieces of dialogue were perfect for a series on which men dressed up as women (Ben Piazza in the third season's "Bond of Fear"), women posed as men (Marj Dusay in the second season's "The Killing Defense"), a ghost committed murder (future *Runaways* regular Karen Machon in "The Black Art of Dying"), and murder victim Ford Rainey was killed by the rattlesnake he found in his liquor cabinet ("Day of the Viper")—no, not the potent concoction that one made with equal parts Coffee Liqueur, White Creme de Cacao, and Heather Cream—

an actual rattlesnake. Not too surprisingly, "Day of the Viper" was one *Barnaby Jones* show its director Walter Grauman never forgot. "I found this big cave up in Bronson Canyon," remembers Grauman, "and we got several dozen rattlesnakes from an animal trainer—a huge, fat man, whose little wife handled them; he wouldn't touch the fucking snakes. Anyway, we put the snakes in a pit. They were either de-fanged or their mouths were sewed shut so they couldn't bite. So we're in this dark cave. We turned on the lights, piled these snakes into this pit, and I was up on this ladder. I directed the whole scene from a ladder, from up high on a ladder. You know I'm no fool. We turned off the lights. The snakes started to come out of the pit as soon as we did. You didn't know where the hell they were. It was kinda scary."

In the second season opener, "Blind Terror," in which guest Christopher Stone played an animal trainer who turns a mountain lion loose on a nosy Barnaby, it was the mountain lion who was scared. "I said 'Action,'" laughs Grauman. "They let the cougar out of the box, and the cougar just looked at Buddy. He was scared to death of Buddy. He wouldn't go near him. But we had to shoot this scene; so I said, 'Buddy take the broom, and poke the cougar. That way it'll look like you're fending him off.' So throughout that whole thing, poor Buddy is trying to get this cougar to move, trying to make it look like this cougar is ferocious. I kept saying, 'Poke him, Buddy. Poke him. Brush him. Brush him,' and everybody was laughing. I mean it was really quite an experience, seeing Buddy Ebsen with this big broom attacking this cougar."

Buddy Ebsen was always willing to do whatever his directors wanted. "Buddy Ebsen was unbelievable," enthuses series director Michael Caffey. "He was a joy to direct, a joy to be around. I used to look forward just to seeing him come in in the morning. He was a supreme professional. He always showed up fully made up and in wardrobe. It didn't matter what day it was, what time it was, how hot it was. He was always there for the other actor. He came in and played the scene for the other person; that's what you're supposed to do. That's the professional thing to do. It helps the other actor. The other actor plays the scene for you so you can look into his eyes and play off of him. Buddy was the only actor I ever ran into that did that. Plus he always connected with the fans. Anybody who walked up and said, 'Hello, Mr. Ebsen,' he'd talk to them eye to eye. Most actors don't do that. That's not all bad, because they're concentrating, but Buddy always did that. Buddy was my hero."

There were a lot of reasons why Buddy Ebsen was Michael Caffey's hero. Ebsen was always doing special things for other people. His behavior during the filming of the fourth season's "Double Vengeance" was a perfect example. "A lot of that was shot in Palm Springs," remembers Caffey, "on the main drag. We had a little scene at a gas station, and here came this little old lady pushed in by a helper. Her arms were folded. She was a hunched over, tiny, wizened little thing. Buddy went over because he was asked to. She whispered something. He leaned all the way over. She tilted her head up, asked him to do his little song and dance thing. He did. Now this was on the corner; cars are going by while he's doing this. This little old lady—her hands come up, she starts to clap, her face comes up, she dropped twenty years. I'm over there with a tear coming down my cheek. Other people were the same way. That's the kind of kindness that Buddy showed to person after person after person. He did it very quietly. It wasn't a big thing. That little old lady was just in heaven. Buddy leaned over and gave her a little hug. He's known for things like that. He's known for doing things for people that cost him money and everything else. Moments like that are what defined Buddy Ebsen for me."

Laughs Lee Meriwether, "We were always having actors coming up to us and saying, 'Gee whiz. Don't you guys get stuck in all the honey around here? It's mighty syrupy sweet around here. Gee whiz. Is it always like this?' We had a wonderful crew on that show, a fantastic crew—but all of that was because of Buddy. Buddy set the tone on that show. He set the atmosphere. It was one of comfort, of love, of support. Buddy was spending a goodly part of his life right there and he was going to make it as close to home as possible. I think Quinn loved that." *Barnaby Jones* guest star Lynda Day George certainly did. "I loved doing that show," raves George. "Buddy was such a funny guy. He was such great fun. He had a great sense of humor, a very dry wit, and he was a very wise person, totally knew the business. He liked to work with performers. He enjoyed meeting the people on the show, always wanted to know how he could make your job easier." "Buddy was the quintessential professional," agrees guest Jonathan Goldsmith. "Most of the time when you do scenes with a star, they're not there for your close-ups. They're gone, and you're talking to a chair. Buddy was always there for you. He's one of the few, maybe one of the only. He was very, very gracious. Just a delightful man to work with." "Buddy worked very very hard," adds Meriwether. "He always wanted to be there for the other actors. I think that's why our crew stayed with us, why the writers stayed with us. I mean, everybody loved him. Everybody wanted to work with him."

Buddy Ebsen was professional in every way. Even when it came to making a wardrobe change. Recalls Michael Caffey, "He'd be in his trailer for such a long time, I'd get to wondering, Geez what is Buddy doing in there? Is he sniffing or snorting? So one day I'm in Palm Springs, and when Buddy went off to his dressing room, I said to the crew, 'Okay guys, I'm gonna find out what the hell he's doing in there.' So I went right over, knocked on the door. He says, 'Come in.' I went in, and I observed Buddy changing wardrobe. Now you have never seen anything like this! He's talking to me. He's saying, 'Mike, would you like to have a cold brew? Would you like to have a little something?' and off comes the coat. Now, you know you have wardrobe men. The coat is put on a hanger. He hangs the coat up. Then comes the shirt. That goes on a hanger. That goes up. Off come the pants. They get put on the hanger. This takes time. He was very meticulous with it. Here come the socks. You don't drop the socks on the floor. You pick the socks up and put them on a stretcher. Well, I was timing this whole thing. It took twenty to twenty-five minutes. He was busy all the time. He wasn't dogging it. He wasn't on the phone. He wasn't playing a big man. So I went and I called up the producers. I said, 'Now look, you get hold of these wardrobe people and in the future, when you change Buddy's wardrobe, just change the coat.' So, the coat would be standing on the set. That way when he pulled off the coat, and put on the other one, he was ready. I have never seen anything like that wardrobe change! It was just classic. You could have done a comedy off of it. I mean when most of us change shoes, we take the shoes off, and throw them on the floor; then we grab the next pair. With Buddy, the shoes were turned. The right one on the right. The left one on the left. Almost as if they were gonna come in and take a picture."

The methodical way in which Buddy Ebsen changed his wardrobe proved him the perfect choice for the role of a private detective who just as methodically assimilates various pieces of evidence until finally putting them together to solve the mystery. Arthur Conan Doyle's classic character Sherlock Holmes operated in a similar fashion. During the run of *Barnaby Jones,* Buddy Ebsen was honored for his characterization by a Sherlock Holmes society.

Quite often, Barnaby Jones found a vital clue through the experiments he conducted in his laboratory. Most TV private detectives never had crime labs. If they did, they weren't shown on television. During *Barnaby Jones'* first few seasons, Barnaby's lab was a very prominent part of each episode. "Buddy liked that," reveals Meriwether. "As a detective, Barnaby's lab was very important to him. So Buddy wanted more scenes in the lab, more scenes where he'd be finding things out in his lab. Quinn agreed with him. He had the producers and writers write scenes for that." While director of photography William W. Spencer found such action-less scenes talky and boring, the lab sequences were one of the show's most absorbing, and realistic, elements. But for some reason, television critics found Ebsen's characterization totally unrealistic. Points out Lynda Day George, "I've had some experience with real detectives, and from my personal experience with detectives, it's been my observation that most of what you do as a detective is just that—you detect. That's what Buddy did on that series. That's why that series was more realistic than most detective shows."

Adding further realism were the details QM Productions regularly brought to each and every prop that was used in each episode. For example, in the series' second episode, "To Catch a Dead Man," guest villain William Shatner created a false identity with an Arizona driver's license which, when compared to his actual California driver's license, was exactly correct in regards to such vital statistics as Shatner's height, weight, etc. The only differences between these licenses were the names of the state registrars and governors, plus the fact that in the one driver's license picture Shatner was bearded, while in the other, he was clean-shaven. Why QM Productions went to such efforts in printing up two licenses was baffling. After all, the close-up of both licenses lasted only seconds, certainly not long enough for the viewers to notice such great detail. Perhaps Quinn Martin was envisioning the day when, thanks to the pause button on their VCRs, viewers could freeze the picture to notice such detail.

There was lots of detail in "Twenty Million Alibis." In "Twenty Million," Barnaby matched wits with reformed jewel thief turned best-selling author Peter Haskell. Haskell hadn't intended on killing the wealthy Marie Windsor's butler when he broke into Windsor's home to steal her jewels. Haskell planned on returning the jewels—

Buddy Ebsen (as private detective Barnaby Jones) in Barnaby's laboratory in a publicity shot for the January 28, 1973–September 4, 1980, CBS-TV series, *Barnaby Jones*.

the theft was all part of an elaborate publicity stunt for his latest book. Fortunately for Haskell, he had an unshakable alibi. He couldn't have possibly committed the crime between the time he was first introduced on 'The Gary Michaels Show' and when he finally walked on to join Michaels' other guests a short time later. He could have, thought Barnaby, if he crawled through the studio's air ducts, ran up three or four flights of stairs to the roof, then shot some kind of rope or wire over from the studio building to the penthouse where Windsor lived. Barnaby would have to prove that, said Haskell. Barnaby did—by retracing Haskell's route through the air vents. "Buddy had a stunt guy [Al Wyatt] who looked just like him," says "Twenty Million" director Michael Caffey, "but Buddy did do some of the crawling through the air ducts in that show. He did some of the running up the steps too."

Being a dancer, Ebsen was in very good physical shape. He hardly hobbled around on the series as the program's detractors claimed. In fact, Buddy Ebsen was to outlive many of the actors who guest-starred on his series. Still, like anyone, Ebsen had his flaws. Chuckles Caffey, "I remember one time on one of the shows, there was a place called Packerville, and he had to put that in his speech. Just as we rolled the cameras, I whispered over to Buddy, 'Buddy, don't say "Peckerville."' Course he did. He got to it and the eyes opened twice their size and out it came. Well, we had a great time. He had trouble with names from time to time. He often couldn't get his own [character] name out. One time, he really had trouble. We were shooting in the Sunset Towers on Sunset Blvd, and he had a whole spiel of things to say. He had gone to lunch, had some drinks. He got to these names, and they just spewed all over." Normally that didn't happen. Ebsen always recorded his dialogue and listened to it again and again until he got it perfect.

Falling asleep on the set was another thing Buddy Ebsen did quite often. "He'd come back from lunch, and in between takes, while we were making adjustments, he'd fall asleep," laughs director of photography William W. Spencer. "I've fallen asleep on the set myself. It was easy to do on that show. It was quieter and there wasn't that much going on. Buddy always seemed to know when we were ready to shoot though. He'd just sort of wake up automatically." "He could go to sleep standing up," marvels Caffey. "He'd tell me, 'These are my cat-naps.'" Adds series director Michael Preece, "I remember one time we were doing this show, and somebody says, 'Where's Buddy?' He had gone just outside the door and he was sitting in the lobby of this set, fast asleep." Whenever *Barnaby Jones* assistant director, later production manager, Paul Wurtzel arrived for work about six or six-thirty every morning, he often found Ebsen's car parked in front of his dressing room, with Ebsen behind the wheel, sound asleep. Wurtzel never blamed Ebsen for sleeping so much. "He lived out in the San Fernando Valley, in a place called Liberty Canyon, and he had a long commute," says Wurtzel. "He had about a forty-five minute drive. He was very tired all the time. He put in a long day. He never made any waves though. He was a very quiet guy."

Co-star Lee Meriwether was by contrast the exact opposite. "What a funny lady!" exclaims Lynda Day George. "I always thought she should have been a comedienne. She was soooo funny! She had a kind of bawdy, raucous humor that was just wunnnnderfullll! We really laughed a lot. We made a lot of other people laugh too. She liked to do accents, liked to tell funny stories. I remember one time the two of us were sitting out behind the truck, cracking each other up. We had some really funny things going on—girl things. It wasn't anything dastardly; but at one point we were overheard by the drivers. We were utterly humiliated. We were just little imps. We didn't do anything bad. It was just fun. Lee was always doing that. I mean when you're on the set, you have to give your mind a break. That was one of the ways she did that, one of the ways that I did that."

"Lee Meriwether had a great sense of humor," agrees casting director Meryl O'Loughlin. "She was a great foil for Buddy. Buddy was like a pixie. He and Lee worked well together." "Lee Meriwether was a very good dramatic actress," declares series producer Philip Saltzman. "We'd used her before on *12 O'clock High* and *The FBI*, and so I was very familiar with her work. When we gave her more to do on *Barnaby*, she handled it very well." "She was a great broad," adds series director Walter Grauman, "a good gal. I liked her a lot. I still like her. She's cute, she's funny, she's bright, and she was good in that role." Unfortunately, during the first few seasons, Lee Meriwether didn't have all that much to do on the series. Despite that, the actress never complained. Nor did she ever expect her children Lesley and Kyle Aletter to receive special treatment during the two or three occasions the two girls did bit parts on the show. Buddy Ebsen didn't expect any special favors for his daughter Bonnie either. Nor did Quinn Martin expect any for his daughter Jill. "Jill Martin was a nice kid," says Wurtzel. "I remember when she did the show, I had to sign a paper to be her guardian because her mother couldn't come to the set." "We had her on the show a couple of times," recalls Meriwether. "She was a good little actress." Even one of the series' director's kids got on the show. Remembers *Barnaby* director

Kenneth Gilbert, "When I was preparing my show, Leo Penn was directing the show ahead of me. Leo comes over to me. He says, 'I read the script for the show that you're gonna be doing. I hope you don't mind.' I said, 'No. No problem.' He says, 'I have a son who wants to be an actor. There's a part in there that he could play. Could he do it?' I said, 'Yeah. Sure.' Well, of course, that was Sean."

Somehow in a series where a private detective's secretary was his daughter-in-law, having the children of the series' executive producer, its two leads, and one of its directors guest star, seemed appropriate. For if *Barnaby Jones* was a family show on-screen, it was just as much a family show off-camera. When Buddy Ebsen and Lee Meriwether threw the annual Christmas party for the crew, they always invited the crew's wives and children as well as guest stars from that season. So, when new series regular Mark Shera joined the cast in the fifth season (as Barnaby's cousin, Jedediah Romano Jones, or, as he preferred, J.R. Jones), it was no surprise that Ebsen and Meriwether immediately befriended him. To this day, all three actors remain in close touch. "Buddy was very helpful with Mark," remembers Ebsen's make-up artist Roy Stork, whom Ebsen brought to the series from *The Beverly Hillbillies*. "Mark didn't have too much experience." "When Mark Shera came to the show we were all kind of surprised," says Kenneth Gilbert. "Nobody was expecting a sidekick kind of thing. We'd gone all those years without one. Buddy made him feel as much at home as possible."

Mark Shera definitely felt at home. "He was just a comedian," laughs director Michael Preece. "He was the class clown. When you'd say, 'Let's roll,' meaning let's roll the camera, he'd start rolling, maybe against the wall, maybe on the floor." "Mark was just fine," adds Michael Caffey. "He was very amenable. He always did what I asked him to do." "He took his time getting to the set," remembers Paul Wurtzel. "I used to tell him, 'You're gonna wind up pumping gas in some gas station if you don't straighten yourself out. Get to work.' Everybody was always ribbing him and kidding him like that. He, Buddy and Lee, all got along fine. That was one of the happier sets I ever worked on. Everybody got along just great."

"*Barnaby Jones* was one of the happiest sets I've ever known," agrees production coordinator Karen Shaw, "but Paul Wurtzel could be a stinker. Paul was too much of a perfectionist. Other than that, it was a very very happy show. It was a happy crew to work with. Lee Meriwether and Mark Shera were always participating in things, and Phil Saltzman was such a nice producer. He was a true gentleman. All of us who worked on that series, we all have such fond memories of that show."

Perhaps there was no one who had fonder memories of the series than Buddy Ebsen's long-time make-up artist, Roy Stork. With Ebsen since the days of *The Beverly Hillbillies*, Stork never forgot Ebsen for "going to bat for me, and getting me paid over scale," during his seven and a half years on *Barnaby*. Nor could Stork ever thank Ebsen enough for the efforts the actor went to when Stork made a special request of Ebsen after working with him for five years on *The Beverly Hillbillies*. "I was in the Doolittle Raid over Tokyo," explains Stork. "We were the first ones to bomb Tokyo after Pearl Harbor. I was in the Tenth Air Force, Seventeenth Bomb

Group, as a co-pilot. Well, this one day I went up to Buddy. I said, 'I got a favor to ask you. We're having our reunion for the Tokyo Raiders at the Balboa Bay Club. Bob Hope was supposed to come out and be our master of ceremonies. He can't make it. Would you be willing to take his place?' He says, 'Sure.' So then he went out and did a lot of research, and when he came in to act as our emcee, he really made a hit. We were all saying, 'Bob who?'"

If there was any particular incident that best illustrated just how close-knit and loving a group the *Barnaby Jones* cast and crew was, it had to be when the series' most frequent director Walter Grauman lost his first wife. "She had a stroke or aneurysm," remembers Grauman's assistant director Paul Wurtzel. "It happened so unexpectedly. She died the first or second year of the show. We worked out the schedules so that Walter could visit his wife's grave. Every morning before he came to the set, he'd go out to the cemetery. You could always tell that he'd been there—the tips of his buckskin shoes would be wet." "Walter was terribly morose and mourning for his wife, and at that time, he was directing a lot of the episodes," adds series producer Philip Saltzman. "Almost a third of the episodes were directed by Walter, and there was a lot of shooting in the Valley; so we worked it out so that all of the morning shots could be done on the west side. That way Walter could go to the grave site early in the morning and then come to the location." Buddy Ebsen also had his bad times. During the series run, Ebsen lost his mother. Lee Meriwether had some unhappy times too. "I had one brief period of time where I lost about five girlfriends in the space of eight months," remembers Meriwether. "I came in and asked permission a couple of times to be written out. That amazed Quinn. I was the first actress who'd ever asked to be written out of a show."

Which made it clear that Lee Meriwether was one actress who had her priorities straight. Almost everyone who worked regularly on *Barnaby Jones* did. Quite a few of the series' directors and guest stars did too. Director Michael Caffey certainly did. As the father of thirteen children, including the "Go-Go's" lead guitarist Charlotte Caffey, Michael Caffey couldn't pick and choose what television shows and things he was going to direct. He had to take whatever was given him. Many times Caffey got lucky. Especially when he was doing *Barnaby Jones*. During the first season, Caffey lucked out when he was handed "Sunday: Doomsday" (a black-comedy in which Gary Lockwood was arranging a special kind of death for Barnaby). That was the same season Caffey got another one of his favorites, "Twenty Million Alibis." "Twenty Million" reunited Michael Caffey with one of his favorite actors, Peter Haskell. When Caffey was assigned the fourth season's "Double Vengeance," he was just as delighted. "Double Vengeance" gave him another opportunity to work with one of his all-time favorite leading ladies, Lynda Day George.

"I directed Lynda several times," reveals Caffey. "Lynda Day was something else! She was an absolute joy. A supreme professional, lovely lady, just terrific. I can't say enough good things about her. She's an excellent actress, a beautiful woman. I remember I did an *It Takes a Thief* with her, and she was a joy then. [Series star] Bob Wagner came up to me at one point when we were filming that show. He says,

'Mike, this is the kind of gal we should have on all of our shows.' Bob loved Lynda. Everybody loved Lynda. She never let anybody be mistreated. She didn't like to see anybody hurt. She was, and is, a very moral person."

That made Lynda Day George perfect for "Double Vengeance." In "Double Vengeance," George builds a false identity which enables her to marry and murder a man in order to get control of his business—a business which he and his slimy partner (Lloyd Bochner) have stolen from her father. The minute she regains control of her father's business, George turns it back to its original purpose, performing good works for the community. The no-good Bochner, however, has other plans. Assisting him in these plans is George's lover (Edward Power). Written by future *Barnaby Jones* producer Robert Sherman, "Double Vengeance" was a perfect illustration of just how talented series producer Philip Saltzman and his associates were when it came to coming up with new and innovative story-lines.

"Phil was absolutely brilliant," enthuses Lee Meriwether. "He led our ship into bigger waters. He really guided us beautifully." Case in point—the fifth season's "Duet for Dying." "[Story consultant] Gerry Sanford wrote that," remembers Saltzman. "Gerry had written some country-western songs, and we were talking about a story area that would allow us to use them; then Gerry started talking about some of the country and western women. I said, 'Gee, wouldn't it be great if there were a couple of country-western women who traveled around together and lured men into some place where they could rob them and kill them?'" Thus was born the Starshine Sisters. "Well," continues Saltzman, "trying to find two actresses who could sing was tough [Cassie Yates and Mary Ann Chinn got the parts], but once we did, we did so well with that story-line we decided to bring 'em back." They did one month later in "Duet for Danger."

During the second season, Meredith Baxter had played a serial killer in "The Deadly Jinx." During the story construction of that episode Philip Saltzman discovered that the much-maligned Adrian Samish was quite clever when it came to improving a story. "Every once in a while," reveals Saltzman, "we'd try to do a closed mystery. In other words, you wouldn't know who the killer was until the end of the show. Now in this show, Meredith Baxter was doing all the killing, and I was planning to hold that until the end. That was to be the big twist, and the big surprise. Adrian had read the story. He said, 'Gee, why don't you reveal that halfway through? Then you've got 'em both ways. You've got the mystery up to the first half-hour. During the second half, you can show why she's doing it, develop all that.' So, I did. I thought that was a very good idea. We opened it up in the second half, and showed why she was doing all these things—how she had been all warped by her mother [Ida Lupino]."

The news-hungry reporter that Robert Reed played in the sixth-season opener, "Death Beat," was about as warped. "Death Beat" made for a great sixth-season premiere. Eager to advance his career, Reed's newsman stops at nothing to achieve this goal, whether it is manufacturing news—such as phony suicides—or committing genuine murder. In fact, Reed is so obsessed with making news, he even asks Lt. Biddle (series regular John Carter—brother of *Combat* regular Conlan Carter) to allow him to report on his own arrest. Biddle agrees. "Death Beat" was one of the finest performances Robert Reed ever gave on television. "I liked Robert Reed," says "Death Beat" director Michael Caffey. "He was excellent in that show. He gave it his all. I remember when I was doing that show, I got a ticket. I was driving through the golf course at Griffith Park, six A.M., in my little BMW 2002, nobody anywhere. Pretty soon a policeman appears. He says, 'You know, you were doing fifty in a twenty-mile zone.' Then he found out I was a director after he'd given me the ticket. Oh, the apologies! 'Oh, if you'd just said something I never would have given you a ticket.' I said, 'It's good you did,' because I tended to daydream when I was driving. When I was driving, I was directing the picture I was about to do. I was going over the day's work in my mind."

That sort of preparation, plus the experience Michael Caffey had gained during his years as assistant director on the hit World War II series *Combat*, made him more than qualified to step in as a last-minute replacement for the eighth season's two-part movie special, "Nightmare in Hawaii." "Whoever was going to do it broke their leg, or had a heart attack or something," recalls Caffey; "so it got fouled up. They called me in a hurry. I went over and did it. Now one thing that happened that I will never forget was before we started shooting, Buddy had the local priest bless the crew and everything. Well, we never had a problem—we weren't ten minutes off on anything we did. The people there loved that; they respected that. They thought it was wonderful that Buddy would do such a thing."

With the exception of the *Barnaby Jones* series theme (Jerry Goldsmith was hired to compose one after John Elizalde's original choice—the soon to be London Symphony conductor Andre Previn—turned him down), nothing was going too well during the eighth and last season of *Barnaby Jones*. Turning production chores over to his co-producers Robert Sherman and Norman Jolley, the series' new executive producer Philip Saltzman had no time to referee the ongoing battles between Sherman and Jolley. He was too busy with the new QM series, *A Man Called Sloane*. So when Michael Preece directed the Kenneth Mars guest shot, "The Killin' Cousin," in which private detective Mars suspects Betty of being "the killin' cousin," Preece was on his own. "That was sort of a spin-off pilot," remembers Preece, "and they wanted comedy in that show, but we never discussed how far they wanted the comedy to go. Now, when you hire Kenneth Mars, you get a very strong-willed actor. Kenneth was basically the star of that show. He went way overboard. It was not a successful spin-off." Nor was the sixth-season's "A Ransom in Diamonds" (Felton Perry and Sam Weisman as, respectively, a black and a white detective), or any of the other pilots that QM Productions was trying one right after the other (either on or off *Barnaby Jones*) throughout the late 1970s.

Thus, *Barnaby Jones* continued to be the company's only asset. "It was kind of the low-man on the totem pole at the network and to some degree with Quinn," notes series director Ralph Senensky, "but it was the real money-maker in the end. It outlasted everything else." Like Quinn Martin's other big hit, *The FBI, Barnaby Jones* was not canceled because of poor ratings. "Nobody could believe it," says

Buddy Ebsen as super-sleuth Sherlock Holmes in an amusing publicity shot for the January 28, 1973–September 4, 1980, CBS-TV series, *Barnaby Jones*.

Michael Preece. "It was still a hit, but I guess it was a hit with the wrong people. Older people loved it." "I think the series ended at the right time," reflects Roy Stork. "I think Buddy was pretty happy about it. Buddy always had his eye on the eight-year mark."

"When *Barnaby* got canceled," remembers executive casting director John Conwell's secretary, Lois Winslow, "they were going to do another show with Buddy Ebsen. I was working with [casting director] Jim Merrick at the time. We were lining up people for a presentation to go to the network. They wanted Buddy to do a twenty-minute presentation. Buddy said, 'No, I won't do a presentation.' I couldn't blame him. The gall of these people. Asking him to do a presentation for a show after he'd been on for so long on their network."

Fortunately for Quinn Martin, Ken Howard, star of the producer's third CBS series, *The Manhunter*, wasn't at all like the CBS network executives. Howard may have had his reservations about doing an action-filled series, but in the end he was glad he did the show. "Out of all the TV producers I've ever worked for," declares the actor, "Quinn Martin was my favorite."

Chapter 12

THE MANHUNTER

You know, Mr. Howard, you are the runningest, jumpingest man we've ever seen.
Manhunter *star Ken Howard's two housekeepers to*
their boss after watching a few episodes of his series

Like its big, tall star, Ken Howard, *The Manhunter* (September 11, 1974–April 9, 1975, CBS) was a big show. It was big on budget, big on locations, big on action. Set in the Depression/gangster era of the 1930s, and airing right after the often action-packed, and still going strong QM series *Cannon, The Manhunter* had no trouble getting good ratings opposite its rather weak competition of *Get Christie Love!* on ABC, and the Barry Newman lawyer drama, *Petrocelli* on NBC. For those viewers who wanted the cerebral crime-drama, *Petrocelli* fit the bill. For those who wanted crime dramas with lots of action, *The Manhunter* satisfied that need.

"It was a year of doing little action movies," says Howard, "mini–big action movies week after week. That was more of an action show than the other shows Quinn had done. You had these biplanes and cars exploding and me swinging on the trains," and gunfire, lots of gunfire. "It was a good fast action show," recalls editor Richard Brockway. "We tried to keep up a good pace on all of the QM series, but that show was really fast-paced. We used lots of submachine guns. I really enjoyed working on that show. It had a totally different look to it." "It was one of the toughest shows we ever did," says production manager Howard Alston. "That series should have lasted longer than it did. But we just didn't have enough money to do it as a 1930s period piece. It was a fun series to do. It had lots of shoot-'em-up stuff, and good old fashioned cars. Quinn really wanted that show to work. The pilot, shot on location in Stockton, California, was really great. We had a good time making the pilot, but when it was made into a series, it kinda went downhill."

Not, however, due to any lack of effort on the part of series lead Ken Howard. Always open to new challenges, future *White Shadow* star Howard had already proven

161

**Mary Cross (as Susan Tate) and Ken Howard (as bounty-hunter Dave Barrett) in the Febru-
ary 26, 1974, pilot for the September 11, 1974–April 9, 1975, CBS-TV series, *The Manhunter*.**

himself a quite versatile actor through such roles as Thomas Jefferson (in the hit
Broadway musical, *1776*), Mark Twain (on *Bonanza*, in "The Twenty-Sixth Grave")
and lawyer Adam Bonner (in the short-lived ABC sitcom, *Adam's Rib*). It was through
Adam's Rib that Quinn Martin discovered Ken Howard. "*Adam's Rib* ran thirteen
episodes," remembers Howard. "Then we were canceled. About a month later, I got
this call that Quinn Martin wanted to meet me. Well, of course I knew who Quinn
Martin was. I'd seen *The Fugitive, Barnaby Jones, Cannon*. I thought, Whoa boy.
I'm goin' in for a meeting with Quinn Martin. So, I didn't expect this guy to come
walking out the door and say, 'Hi Ken. Quinn Martin. Come on in. Have a seat, and
let's talk.' There was nobody else there. Nothing in between. It was just man to man,
just the two of us. He says, 'I've got this show called *The Manhunter*. I'd like you
to do it. I think you're gonna have a good career in front of the camera. You're a tall
guy, you're athletic, and you're the right age for this character. I'd like you to read
this treatment. If you want to do it, it's yours. Now you should know that this will
be a tough shoot. My shows are long hours. They're very tough. It's not high art.
It's action-adventure stuff, and I want you to know this going in. At times this will
be frustrating for you, because a lot of days you'll be saying nothing but 'Drop the
gun,' or 'Let's follow those guys.' Now for an actor with your kind of background,
with the kind of work you've done on stage, this will be frustrating. So, if you don't

want to do it, that's fine.' I said, "No, no, I'm interested in action stuff. I've never done anything like that. It'll be another interesting aspect. I'd love to get into it. I'd like to give this a shot. Thank you for being so candid about it.'"

Never having done an action-adventure television series, much less television guest-work (in addition to his *Bonanza*, Howard's only other TV guest credit was a *Medical Center*), Ken Howard quickly developed an appreciation and admiration for the hard life regularly faced by the dramatic television actor. Unlike some actors, Howard never considered television crime-drama beneath him. "I always had a kind of different view, maybe because I started on the stage," reflects Howard. "I always thought I could have a career that was pretty multifaceted. I wanted to be versatile, rather than become well-known. Doing *The Manhunter*, that was a whole new world to me. We'd shoot in Newhall and Piru. Those were tough shoots. It was like being in the Army. You'd go from the crack of dawn till night. I spent that whole year getting up in the dark, coming home in the dark. You'd shoot six days a week in the heat, in the rain, in the cold."

Like Burt Reynolds, Ken Howard liked to do his own stunts. "When I had done the pilot, I had done all my own stunts," states Howard, "and it was fun for me. Quinn didn't like that. He said, 'Look, we have really good stunt-men like Tony Epper,' who moved like a cat, 'and Dick Durock. Let them do the hard stuff. You do the minimum of stunts.' But a lot of times I wanted to do the stunts. I ran well. I jumped well." In the series' premiere episode, "The Ma Gentry Gang," in which Ida Lupino guest-starred as a Ma Barker–type gang-leader who pulls off a series of daring train robberies, Howard performed one of his most life-threatening stunts. "We shot that in Colorado," remembers Howard, "and there was this scene where I'm supposed to swing in into the train—you have this scene of me climbing and swinging—and this was on a moving train! Quinn was in the dailies, he saw my feet come down and then my body swinging with the train with the background rushing by, and my back's toward him in this shot. Then I swing around and there I am, swinging with my one hand and holding my gun in the other. Quinn came right out of his seat. He says, 'No! No! No! You promised. I don't want you doing that.' Well I couldn't resist it. It was too much fun. Another time I dove off of this high docket. Maybe fifteen feet up. It was one of those things, diving through the air, firing off a shot, and hitting the water. He'd sigh, 'Well all right. But don't do too much of that. I don't want you getting hurt.'"

While Ken Howard enjoyed enacting the action-filled portions of *The Manhunter*, playing the actual role of ex–Marine turned gangster-hunter Dave Barrett was less than satisfying for the actor. "I was playing a role that I wasn't suited to," explains Howard. "If you were to pick somebody to play the Manhunter, it would be a Clint Eastwood. Kind of a stony-faced man of few words, which is not my own measure of what I had done as an actor up to that point. I tried to be that as best I could. Quinn and the writers tried to adjust the character a little bit more to me as we continued in that series. I remember him telling me, 'You're more like Jimmy Stewart. You're verbal and laconic, and you have this thing that we're trying to get,' which was good because the way it was originally intended—it was to be a guy who would say very little and who would be super-macho. So, Quinn and I would have dinner, usually about once a month at Musso-Frank's, with lots of martinis and big steaks, and we'd talk about how we could improve the show and what parts of the show he liked. I mean he took the time to improve the show creatively. The show actually had good ratings. It did well. It was just very expensive. I think that's why it went off. That character wasn't exactly who I wanted to be. I didn't want to get locked into that role at that time. But had it gone another year, I still would have done it."

"When the show went off," remembers Muffet Martin, "the ratings were actually pretty good. It was building an audience, but it was approaching that time in television where if you weren't an instant hit, you would get cut off. Plus it was kind of a rural show, and I think that may have made Ken Howard ill at ease. Because he was a New York actor. I'm not sure that he was the right actor for that part. That show just didn't seem to click, which was too bad. It was a good show." Adds the series location manager and Howard's friend, Robert Goodwin, "Ken had done all these urbane, witty comedies, all these sophisticated New York comedies. Now here he was clumping around in a 1932 Chevy, chasing all these gangsters." "I'd worked with Ken Howard on *Medical Center*," recalls series director Michael Caffey, "and I think that that was his first show. He wasn't used to shooting things out of continuity. You always shoot out of continuity in television, nothing's in continuity in television, not even the sequences. Eventually Ken got comfortable with that."

Ken Howard grew even more comfortable in the role of Dave Barrett as the series progressed. Recalls Howard, "Later in the year, they brought in this guy, this funny, hard-nosed guy, and he started changing it around. The Manhunter became more verbal, and this guy had me wearing kind of a three-piece, tweed suit. He started writing the character to me. I enjoyed that. It's always good in television, when the character you're playing melds with the person that you are because you're playing that part every day, and, as with most acting that's good, what comes out is you. That's really what they want. So they were adjusting it so that more of who I was would come out in that character. This writer was making me more of an FBI type, not a country guy," which therefore allowed for the show to continue its strong suit—the blazing gun battles between Barrett and his foes.

The fine working and personal relationship Ken Howard had with his executive producer Quinn Martin was another thing the star enjoyed about doing the show. Remembers Howard, "The one thing that Quinn said to me, and this is so unique in this business ... he said, 'Look, you're the star of the show. I'm the producer. If something really bothers you, if something's going wrong and you're not happy, just pick up the phone and call me and we'll talk about it. I will do whatever I can to address it and take care of it.' Well in the course of that season, I called him three times, and every time it was taken care of. Now when you're working a show like that, you get very close to the crew—it's just you and the crew. So whenever I called Quinn, it was because I wanted him to change the caterer, or tell him that the assistant director was making people crazy, or something like that. And, at the end of the season, I told him, 'I so appreciate that each time I called you, you took care of it.' He said,

'Look, you only called me three times in the whole season. Some actors call three times a week. I was happy to do what I could because you weren't overusing that.' I mean, Quinn was great. He was a real straight-shooting guy. He was a lot of fun."

Not fun was the series' pilot film. "That was one of the toughest pilots I ever worked on," recalls assistant director Paul Wurtzel. "We had fog, rain, everything went wrong." "We did it in eighteen straight days," adds unit production manager Bob Jeffords. "We shot it up in the Gold country in Stockton. The weather was terrible. The only days it didn't rain were the days it snowed. We had the worst production manager I've ever worked with in my career. He wouldn't determine the next day's work until we finished that day's work. That's unheard of. It's almost criminal. I didn't get much sleep on that show. The most sleep I got on any night was five hours."

Creating the 1930s Depression era Midwest in a 1970s California town was none too easy either. "We had five carpenters on that show," continues Jeffords. "There were so many sets that had to be built. The basic picture cars came from Movieworld [a frequent supplier of such vehicles to television and movie production companies], but most of the cars were extras' cars. We found a tremendous supply in the Gold country. We just used local people, dressed 'em up, used them in their cars." "We had to be careful with the cars," remembers Alston. "You can't really beat up those cars a lot. We had to hide the parking meters that were on the streets too."

The TV antennas in the towns definitely had to go. Trying to explain that to the people in the town of Locke was rather difficult for location manager Goodwin. "The town was virtually unchanged with the exception of all these TV antennas," recalls Goodwin, "and part of my job as a location manager was to go in and get them to take down all these TV antennas so that we could shoot there. Well, it turned out that the entire population of this town was Chinese. Most of them didn't speak English. I went in. I told them, 'I'm with QM Productions.' They all shook their heads. They didn't understand what I was saying. Then through sign language, they told me to wait. Somebody ran off to get the one guy in the neighborhood who spoke English. He comes in, and by now there's quite a few people who are gathered there. I explained to him that I was with QM Productions and that I was there to make a television show. He turned to the others and repeated that in Chinese. They all looked at me and went, 'Quinn Martin! Quinn Martin.' They couldn't speak English but they sure as hell knew who Quinn Martin was because one of the things that Quinn always did—one of the hallmarks of his series—was whenever they'd show the main titles, the announcer would say, in this real loud voice, 'A Quinn Martin Production. *The Manhunter*. Tonight's Episode.' That just cracked me up. Here are all these people who don't even speak English, but to them Quinn Martin was like a household name."

Director Walter Grauman really had his hands full during the two weeks and a half he shot the pilot of *The Manhunter*. "Walter did a hell of a job on that," Wurtzel says in praise of him. "He was under tremendous pressure. We'd gone up and scouted all this stuff ahead of time, went down this main blacktop road to this farmhouse, and there was this dirt road. It was perfect. Well, when we came back to shoot it, somebody had built on the corner—where you make the turn into the farmhouse—

a double wide mobile home. Nobody had told us. We had scouted it and everything, and we'd made plans to use this location, and it was too late to try to find another one. We knew we couldn't tear the mobile home down. So [art director] George Chan built a whole new framework—sixty feet long, forty feet wide; he got camouflage netting from the Army and draped it over the whole thing. We put trees and brush in front of it, so, when you followed the car turning in on this road, you never saw that mobile home."

Like everyone else on *The Manhunter* pilot, director Walter Grauman caught a cold during the filming, a bad cold. Grauman lost his voice. Therefore, trying to tell Ken Howard what he wanted him to do in the scene where Howard was chasing bad-guy Gary Lockwood through the slag piles near Lockwood's hide-out proved rather difficult. "So," laughs Grauman, "finally I just indicated, like charades, 'Watch me,' and I threw myself and I rolled all the way down the hill. Gary Lockwood has never forgotten that. Every time he sees me, he says, 'There's that crazy Grauman. Son of a bitch always does his own stunts to show you what he wants.'"

There was one stunt however that Walter Grauman hadn't expected to perform, chuckles location manager Goodwin. "We needed this farmhouse—found this charming little turn of the century 1880s farmhouse outside of Modesto somewhere. There was this great big fenced-in area, like a pasture, in front of the house. Walter wanted to go inside the pasture to get a couple of angles of the house, and there was this enormous pig being kept in this pasture. We said to the woman who owned the house, 'Is it safe to go out there?' She said, 'He's like a pet. Don't worry. Go right ahead.' The pig must have weighed about six hundred pounds. He was a huge animal. So we all climbed over the fence, and got into this pasture. This pig took one look at Walter Grauman, and he just attacked. He was charging Walter from one side of the fence to the other. All of a sudden this lady comes running out of her house with a baseball bat, chasing this pig, trying to keep the pig from attacking poor Walter. Walter was kind out of breath, and sweating by the time she got that pig under control. Well, when Walter finally caught his breath, he comes up to me. He looks around. He says, 'Where's George [Chan]?' I said, 'He's out back mixing up the sweet and sour sauce.'"

Today a successful producer, Robert Goodwin credits Quinn Martin with getting him started on his road to success. It was hard for Martin not to admire the at-times brash Goodwin. "I was a very forward young man," laughs Goodwin. "I actually walked up to Quinn Martin's office. A lot of people in the company didn't even know there actually was a person named Quinn Martin. Some people [like *Barnaby Jones* make-up artist Roy Stork] thought it was two different people—Mr. Quinn and Mr. Martin. But I was ambitious. I just walked up to his office and introduced myself, and we became friends. After I did that pilot, Quinn was impressed with me. He even paid me while I wasn't working. I got paid to do nothing. He made a big excuse. He had me going out and taking photographs of little towns all over California in case *The Manhunter* got picked up. So he noticed me, and I became the fair-haired boy there. I even wrote a couple of scripts for Quinn. I actually wrote a script for *The Manhunter* ("The Carnival Story"). When they picked *The Manhunter* up, I was one of two location managers for the show." Goodwin appreciated that work. At the time he was a single parent with a one-year-old child. "Quinn gave me this car and this camera," continues Goodwin, "and I drove all over finding towns that were the right period. I found a place in Santa Maria with a back country road and a church built in the 1890s. They actually wrote an episode around the location. I showed it to [series producer] Sam Rolfe, and we did an overnight with Marj Dusay, shot in this tiny little church. We created all these files of these great spots we could use for locations."

Series director Lawrence Dobkin was quite resourceful as well. Remembers Ken Howard, "I was inside this big country store, trapped in there with bad guys outside, but I didn't have any dialogue. They didn't have a script yet. So we spent a day shooting what we figured was pretty good stuff. Larry said, 'I don't know what we're doing, but I know how these shows go.' Well, almost everything we did was usable."

The Manhunter being an action-filled show, it only made sense that the series employ directors who were quite skilled at elaborate action pieces. Lawrence Dobkin's *Rat Patrol* work proved him more than qualified. Ditto George McCowan's number of *Cannon*s. Walter Grauman's many *Untouchables* certainly proved his worth. "Wally Grauman really helped me in the pilot," recalls Howard. "Some of the things he told me had to do with acting on film. He wanted me to do less; he wanted me to do almost nothing. He told me, 'Keep it all inside.' I learned a lot by holding it very tight inside. I use pieces of that even now when I work." Howard was no less impressed with Paul Stanley's direction of *The Manhunter* episode, "Man in a Cage." Stanley had directed a number of episodes of *Mission: Impossible*. In "Man in a Cage" Stanley was reunited with *Mission* regular Greg Morris. "It was sort of a *Cool Hand Luke* kind of thing where Greg Morris and I were chained together," remembers Howard. "Michael Constantine played this prison boss with a Southern accent. Paul Stanley was a kind of lanky guy with salt and pepper blondish hair. He was a technical guy, just said a few things to me. When I saw that show all put together, it was like a big film. He'd shot me from all these angles, from a distance. He'd done all these camera things to make the stuff look good."

Adding further tension to the elaborate action sequences were the background scores of series composer Duane Tatro and other musicians. "The most fun I ever had was with *The Manhunter*," states Tatro. "I got to stretch out musically on that show. I had sort of a twelve-toned score which was very helpful in creating edgy music and slipping into country themes. We used lots of guitars in that series. I used a gut-string guitar on the pilot, interrupted it with an orchestra when they'd get to a roadblock. The series theme came from the theme I'd written for Ken Howard's character in the pilot. It combined country with a contemporary sound. Quinn was very pleased with the score I did for *The Manhunter*."

Apparently, somebody was not pleased with *The Manhunter* series. Despite its good ratings, despite the commitment and likable quality of its star Ken Howard, the series was canceled after one season. Ken Howard learned about the series' cancellation from Quinn Martin himself. "At the end of the season," remembers Howard, "I went to do a show, a new experimental play at the Vivian Beaumont in New York called 'Little Black Sheep.' I was staying at the hotel in Philadelphia near the University of Pennsylvania campus where the Annenberg Theatre was located. We were doing out of town before we went to the Beaumont. Quinn called me. He says, 'I know you have conflicted feelings about this. I'm calling to tell you the show wasn't picked up. I know that part of you is relieved, but I want to thank you for staying the course and for staying committed to the show. I know you would have if we'd continued.' He was very nice about it. He says, kind of laughing, 'I wouldn't be surprised if after we hang up, you'll go celebrate.' I did that very thing. When we hung up, it made me laugh, and I ordered a bottle of champagne, and shared it with a couple of friends. Quinn was just terrific, he was really good about stuff like that. I mean here I was. I was only thirty and he was such a powerful producer. But he didn't have the sort of arrogance that goes with that kind of producer. He didn't have that, 'Listen, you're just an actor. You just do what you're told' attitude. He treated me with real respect and friendship. He was very consistent that way. He was more the exception than the rule."

Unfortunately, feelings were less than cordial between Quinn Martin and some of the other talents who were to be involved in the producer's next series, *Caribe*. From start to finish, *Caribe* was a disaster. To many at QM Productions, it was also something else. *Caribe* was the beginning of the end.

Chapter 13

CARIBE

The only show I thought Quinn really screwed up on was *Caribe*. It was an awful show.

Caribe *guest star Marlyn Mason*

If it hadn't been so expensive, the people at QM Productions who were involved in *Caribe* (February 17–August 11, 1975, ABC), might have found themselves laughing about the show. Maybe they were laughing about it anyway. QM's version of *Hawaii Five-O* (with Stacy Keach and Carl Franklin as a pair of cops whose beat is Miami and the Caribbean), *Caribe* was QM Productions at its absolute worst. Nobody who was involved in the making of the show knew what anybody else was doing. Creator-producer Anthony Spinner was writing episodes for a Robert Wagner/Cary Grant–type character; ABC's Michael Eisner was insisting that Quinn Martin cast Stacy Keach. Martin cast Keach; ABC didn't like Keach. ABC could forget about hiring Quinn Martin's original choice—Robert Wagner. Wagner's wife Natalie Wood didn't want Wagner going to Miami.

It didn't help that Anthony Spinner was producing *Caribe* at the same time he was producing *Cannon*. "I never understood why *Caribe* was canceled," says the producer. "We were so high in the ratings. It wasn't a great show by any means, but they wouldn't give Quinn the money to make it. We were shooting in the Caribbean, and it was costing a bloody fortune—flying actors back and forth [from L.A. to Miami]. Plus Quinn wanted Stacy Keach to live on a boat. I said, 'Well, that's terrific, Quinn, but you see, these islands, all through the Caribbean, some of them are 1200 miles from each other, or from the Florida coast, so, if there's a murder on Tuesday, and the guy takes his boat, he won't get there for a week. By that time, the body would have rotted.' 'I don't want to hear that,' he says. 'He's gonna be on a boat!' So by God, he was on a boat."

Of course, Stacy Keach was nothing like the character Spinner had created.

"Quinn told me to think R.J. Wagner," reveals Spinner, "so I wrote the first show for R.J. Wagner. He was gonna be this playboy living the grand life on this boat with all these gorgeous girls; he was very slick and smooth, and his sidekick was supposed to be [future *Most Wanted* regular] Hari Rhodes, who was, at that time, a very well respected, middle-aged black actor. Rhodes was gonna be this Bohemian. So I'm writing these shows. Quinn calls me. He says, 'I've got Stacy Keach for the lead. I just talked to him in London. It's all set.' I said, 'For what show?' He says, '*Caribe*.' And my head was swiveling like in *The Exorcist*. I said, 'Quinn. I've written nine shows for R.J. Wagner—all slick, sophisticated, superficial, wise-guy charm, with millions of girls. How does Stacy Keach play R.J. Wagner? I'll have to rewrite every single script now.' He says, 'Yeah. Let me tell you who the black guy is.' I said, 'It's not Hari Rhodes?' He says, 'No, it's Carl Franklin.' I said, 'Quinn, this is supposed to be a Bohemian. Carl is a street kid from South Central, a nice street kid, but who's gonna believe him as a Bohemian?' So, I had to rewrite every script, and Stacy Keach would complain, 'Hey. I thought I was gonna be a lover, and have all these girls, and be charming, and have a great wardrobe. What happened to all of that?' I was kinda stuck for an answer."

Already a disaster by this point, *Caribe* grew even worse as production started. "It was so frantically done," explains Spinner, "that unbeknownst to me, Howard Alston had gone to Florida and built a police headquarters set. So, when I found out, I called Howard. I said, 'Howard, what is this? I hear that you've built a police headquarters.' He said, 'Well, yeah. We always have a police headquarters set.' I said, 'Howard, I'm the producer of this show. I'm the writer on this show. We have nine scripts at work now. There's not a single scene set at police headquarters in any of these scripts. So, what are we gonna do with a police headquarters?' He says, 'Well, I told Quinn we're gonna have a police headquarters.' I said, 'Yeah, but Quinn doesn't really know what this show is about. I haven't had the time to explain it to him.'"

Nor did Spinner have the time to visit any Florida and Caribbean locations, at least according to unit production manager Bob Jeffords. Somehow Spinner did find the time to visit locations during the filming of the series' second aired episode, "Vanished." Spinner recalls, "The first day we shot down there, a hurricane hit. All of the equipment got stuck in the mud. It was pouring rain. The crew got lost for a while. Then, when we started to shoot, Jason Evers and Joanna Pettet were playing this love scene—it was supposed to be a gorgeous day in Nassau, and it was pitch dark. The generators were blasting; you couldn't hear the dialogue. Joanna's hair was all over her face, soaking wet; Jason's hair was the same, and it just looked like … God help us! Now this was Michael Eisner's big show at ABC, and the next day I got a call from Quinn. He says, 'We gotta meet Michael Eisner for lunch.' I said, 'I don't know Michael Eisner.' He says, 'He's the guy who wants to see us about *Caribe*.' I'm thinking, Oh God! So we went and had lunch with Michael Eisner, and he was the coldest man I ever met. I'd say it to his face! I mean, he was an alien. He should have been in *The Invaders*! And I'm tryin' to explain to this guy, 'You see there was this hurricane, and in television, we don't have the money to sit around at $40,000 an hour, and wait for the rain to go away. But don't worry about it. In post-production the sounds will be gone. There'll just be the rumbling of the thunder and the surf, and I will stick in a line where somebody says something about the weather, and that'll be that.' He says, 'I don't believe you.' I said, 'You don't believe me about what?' He says, 'That you can get rid of all that noise.' I said, 'Yes, we can. It's not brain surgery.' Well, that was the worst lunch! We got in the car. Quinn says, 'You handled that very well.' I said, 'Quinn, you're always the boss, and I'm the underling. All of your producers are the underlings until there's trouble, and there I was dying.' He says, 'Ah, you did very well. Don't worry about it. Fuck him.' But that was the way that whole show went. I mean, that whole show was crazy.''

"Quinn had wanted to shoot *Caribe* all over the Caribbean," adds Muffet Martin, "but the show was hard to control. There was bribery, corruption, kickbacks, payoffs. It just was difficult to keep it under control cost-wise, and of course there was always the weather." "Quinn had sold the series based on the idea that it would be shot all over the Caribbean," recalls Alston, "but he didn't share that information with us. You never knew the full story. They'd give you the scripts and say, 'This is what you have to do.'" "The first show was done in the U.S. Virgin Islands," elaborates Jeffords. "It ended up being the only show that was shot off the mainland, that is if you consider Key West the mainland. They finished shooting on a Friday or Saturday, then sent the cast and crew back to Miami. Some of the crew didn't arrive until Tuesday, they were scheduled to start another show that Monday. They got routed and re-routed. Some were stranded in the Virgin Islands. Some were stranded in Puerto Rico." One of the episodes was shot in Puerto Rico. After three days of filming, the director was still doing the first day's work.

As the original plan had been to shoot throughout the Caribbean, "we'd ordered a barge, with a second set of camera grips and electric equipment, so that the barge could be sent off somewhere and wait for the rest of the company to get there," continues Jeffords. "It was down there for several months going between islands with a separate production manager [Lou Place], but it was never used after that first show." "Quinn got upset because we weren't able to go through the whole Caribbean for locations," remembers Alston. "He didn't understand that you don't just move into other people's countries. You need to get visas. You have to get your equipment over there six months before you use it. You can't travel around the world and do a show. You can, if you have a year to set it up. We didn't have a year."

Realizing they had neither the time nor the budget to shoot throughout the Caribbean, the company did the next best thing; they recreated the Caribbean in Miami. Even that had its share of problems. "Miami was not an easy place to shoot film," discloses Jeffords. "Some of the unions there, like the Teamsters, were more interested in what they could get from the show, not what they could do to help the show. We used a lot of Florida people who were accustomed to doing commercials. They'd never done a television show. The first time they did a car-mount, it took them two hours. In Los Angeles, that usually takes fifteen minutes. Then Tony Spinner wouldn't go to Florida; so that complicated things. That show was so location oriented."

The series' associate producer Dick Gallegly took Spinner's place. Having served for so long as production manager on *The Streets of San Francisco* and *The FBI*, Howard Alston thought Gallegly might be able to help *Caribe*. Prior to assigning Gallegly to the series, Alston had gone down to Florida and first set up those parts of the series which were for Alston the most difficult. When Alston went back to California, he'd left behind all of those things that were for him the easiest. What was easy for Howard Alston was not necessarily easy for Dick Gallegly. Dealing with series star Stacy Keach certainly wasn't easy for Gallegly. "Dick hadn't been given the power to be equal to Stacy Keach," explains Jeffords, "and somebody needed to control Stacy Keach. Stacy felt that it was his show; he tried to produce it himself. That created lots of conflict. QM didn't work that way. I think Stacy hurt that show tremendously, mostly because of his own ego. There were aspects that suffered because he was trying to make himself look good. He just rode over Carl Franklin, never gave him a chance. Carl was very unhappy."

Jeffords wasn't in the best mood himself. "I had just come back to L.A. from *Streets* because I'd been offered a job in L.A.," says Jeffords, "and I was glad to take it. I'd been out of town for four years. I was home for about a week; then Howard Alston told me he needed me to go down to Florida for a week to ten days to help Dick Gallegly on *Caribe*. I went down there two days before Christmas. I was only supposed to be down there a week. I wound up being there for four weeks! When Howard came down the third week, I said, 'Listen, I've been out of town for four years. The last time I talked to you, you promised me I'd be back at home.' I talked him into letting me go back to L.A. I felt so sorry to leave Dick Gallegly with that show. That whole thing was just so hopelessly confused."

Guest star Marlyn Mason never forgot the unpleasant conditions she and fellow guest Rudy Solari faced while shooting episode #4—"The Mercenary" in Puerto Rico. "There were no rest-rooms!" exclaims Mason, "and poor Stacy Keach. We were all using his trailer. I remember Rudy and I, we sat Stacy down, we said, 'Hey man. If you're gonna do a series, you gotta get a bigger dressing room. You can't have people tromping in and out like this.' I mean Stacy was a good sport; the conditions in Florida were just awful. There were no chairs, no nothing, and it was so hot down there. I couldn't wait to get out of that show. That was really a take the money and run show." Series director Virgil Vogel was adversely affected by the weather. Vogel got so sick, his assistant director David Whorf had to take over and direct the rest of the episode Vogel had started.

Whorf's sense of humor got him through *Caribe*. Remembers director William Hale, "There was this restaurant in Miami where you had to have a two-week reservation, and David got this idea—he called them up, he says, 'Would you have a table for two for Commissioner Hale?' They said, 'Yeah, sure.' So, we drove up there in David's Volkswagen, the parking attendant took the car, the owner comes up. He looks at me. He says, 'Oh, Commissioner Hale, how are you?' So we went in, had dinner. Then we left the restaurant, and the owner's walking out with us. Well, we're waiting on the car; then we realize that the parking lot attendant is gonna deliver a little dinky

Volkswagen to Commissioner Hale. So we were sweating bullets. Fortunately, the owner walked back inside before the car was delivered."

Considering all of the troubles ABC and QM had in doing *Caribe*, the network might have been better off had they gone with the version that was being done by Quinn Martin's friend Don Brinkley and Brinkley's partner, Frank Glicksman. "We had this series idea which we took to ABC, having to do with a cop stationed in the Caribbean," remembers Brinkley. "After we started working on it, we heard that Quinn was doing a show set in the Caribbean. We called ABC. We said, 'Is this true?' They said, 'Absolutely not. It's absolutely untrue.' So we worked our tails off on it, and got our scripts ready.' Next thing you know, *Caribe* was on the air. It was a terrible show—absolutely phony—the thing lasted about twenty minutes."

Apparently, the only good thing about *Caribe* was its opening credits. "They were great," enthuses editor Richard Brockway. "You had these credits of the various islands, the natives, pretty girls in bathing suits, fast motorboats. I thought Howard Anderson did a wonderful job on those main titles. Those credits sort of anticipated the ones on *Miami Vice*. The cuts on those main titles were marvelous, they were weird, far-out things. You had the titles popping, popping, popping. *Caribe* had a great look about it."

In the opinion of Paul Sorvino, star of Quinn Martin's next series, *Bert D'Angelo, Superstar*, he was the greatest thing about that series. At least that's how Sorvino struck *Superstar*'s directors.

Chapter 14

BERT D'ANGELO, SUPERSTAR

> There was a toilet in the prop room, and when you went in and raised the lid, Paul
> Sorvino's picture was at the bottom of the toilet. Which pretty much summed up
> how we all felt about *Bert D'Angelo, Superstar*.
>
> Bert D'Angelo, Superstar *director Michael Caffey*

While a lot of potential QM series pilots were tried out on *Barnaby Jones* as episodes of that series, *Barnaby* wasn't the only QM series to air pilots. On March 4, 1976, *The Streets of San Francisco* aired an episode called "Superstar." In "Superstar," Lt. Detective Mike Stone (Karl Malden) and Inspector Steve Keller (Michael Douglas) clashed with maverick New York cop Bert D'Angelo (Paul Sorvino) who had followed a suspect from New York to San Francisco. After the three solved the case, the NYPD transferred D'Angelo to the SFPD so as to acquaint the San Francisco Police Department with the way things were done back in New York City. Thus was born the new QM series, *Bert D'Angelo, Superstar* (February 21–July 10, 1976, ABC).

QM Productions' version of the long-running hit series *McCloud*, featuring the same kind of heated arguments between the title character and his new superiors, the same sort of clash between the West and the East, the same inevitable triumph that the title character always enjoyed by employing his own methods, *Bert D'Angelo, Superstar*, was sorely lacking in three other elements which, when combined with those things previously mentioned, made *McCloud* so much fun—the unconventional wardrobe for its title character; the always outrageous, and lengthy, pursuit and capture of the criminal; the never ending supply of gorgeous women for the leading man's romances. Not that *Bert D'Angelo* guest actresses Stefanie Powers, Barbara Luna, Jo Ann Harris, and Leslie Charleson were lacking in pulchritude.

One reason *McCloud* lasted as long as it did, some said, was that it only ran once a month as one of the rotating segments of *The NBC Mystery Movie*. Whether a similar practice with *Bert D'Angelo, Superstar* would have saved that series is of course open to question, but chances are, probably not. As almost everyone agreed, *McCloud* star Dennis Weaver was a very nice guy. His likable personality added to his character, and thus to the show's draw. Few who worked with *Bert D'Angelo, Superstar* lead Paul Sorvino found him likable.

Bert D'Angelo director William Hale had no kind words for Sorvino and remembers him as very difficult to work with. "I remember on the one show I did, we were standing out in the rain. Up on top of a 'parallel' —

Title card for Paul Sorvino's February 21, 1976– July 10, 1976, ABC-TV series, *Bert D'Angelo, Superstar.*

one of these things that raises the camera higher than eye level — and Sorvino was entertaining some friends in his trailer. The a.d. went to his trailer. He says, 'Mr. Sorvino, they're ready for you.' So, me and the crew we're standing out in the rain, getting soaked, Sorvino doesn't come out. The a.d. goes back a second time, 'Mr. Sorvino, they're ready for you.' About twenty minutes later, that son-of-a-bitch comes out, and the show wasn't well established at that time. It was still almost like a pilot. So he was being nasty to us. To those of us who at that time were trying to put him over, put him over as an actor. There's no excuse for that."

Having worked with Vic Morrow on *Combat* and William Conrad on *Cannon*, director Michael Caffey was accustomed to dealing with troublesome actors. Michael Caffey had very few problems with Paul Sorvino. "It could get to be a pain if you were around him for a while," admits Caffey, "but he did pretty much what I asked him to do. He knew everything. He was really full of himself." Opera stars were said to be that way too. Sorvino auditioned for the role of Bert D'Angelo by singing an aria. "He was a character," laughs series creator William Robert Yates. "He loved opera, loved to sing opera. So he interviewed by singing a song. I said, 'I don't think we can use that particular talent in this episode of *The Streets of San Francisco*, but I'm delighted to know that you can do it.' His personality made that part. I think that's why the network bought it."

"Men with No Past" guest star Collin Wilcox-Horne shared the network's admiration of Sorvino. "She was a method actress," laughs Caffey. "She worshipped Sorvino. She kept saying to me, 'Oh! Isn't he the greatest actor you've ever seen?'" Unit production manager Bob Jeffords hardly thought so. "He was a very demanding actor," says Jeffords. "He wanted to be told what the show was about; he wanted to know about the look of the show. That was not part of the Quinn Martin shows. That was not a happy set." Sorvino's co-star Dennis Patrick (D'Angelo's superior, Captain Jack

Breen) didn't make the set any warmer. "He was very acidy," says Caffey. "He was sharp-tongued. This was not your friend." The series' other regular, Robert Pine (Inspector Larry Johnson) was a nice person, however, as was "Men with No Past" guest star Glenn Corbett. "Glenn Corbett was a likable guy," says Caffey. "He was a pleasure to have on the set."

Having been in the business for years, "Flannagan's Fleet" lead guest Peter Mark Richman was no problem either. "I think I played a spy in that show, and we were shooting on location in these terrible neighborhoods," recalls Richman. "It was a dilapidated area. I think I limped in that show—I always tried to do something physical like that whenever I played a character. I was only there that one day. I had to get back to L.A. that night. I had to do a voice-over for Oldsmobile. I did the voice-overs for Oldsmobile for three years."

By the time Richman's June 5 "Flannagan's Fleet" episode aired, *Bert D'Angelo, Superstar* was pretty much of a goner. Premiering on February 21, 1976, the show had temporarily halted its broadcast after the April 3 episode, "A Concerned Citizen." Only three more episodes aired following the broadcast of Peter Mark Richman's "Flannagan's Fleet." One episode, "Requiem for a Rip-Off" never made it to the air.

Quinn Martin hadn't lost his touch for making hit series though. The incredible ratings amassed by the March 21, 1976, broadcast of the *Most Wanted* pilot had convinced ABC to immediately schedule that new QM series for the 1976-77 season. What with a popular series star like Robert Stack for its lead and a very talented series producer like Harold Gast for its producer, *Most Wanted* was unquestionably the next hit series for QM Productions.

Chapter 15

MOST WANTED

Ordinarily, working on a Quinn Martin series was just a wonderful experience. On that show, it always seemed like everybody had just come back from lunch. In this business, when everybody comes back from lunch, everybody's full, warm, and tired. So, when you start shooting after lunch, it's very slow for the first couple of hours. That's the way it was on that show. All the time.

Most Wanted *guest star Lynda Day George*

Most Wanted (October 16, 1976–April 25, 1977, ABC) should not have been the disaster that it was, not when its series lead was Robert Stack, not when its producer was *Judd for the Defense*'s Harold Gast, not when its creator was *Mission: Impossible*'s Laurence Heath. Laurence Heath had written some of the better episodes of *The Invaders*; he'd written a number of good *Mission: Impossible*s. Given that, given a series theme by *Mission* composer Lalo Schifrin, directors like Virgil Vogel and Don Medford, a guest roster including Harris Yulin, Ed Nelson, Mariette Hartley, Rip Torn, plus the very clever, tongue-in-cheek guest casting of *Mission: Impossible* regular Lynda Day George, leading her own (criminal) team, *Most Wanted* should have been a hit series. It certainly had been a hit pilot.

Mixing elements of *The FBI, Mission: Impossible, The New Breed,* and Walter Grauman's *The Silent Force, Most Wanted* starred Robert Stack as Captain Linc Evers—leader of the LAPD's Most Wanted unit. That unit included just two other members, Sgt. Charlie Benson (Shelly Novack) and Officer Kate Manners (Jo Ann Harris). As its title implied, the Most Wanted unit had been established for just one purpose—to track down and capture every one of the criminals whose names appeared on the personal most wanted list of Los Angeles city mayor Dan Stoddard (Hari Rhodes). The role of Mayor Stoddard was obviously inspired by then current Los Angeles city mayor Thomas Bradley. As both the real Bradley and fictional Stoddard were black, the series therefore had an air of reality. According to Quinn Martin's secretary, Sally Richman Manning, the realism was intentional.

Title card for the March 21, 1976 movie-pilot for the October 16, 1976–April 25, 1977 ABC-TV series, *Most Wanted*.

"It was almost a reality series," notes Manning, "but in those days we didn't have reality series. The show had them going after top ten criminals, child abusers, and so forth. There was always some basis of fact in the cases." If the stories were indeed based on real incidents, then that was truly frightening. Like the criminals in *Cannon*, the villains of *Most Wanted* were very dangerous people. In the March 21, 1976, movie-pilot, the team had pursued a fanatic who raped and murdered nuns. In the February 5, 1977, episode, "The Hit Men," they were after a gang of professional killers.

While not all the criminals in *Most Wanted* committed murder, they certainly committed some unusual crimes. "The Two Dollar Kidnappers" were a gang who, if someone wanted a number of people kidnapped, would do so at discount rates. As "The Dutchman," ex-con Rip Torn and his gang used stolen laser rifles to hold up supermarkets. In the series premiere episode, "The Sky Killer," Harris Yulin portrayed a skyjacker who conducts an airborne "trial" of the congressman who convicted him, with twelve hostage passengers as his jurors. One of the most realistic episodes in the entire series was the December 25th Lynda Day George guest shot, "The Ten Percenter." As the title character, George played a brainy attorney whose gang only robs the people and places she herself picks through her position. The following week, the Most Wanted team went undercover in a minimum (not maximum) security prison in order to solve a series of white collar killings ("The White Collar Killer").

Airing two of the series' more realistic stories on Christmas Day and New Year's Day was nothing short of foolish, but considering some of the other things that were going on at QM Productions at the time, it was understandable. Right about the time *Most Wanted* began, QM Productions took on a new production head, Marty Katz. "Marty Katz had a great opinion of himself," laughs *Most Wanted* series producer Harold Gast. "He knew everything about everything. Now, one time, the director I'd been planning to use was offered a TV movie, and when that happens, you usually let the director go. So I was looking around for a director. Marty Katz says, 'I know a very good director who's available. Why don't you use him?' I said, 'Who?' Well this guy hadn't done a whole lot, but Marty knew his work from I don't know where. He assured me this guy was a very good capable director." Gast hired him, and he started making the picture. "It was like there was no director there. It was like some kid in high school making believe he was a director. I mean there was one scene which involved four or five people in an office talking over some problem. [The director] lined them up in a totally artificial way, a way that they would never stand in, and he had them say their lines so he could get them all in one shot. I saw this in dailies. I said, 'Oh my God, that's awful.' I got up and went forward three or four rows to where Marty Katz was sitting. Marty said, 'You don't like him?' because I had complained to Marty about this guy before, and this was the fourth or fifth day of this show. I said, 'Marty, now do you see why I say this guy is a terrible director? The way he lined up those people—having them standing against a wall?' He said, 'Well how would you have done it?' I said, 'Differently!' and went back to my seat. I mean, Marty Katz was a phony. He didn't know anything. He didn't know a good director! I haven't heard of this guy since."

Of course, after *Magnum, P.I.*, everyone knew who Tom Selleck was. Selleck had played the computer expert of the Most Wanted unit in the series pilot. Laughs editor Richard Brockway, "When we were making tests for the show, Quinn asked me what I thought of Tom Selleck. I said, 'He looks great, but my God, that voice!' Well, I never lived that down." QM Player Leslie Charleson had also appeared in the pilot. She'd played the psychiatrist member of the team. "She was nice," recalls pilot director Walter Grauman, "but a very nervous actress. Very nervous as if it were her first role." The other member of the team in the pilot was Shelly Novack. Like Robert Stack, Novack was the only member of the original cast to reprise his role in the short-lived series.

"Shelly Novack had to go to the bathroom more than any other actor that I ever knew," recalls series director Michael Preece. "We'd get them all there, be ready to shoot, then he'd say, 'Excuse me, I have to go to the bathroom.' So he goes to the bathroom, we shoot the scene, it would drive you to distraction." "Novack was a problem child," adds assistant director Bob Jeffords. "He wouldn't do anything until he had to go in front of the camera. He became a sign for when we were gonna be ready on the set." "Shelly was a good guy," states sound mixer Dick Church. "He came from a pretty wealthy family. He was always cooperative, but really insecure. I liked him a lot. I was sad when I heard that he died," as was series guest Lynda Day George. "I was really sorry about that," says George, "because Shelly Novack had a brain in his head. He was a person who had a thought pattern going for him somewhere along the line. I guess that got eaten up by the drugs."

Novack's drug addiction made things difficult for series star Robert Stack. "Shelly and Robert didn't get along," remembers the series' production coordinator Debbie Yates Marks. "Bob Stack had as much class as anyone I've ever met. He tried to teach Shelly and Jo Ann Harris the way the business worked. He tried to keep the both of them under his belt." Harris however had her own ideas in regards to her performance. The actress frequently tried to change the scripts. "The scripts were written by older people," states Preece, "and she would change them, because she knew that's not the way young people talk. She had a very good figure, and they always had her wearing tight jeans so they could show it off. We were always starting shots on her butt." Being what assistant director Bob Jeffords calls "a solid professional," Jo Ann Harris

Tom Selleck as computer-specialist Tom Roybo and QM favorite Leslie Charleson as police-psychiatrist Sgt. Lee Herrick in the March 21, 1976, movie-pilot for the October 16, 1976–April 25, 1977, ABC-TV series, *Most Wanted.*

was less than satisfied with her role. She wanted to do more. "Stack was always sending the kids out on assignments, but neither of them had much to do," recalls Preece. "He didn't either. When I pushed him for a reaction, he'd say, 'I've got two. Which one do you want?'

Like *The FBI, Most Wanted* was structured to showcase the guest stars. As a result of that and Harold Gast's writing credentials (the 1940s radio drama, *Front Page Farrell*; the critically acclaimed Reginald Rose series, *The Defenders*), it was a good show. "We had a lot of very good actors on that show," states Gast. "We almost had an embarrassment of riches." Among the guest stars were Pernell Roberts and Rip Torn. For Gast, both were "a pain in the ass," especially Torn. "In order to get Rip Torn, we had to send him a script," remembers Gast, "so we sent him an earlier draft of this show (the aforementioned "The Dutchman"). Rip Torn accepted the part from that script, but that script went through a number of revisions before we got to the final shooting script. Now, in the draft that went to Rip Torn, he plays a middle-aged man who's involved with a young woman, and they have a scene in which they kiss quite passionately. By the time we got through polishing that script, that kiss was eliminated. Rip shows up for work. He objects violently to the fact that he's not gonna get to kiss the girl. He took it as a personal reflection. We had offered him this part where he was a very virile man, and all of a sudden we had emasculated him. I had I don't know how many conversations with him trying to persuade him not to be upset about that because I wasn't gonna put it back. I didn't like it, Quinn didn't like it either. Rip had a number of problems with the script. He was very picky. We negotiated our way around everything except that. I said, "If you feel so strongly about it, you are welcome to talk to Quinn and see if you can persuade him.' So he talked to Quinn, and with no trouble at all, Quinn was persuaded to let him do it. Then Quinn said to me, 'I said to him he could do it, and that we would shoot it, but I'm gonna cut it out of post-production.' So that's what happened. We shot the kiss and it disappeared."

Gast wasn't too upset about that, but he felt terrible about what happened to long-time QM production manager Howard Alston. "When I came back to work for Quinn on *Most Wanted*, he had changed quite a lot," reveals Gast. "He was sort of captured by some other people

Shelly Novack (left, as Sgt. Charlie Benson), Jo Ann Harris (as Officer Kate Manners) and Robert Stack (as Captain Linc Evers) in a publicity shot for the October 16, 1976–April 25, 1977, ABC-TV series, *Most Wanted*.

who impressed him very much. He did some very peculiar things, like firing Howard Alston, who was the best person working on his staff. He was persuaded by these people that Howard was no good, and Howard was the best, absolutely the best. I was heartsick about that. I remember being at a dinner party that Quinn gave in some restaurant, and Howard was sitting next to my wife. He sort of cried on her shoulder the whole evening about Quinn's firing him when he'd been so loyal. I later mentioned that to Quinn, and Quinn said he had carried Howard for a long time, but had gotten rid of him because Howard had changed. He said Howard had had a nervous breakdown. Which was not true. That was very much against Quinn that he would do a thing like that."

Bringing in Marty Katz to replace Alston was, by all accounts, not a good idea. "As soon as Marty Katz came in, he had to have an assistant [Edward Teets]," groans

Shelly Novack (left, as Sgt. Charlie Benson), Jo Ann Harris (as Officer Kate Manners) and Robert Stack (as Captain Linc Evers) in a publicity shot for the October 16, 1976– April 25, 1977, ABC-TV series, *Most Wanted*.

Gast. "Howard had never needed an assistant. Marty Katz would send Edward Teets to sit in on production meetings for each show, as though Katz was too busy to attend them. I never saw Katz really working. I don't know what the hell Marty Katz was doing." Assistant director Bob Jeffords was no fan of Katz himself. Jeffords remembers, "Marty Katz brought in this production manager named Ron Fury, and he was one of the worst production managers I've ever worked with. We had all kinds of problems." Which was why sound mixer Dick Church left halfway through the series. "I wanted out of there," states Church. "I hated to leave Bob Stack though. I really liked Bob Stack and his wife."

Series regular Hari Rhodes was another pleasant memory for those who did the show. "I always enjoyed working with Hari Rhodes," says Jeffords. "He was a QM Player. He was just a pleasure to work with." The series' director of photography Jack Swain was another good thing about the show. "Jack Swain was a nice man," Lynda Day George says enthusiastically, "a really bright guy. Not until you had a conversation with him on the set would you realize just how really intelligent this guy was."

For a series with a very unhappy set, a good-humored, always optimistic guest like Lynda Day George was a welcome sight. But even the upbeat George was quickly deflated when she guest-starred on the show. "Robert Stack was very concerned about the show, but it seemed like he was tired all the time," muses George. "That was not a pleasant shoot. We were at this hotel, which had these great grounds, but it was absolutely, miserably hot. Everybody was practically passing out from the heat. We were all sopping wet. It was just miserable. Every time they turned off the lights, we all ran off to get cool. That whole show was a very tired experience. I've always been one of these people with a real high energy level, but I remember that when I first walked onto that set, I felt like I'd walked right into a wall. There was no excitement on that show, no laughs on that set. I had asked Chris to come and visit at one point because there was nothing going on; so he brought the kids to the set, but he didn't want to stay there very long. He had planned to come and spend the afternoon with me while I was working; however, it was so dreary on the set he felt that was not the way he wanted to spend his afternoon."

Despite the lack of enthusiasm of Lynda Day George and so many other people who worked on *Most Wanted*, series producer Harold Gast enjoyed doing the show. More than likely, Gast's enthusiasm was what kept the series going as long as it did. "It was strange that that show didn't work," reflects Howard Alston. "Quinn was bound and determined to make the show work. He gave them carte blanche to do whatever they wanted to do. He spent a lot of money. Quinn pulled out all the stops to make it work, but it wasn't nearly as good as the series we'd made before. It was too commonplace. It was the wrong combination of everything."

There weren't any problems with Quinn Martin's next series, *Tales of the Unexpected*. Quinn Martin was very excited about that series. At long last, he would get to make a series that wasn't a crime drama.

Chapter 16

Tales of the Unexpected

It was a chance to do a more bizarre show. Not just cops and robbers.
Muffet Martin

As the 1971 motion-picture *The Mephisto Waltz* had shown, Quinn Martin was certainly capable of doing more than crime dramas. Quinn Martin had always wanted to do more than just crime dramas. Throughout his career, Martin was open to all kinds of concepts. He tried all kinds of genres, sitcoms, Westerns, lawyer dramas, secret agent series. One of the reasons Martin so liked producers John Wilder and Philip Saltzman was that both men were quite versatile when it came to devising such series concepts. Saltzman's range was astonishing. Wilder's was too.

"Quinn was so generous," praises Wilder. "We spent a lot of time together. He loved to teach me what he knew. After I left *Streets* at the end of the third year, he wanted me to come back and set up a feature department. He even offered to underwrite a company for me if I would. I loved working for Quinn, but I didn't want to do any more television series for QM. I wanted to do my own shows." John Wilder had done more than one television series for Quinn Martin. In 1976, he'd brought the producer a new TV series concept called *Nightmare*. *Nightmare* was a science-fiction/horror anthology series, and "Quinn thought it was terrific," remembers Wilder. "He loved that genre." Yet, when Martin and Wilder pitched it to the networks, no one was interested.

One year later, NBC approached Martin with a new series concept entitled *Quinn Martin's Tales of the Unexpected*. "We were up at the San Francisco Film Festival, walking along by the water, when he told me," recalls Wilder. "He said, 'You're interested in doing a thriller kind of a series, and NBC has asked me if I would do something, put my name on it, like *Quinn Martin's Thriller*, or *Quinn Martin's Tales of the Unexpected*.' He was flattered by the prospect of putting his name on top of a show like that." John Wilder was more than happy to turn *Nightmare* into *Quinn Martin's*

Tales of the Unexpected. The new series had an exciting concept—Quinn Martin would himself appear on screen to introduce the stories.

"I wrote something for him that we never shot," reveals Wilder. "It was an introductory piece where he walked through the different sets, and introduced the film. I wanted him to do that every week. I was excited about him doing that. I was excited for him. I felt that he was the best TV producer in the game. I don't know why we didn't go forward with that approach. He may have just pulled back for personal reasons."

Unlike *Caribe* and the fourth year of *Cannon*, *Tales of the Unexpected* (February 2–August 24, 1977, NBC) went into production with story concepts already in mind. "When we did *Tales of the Unexpected*," explains Wilder, "I went back to stories that I had lined up for *Nightmare*. "A Hand for Sonny Blue" was a story I had adapted from a short story about a concert pianist who loses his hand in an accident, then gets a replacement for that hand. Only it's a criminal's hand. In my version, the pianist was a baseball pitcher. Put a criminal's hand on a baseball pitcher, it becomes a lethal weapon. I made one change from my original script for *Nightmare*. When I had written the original, Sonny Blue was black. Well, we started thinking about casting, and Rick Nelson and I had grown up together as pals. Rick had played the pied-piper child molester on *Streets*, and I think that had given us the number-one show of the week. So I made Sonny Blue white. That way I could cast Rick. Rick was a terrific athlete. I made his catcher black. We cast Carl Weathers in that part."

Premiering on Wednesday February 2 at 10:00 Eastern time, *Tales of the Unexpected* kicked off with "The Final Chapter," guest-starring *The Invaders*' Roy Thinnes. "That was the first hour we shot," remembers Wilder. "Roy played an investigative reporter who got himself put on death row. R.G. Armstrong was a warden, Ned Beatty a jailer. [Art director] Herman Zimmerman designed the death row set. Herman was a wonderful production designer."

John Wilder would have been happy to continue with the series, but when he got an offer from Universal Studios to produce the epic miniseries *Centennial*, he accepted that offer. *The Streets of San Francisco*'s William Robert Yates became *Tales*' new producer. "Quinn asked me if I could take over the series, and it was pretty easy because the scripts already had been rewritten," says Yates. "I just finished what was left. So for a while I was producing two series at once. I remember thinking if I get through this season alive, I'll be really lucky." Yates did.

Tales of the Unexpected wasn't as fortunate. After five weeks on Wednesdays, the show concluded its run with a special two-hour episode that aired on Sunday. Five months later, in August '77, the series returned to its original time slot for two weeks, during which time two new episodes aired. More than likely, the expense of the special effects and special sets were what killed the series. "It was hard to edit because there were so many weird special effects," reveals editor Richard Brockway. "Each week there was a different kind of special effect. In one show we had these big black wild dogs, ["The Devil Pack"], their eyes glowed red. The red had to be right in the eyeball. If it was off just a little bit, it looked stupid. Quinn checked everything like that. He never let anything go. So everybody was working night and day. Nowadays you could do that kind of effect in a matter of minutes on tape machines and special machines. But back then everything was on film. It took days to do it. The optical house would bring the shots over that they were gonna use; if they weren't right, man we were in a lot of trouble. They'd have to take it back and redo everything. It was all just hit and miss when you were doing those special effects. You'd try something and hope it was gonna work."

Such experimentation was expensive, as were productions like Walter Grauman's "No Way Out," in which naval officer Bill Bixby sails through an unusual time warp twenty five years into the future. "Quinn was trying to save the show," explains Grauman, "and he needed some help so he asked me to do it. We did this storm at sea, had this huge tank, dumped thousands of gallons of water in the tank, made these giant waves, created artificial lightning with these arc lights, and thunder with these huge tins that we rattled. I was on a big crane, sitting on the arm of a crane in a wet suit, my script covered with plastic. I said, 'Okay, action!' and the water dumped down, and they rattled the tins, and the lighting crashed. I kept saying, 'Lighting! Thunder! More waves! Stir it up! Make it rougher!' and all of a sudden, I said, 'Stop! Cut!,' and everything stopped. I said, 'You know, I feel like God.' Everybody broke up. That was a good experience."

Guest star Marlyn Mason was very amused by her *Tales of the Unexpected* guest shot, "Mask of Adonis." "Robert Foxworth was playing kind of a Darryl Zanuck character who's very vain and wants to stay youthful and live forever," laughs Mason. "I had this institution that kept people young and alive, and I spoke in this phony European accent. That was such a stupid show. Robert and I just laughed."

Slotted opposite ABC's runaway hit of the 1976-77 season, *Charlie's Angels*, starring television's hottest new personality, Farrah Fawcett-Majors, *Tales of the Unexpected* never even had a chance. Quinn Martin's next series, *The Runaways*, might have, had it not been for its leading man, Robert Reed.

Chapter 17

THE RUNAWAYS

Quinn liked *The Runaways*. He thought it was relevant. It was an ongoing problem—kids running away. He thought they could do a lot with it.

Muffet Martin

Like any parent, Quinn Martin was always concerned about the welfare of his
children, and in the late 1970s, the producer brought to TV viewers a series that
tapped into such concerns: *Operation Runaway* (April-May, 1978, NBC), later *The
Runaways* (May–Sep 79, NBC). Playing the role of L.A. psychologist David McKay
in *Operation: Runaway* was *The Brady Bunch*'s Robert Reed. The fame Reed had
gained from that series made him perfect for the Martin series; in *Operation: Runaway*, Reed's character tracked down missing children. Unfortunately, shortly after
production started on *Operation: Runaway*, Robert Reed began causing problems.

"Reed wanted script control," reveals series director Michael Preece. "He was
always making demands." "He wanted to change stuff all the time," adds production
manager Paul Wurtzel. "Quinn told him, 'Let's do it before we start shooting. If you
have changes, we'll go over it. Don't do it when we're in production. It slows everything down.'" Known for causing problems during his five years on *The Brady Bunch*,
Reed continued to alter the scripts on *Operation: Runaway* in spite of Quinn Martin's
warning.

Because the socially conscious program was so important to Martin, the producer was willing to tolerate Reed's behavior—to a point. Series production coordinator Karen Shaw remembers, "We did this one show, and Reed refused to do it
because it had a homosexual theme to it. He disagreed with it, and went up against
Quinn. Quinn shut the show down."

"Quinn said, 'Let's get rid of him,'" recalls Preece. "We shut down the whole
production. I loved it. I was on salary all that time." Preece also loved *Operation:
Runaway*. So much so he turned down his friend Leonard Katzman's offer of another

series. "I said, 'No thanks,'" laughs Preece. "'I'm working on the best series you ever heard of in your life. It's called *The Runaways*. The stories are wonderful. We've got the best writers that you could imagine.' After our show was canceled, it took me about a year to get hired for *Dallas*. That was the show Leonard offered me."

Michael Preece was right. With William Robert Yates as its producer, *The Runaways* did have good writing. "He was one of the brightest men I ever came across," says the director. "You didn't think he was doing anything, then you'd leave the room twenty minutes later with the pages of exactly whatever you'd talked about in your hand. He would have written out exactly what I was thinking about. He would be smoking all the time we were talking. He smoked like crazy. The ashtray would be so full, you had a hard time finding an empty spot to put the next cigarette."

When *Operation: Runaway* returned one year later as *The Runaways*, it was now Alan Feinstein who was playing the psychologist. (The name of Feinstein's character was Steve Arizzio.) Continuing in the role of Karen Wingate, Dean of Women at Westwood University, was Karen Machon. Joining the cast for the new version of *Operation: Runaway* was QM Player James Callahan. "I was starving to death this one summer," remembers Callahan, "nothing going on, nothing happening; then my agent calls me. He says, 'Quinn Martin wants to see you. Do you know him?' I said, 'No. I've worked for him, but I don't know him.' Well, I went to Quinn's office, went into this huge, cathedral-like office. I'm gulping and looking around, and behind the desk is Quinn. 'Jim,' he says. 'Sit down.' I said, 'Okay, Mr. Martin, I will.' He says, 'Well, Jim. How are you?' I couldn't think of a thing to say. I thought, What's going on here? I said, 'Fine. How are you?' He says, 'Good. I'm doing a new series called *The Runaways*. I want you to play the police detective. Will you do that for me?' I said, 'I'd love to do it. Are you serious?' He says, 'Yeah. I'll call your agent and work out a deal. Thanks, Jim, and God, you look good.' So, out I went, and I got the part. I couldn't believe it. I could not believe it."

"James Callahan had the greatest sense of humor," chuckles Michael Preece. "I remember one time we had this softball game. I got a double or something, I was rounding second, fell down. Callahan screamed, 'Preece! Age is an ugly thing!' He came to my house quite a few times. I remember one time I was making something, and ran out of flour. I looked around. I said, 'We don't have any fucking flour.' He says, 'Maybe your neighbors do.' He goes next door to my neighbor lady. He says, 'Do you have any fucking flour?' She says, 'What?' He says, 'Well, that's what he said.'"

New QM secretary Debbi Lahr Lawlor very much enjoyed helping her boss, associate producer Andy White, get scripts ready for *The Runaways*. "It was kind of fun to work on," says Lawlor. "Andy White would churn out the scripts. I would edit and type them. Andy White was a very nice man. He was quiet, did his work; he had a nice wife." Yet, despite its good off-set feelings, and despite its more pleasant leading man Alan Feinstein, *The Runaways* was heading towards cancellation. "If Robert Reed had stayed with the show, it probably would have run longer," believes Preece. "Alan Feinstein was a good actor, but he didn't project the compassion when dealing with issues like runaway children, and runaway grandfathers, which Reed did. Quinn was very concerned with the issue of people who ran away. I remember I did an episode with Barry Sullivan where he played a runaway grandfather. I liked that show. The shows I did on that series were some of the best shows I've ever done."

"Quinn was really disappointed when the series was canceled," says Muffet Martin. "He was really sorry they gave up so easily, and so fast." "It never really got the ratings it needed, and we'd also had a network change," adds William Robert Yates. "I think that was when Fred Silverman came in. Fred didn't like the idea, but he didn't want to cancel the show. He didn't want to make Quinn angry. Fred never particularly supported the show. I'm sure that's the reason why it was canceled."

If such was the case, then Quinn Martin and *A Man Called Sloane* series creator-producer Philip Saltzman had nothing to worry about when they launched that series in the fall of 1979. Loaded with high-tech gadgetry, bizarre villains, and gorgeous women, *A Man Called Sloane* starred Robert Conrad as secret agent Thomas Remington "T.R." Sloane III. The combination of high-tech gadgetry, bizarre villains, gorgeous women, and Robert Conrad had given CBS-TV a hit series in the mid 1960s called *The Wild Wild West*. Finally, at long last, QM Productions had the makings of another series hit. With NBC boss Fred Silverman backing *A Man Called Sloane* all the way, that was a guarantee.

Chapter 18

A MAN CALLED SLOANE

It started out great. Bob Conrad had grown this mustache, and he looked great, and he was all for changing his image. Then Silverman told him to get rid of the mustache. So he did, and as the show continued, it got to be more and more a Conrad and company show.

A Man Called Sloane *creator-producer Philip Saltzman*

As the ratings were proving, QM Productions had finally struck gold with the Robert Conrad spy adventure, *A Man Called Sloane* (September 22, 1979–September 12, 1980, NBC). Now down to just one prime-time series, the ever-popular *Barnaby Jones*, QM Productions really needed a successful series, especially since its founder Quinn Martin had sold the company the year before. Martin was still keeping his hand in though. While he was busy setting up Quinn Martin Films and involving himself in other projects, he still had some say when it came to casting and series projects, including *A Man Called Sloane*.

"I had talked to Quinn about doing a spy series, a kind of James Bondian thing, and when I'd first suggested it, he wasn't interested," remembers *Sloane* creator-producer Philip Saltzman. "Quinn was wonderful. You'd make these suggestions, and he'd say, 'No.' Then later, he'll call you up and say, 'Hey. I've got this great idea for a show,' and he'd tell you about the show you'd suggested to him earlier. Anyway, he told me that NBC was interested about doing this spy show, that Cliff Gould, who was a writer I had worked with, had shown interest in the idea, and that Cliff [with John Wilder] had come up with this black character with a steel hand [played by Ji-Tu Cumbuka]. So Cliff and I got together and wrote a script."

In the Saltzman/Gould script for the series' pilot, *T.R. Sloane* (later released as *Death Ray 2000*), the Cumbuka character was a villain. NBC liked Cumbuka. In the series, Cumbuka played Conrad's partner, Torque. Starring former *Daniel Boone* regular Robert Logan in the role later played by Robert Conrad, *T.R. Sloane* was shot in Colorado. Directing the two-hour movie pilot was Lee H. Katzin.

"Lee Katzin had been ill and he had had some kind of a heart problem; so we had trouble getting him okayed by the insurance company, but we finally got him," reveals Saltzman. "They had all kinds of problems while they were shooting in Colorado. Lee had developed a very bad cough and he was close to pneumonia. The minute he'd finish shooting a scene, he'd run into this trailer that they kept heating up. Cliff Gould kind of oversaw the whole shoot."

Once the pilot was completed, it was then previewed for NBC programming boss Fred Silverman. Remembers Saltzman, "He said, 'The show's great. But who's the lox?' [referring to Logan]. Silverman wanted us to replace Robert Logan; so we went on a big spree looking for this new James Bond type character. We interviewed a lot of actors; they always turned us down. Nobody wanted to be compared to James Bond. We offered the part to Stephen Collins and Armand Assante. We were very excited about Armand—he had an accent. We figured he could be a good Bondy character. He turned us down twice. We kept looking; then Silverman says, 'There's always Bob Conrad.'"

At the time however Conrad was starring in the NBC crime drama, *The Duke.* "Silverman said, 'I'll cancel that, and put him in your show,'" recalls Saltzman. "We said, 'Bob isn't right for this part. He's stocky and heavy and very American,' and on and on and on, so we kept looking. Then one day, Silverman calls. He says, 'I've made a decision. You're gonna get Conrad!' So, Bob came in. I met with him. I knew him from *Hawaiian Eye* [Saltzman had written for that series and for *Wild Wild West*], and we talked about the character. I said, 'You really should change your image for this show.' He says, 'Absolutely.' So, I got a big budget from the company; then I took Bob to Beverly Hills, and we went to Gucci, and all these Italian stores, and I got him a complete new wardrobe. Now this entailed getting him at least three of everything—suits, slacks, coats, sweaters, everything, because you use one on the show, then you have a backup, and also a third backup, just in case the other two get ruined. So we spent a lot of money." The production also bought a sports car for the Conrad character. "It was a Cord. It was like a two-seater, with supercharger engine," says Saltzman, "and again, we had to have three of these. The cars were kind of a yellow-cream color and we have to have them painted and restored, and they were murder to drive. They didn't have power-steering. So you had trouble turning the wheel. They were gorgeous to look at though." Robert Conrad had his own ideas regarding the character's image.

"He said, 'I'm gonna grow a mustache,'" remembers Saltzman. "I said, 'Yeah, let's try that.' So we had this great mustache on Bob, and we shot all these commercials and previews for the new series, and I was in the commercials because they had the executive producer talking about it, and we had fun ideas, like Bob's kissing a woman, then he turns to the camera, and says, 'Oh, excuse me. I'm just practicing for my new role.' He looked different with the mustache, just slightly different, and we were gonna run these; then the first day of the first day's shoot, Bob comes in without the mustache. I said, 'What the hell happened?' He says, 'Fred called last night. He thought it over. He said, 'The audience wants Bob Conrad; so get rid of the

Robert Conrad (as secret-agent Thomas Remington Sloane III) and friends in a tongue-in-cheek publicity shot for the September 22, 1979–September 12, 1980, NBC-TV series, *A Man Called Sloane*.

mustache,' So Bob said, 'I always listen to the chief, and the chief said get rid of the mustache; so I did.' Well, after that, it quickly deteriorated into a typical Bob Conrad project. Bob brought in his own stunt-man, who was like his double; so we would have two minutes of fist-fights in the show. He was always knocking guys down, knocking guys out, and that wasn't James Bond."

Installing Gerald Sanford as the series' producer (one of Quinn Martin's people had suggested Sanford) didn't help matters at all. "Gerry was having emotional problems with his girlfriend because he was working so hard. She had decided to go back to New York," explains Saltzman. "Gerry would fly to New York on the weekends to try to lure her back; so he was abandoning the scripts over the weekend. We needed him to rewrite and write the scripts on the weekend." Worsening this already bad situation was NBC boss Fred Silverman. "He'd tell you, 'Make this show a two-parter,'" remembers Saltzman; "so you'd add all this new material and develop the thing, and rewrite it. Then, at the last minute, he'd say, 'No, make it a one-parter.' Well, between our problem with the network and Gerry Sanford's problem with his love-life and the problems I was having with Bob Sherman and Norman Jolley on *Barnaby Jones*, it was very hectic."

Bringing in script supervisor turned director Michael Preece as one of the series' regular directors seemed to be one way to obtain some control. It wasn't. Recalls Preece, "I'd been signed to do every other *Barnaby Jones* for the season; then after about one day on that show, Quinn called me in. He says, 'We've got this series, *A Man Called Sloane*. We need somebody to do it.' So I went on that thing, and the very first day, Robert Conrad came up to me. He says, 'I know I have a bad reputation for being difficult, for drinking, and all that sort of thing. Well, that's all changed. I'm totally different now.' Well he hadn't changed. The first day of shooting he was two and a half hours late. He came running down the street, trying to get back in condition, in full sweats, with a motor home following him. He gets to the set. He says, 'All right, what do you want me to do.' I told him. He says, 'Okay, fine.' But he could not stop sweating. He was just pouring sweat. We had to wait another forty-five minutes for him until we could shoot. He was a belligerent, cocky guy, just like in the [Eveready] commercials. Whenever he'd have a party at his house, he was very very competitive. I remember stepping off the steps at his beach house onto the sand one time, and when I did, he says, 'How far can you jump out there?' He was a pistol, a pain in the neck. He'd tell you he wanted to do his own stunts; then he'd change his mind. Ji-Tu, on the other hand, was very good. He would do whatever you asked. Conrad was very rough on him. But whenever they interviewed him, he'd say Ji-Tu was his best friend."

"It was a horrible show," continues Preece. "Just awful! Conrad drank wine all day long, and when we were doing the episode "The Seduction Squad," the very first day on that show, we started very early in the morning. It was a huge day, and Robert Culp was the guest star, and he took himself pretty seriously too. I had worked with him before. I'd done all the episodes of *I Spy* as a script supervisor, so I knew what to expect from him. Well, we'd shot a little bit downtown at the L.A. Athletic Club, at the jewelry store next door, and after Conrad arrived and got down to the set, he says, 'Oh, by the way, I've got to leave by 4:30. I'm doing *Johnny Carson;* it'll be great publicity for the show.' So I ended up having to double him, and shoot as fast as I could so I could get him out.' Preece also had his problems with guest star Laura Johnson, who was playing villain Culp's accomplice. "Laura Johnson was very pretty," says Preece, "but she was always complaining about being too fat. I wanted her to wear tight pants, but she thought they'd make her look too big. She looked great."

Even the post-production people had problems with Robert Conrad. Says editor Richard Brockway, "He was a tough little guy to work for. He could really be a bastard when he wanted to. When we were doing the show that he was directing, we were way under footage on the show, so everybody was worried about it. But the producers were too afraid to go down to the set and give him any kind of guff, or ask him to do something, because he was a little snot. Well, [QM executive] Merrill Karpf comes in to my office. He says, 'Dick, will you go down to the set and tell Robert we need more footage?' So I went down there. I said, 'Robert, we're really under footage. We need some longer scenes to get us through. I don't think the network will take a show that's this much under.' He says, 'Don't worry about it. Don't worry about it.' This is on a Friday night and we were supposed to finish up shooting on Friday. He says, 'I'm not shooting any more film. You've got plenty there. We're cutting it tonight. I want you to come in tomorrow with your editor. I'll meet you at eleven o'clock.' I said. 'Okay.' So on Saturday, my editor and I went in about eleven. We sat in the projection room, and we sat and we sat and we sat. About two, we're wandering around, wondering where in hell Conrad is. He drives in, and we see him go across the lot. He goes into his dressing room, sits over there, has a couple of drinks; he has about three girls with him. He finally moseys over with the girls. He doesn't say, 'I'm sorry. Thanks for waiting,' or anything like that. He just sits down. They all have their cocktails in their hands, and we run the film. He sits there watching. He says, 'Oh no no no. Let that run longer. Let that run longer. This show isn't short. You just cut it too short, too quickly.' So I had to put all kinds of footage back in to stretch it out, and get it to where it was passable for the network."

Brockway didn't care for the way executive producer Philip Saltzman produced the show either. "He had a lot of ideas that Quinn never used," exclaims the editor. "He changed the whole design. He didn't have the Act I, Act II stuff. He used old fashioned dissolves and fades and irises, spiraling effects, wipes—stuff they'd used years and years ago. Quinn didn't even have an opportunity to look at what he was doing. I remember we were walking out of dailies one day. Quinn said, 'Dick, you know I haven't seen a foot of dailies on *A Man Called Sloane*. Do you suppose I could look at a cut of it?'"

While Quinn Martin may not have approved of Saltzman's visuals, he certainly had no complaints about *A Man Called Sloane*'s success. The series was killing its competition. CBS had already dropped the James Earl Jones–Stephen Bochco drama *Paris* from its Saturday 10 P.M. time slot; ABC had moved their Saturday 10 P.M. entry, *Hart to Hart*, to Tuesday nights at 10. For all his faults, series star Robert Conrad was putting a lot of effort into the series. His *Black Sheep Squadron* co-star Denise DuBarry guest-starred in the episode, "Tuned for Destruction." Conrad had suggested her for the show. He suggested other things as well. Explains Saltzman, "Bob would go to Gerry Sanford, and say, 'So and so's a good writer.' So we used a couple of writers that Bob liked. I'm all in favor of that because I feel it makes the set more comfortable, and people have a better time. Sometimes the shows are better because of that."

A Man Called Sloane did seem to be doing better, and had the competition on the other networks remained as weak as they had proven in the fall of 1979, the series could very likely have been QM Productions' next big hit. After ABC put Aaron Spelling's hit series *Fantasy Island* back in its regular Saturday 10 P.M. time slot, however, there was no chance of that. QM Productions wasn't through trying to launch new series though. In its last two years of operation, the company would attempt a wide variety of series pilots. This time, unfortunately, nothing worked.

Chapter 19

PILOT ERRORS

Quinn wanted to do a lawyer show and a newspaper show. He always wanted to
do a Western. They kept saying, "No. We want action-adventure."

Muffet Martin

In 1971, QM Productions aired three TV-series pilots, *Incident in San Francisco*
(2-28-71, ABC), *Travis Logan, D.A.* (3-11-71, CBS), and *Cannon* (3-26-71, CBS). Only
Cannon made it to series—a successful series at that. Script supervisor Michael
Preece was not surprised by the failure of *Travis Logan, D.A.* The pilot starred Vic
Morrow. "When I heard who was gonna be in the pilot, I thought, 'This'll never go
to series,'" chuckles Preece. "I didn't think Vic Morrow was the kind of person people would want in their living room every week."

Shot on location in Santa Barbara, and for some sequences, the Lincoln Heights
Jail, *Travis Logan, D.A.* starred Morrow as a California district attorney trying to
disprove killer Hal Holbrook's plea of temporary insanity. Director Paul Wendkos
viewed the assignment as "routine." His camera angles and slow-motion sequences
made the movie anything but. While Michael Preece was none too enthusiastic about
working with Vic Morrow, the movie had its high points for the script supervisor,
especially during the filming of the confrontation scenes between Hal Holbrook and
(wife) Brenda Vaccaro. "Paul Wendkos was partially responsible for me becoming
a director," reveals Preece. "He let me direct a scene between Hal Holbrook and Brenda
Vaccaro in that movie."

Sound mixer Dick Church considered *Incident in San Francisco* the show that
inspired Quinn Martin's successful *Streets of San Francisco* series. Starring Christopher Connelly as a young reporter who tries to clear a Good Samaritan of a murder
following a mugging, *Incident* was shot on location at the San Francisco Chronicle
by Don "Midnight" Medford. "When you work with Don," laughs Church, "you work
long hours. That's why we called him 'Midnight' Medford. We were three weeks up

in San Francisco. We shot under all kinds of conditions." "We did an awful lot of night work," adds director of photography William W. Spencer. "We shot a sidewalk scene in that awful section of town, Haight-Ashbury, and we had a lot of rain. When we were working in the 'Chronicle,' we just used their lighting. They had fluorescent lighting. We were in a huge room with dozens and dozens of desks. They had a very large city desk."

William Spencer was again director of photography on QM's next unsold TV movie pilot, *Murder or Mercy* (4-19-74, ABC). Starring Denver Pyle and Bradford Dillman as a father-son lawyer team who defend Melvyn Douglas for the mercy-killing of his wife, *Murder or Mercy* was filmed on location in San Diego. "That was one of my favorites," says Spencer, "mainly because of the director, Harvey Hart. I remember there was an actor in the show who whenever he got to the word 'euthanasia,' could never say it. So Harvey took him aside. Harvey says, 'It's easy. Whenever you get to that point in the dialogue, Just think of the youth in Asia.'"

Two years later, QM Productions aired two more series pilots: *Most Wanted* (3-21-76, ABC), and *Law of the Land* (4-29-76, NBC). *The Streets of San Francisco*'s John Wilder produced both. Wilder succeeded in launching a series with *Most Wanted*, failed with *Law of the Land. Law* had been in development for quite a while. "They were all ready to start shooting that [in the early '70s]," recalls Muffet Martin, "when ABC slapped Quinn with a lawsuit; so everything got stopped. ABC said Quinn was not honoring his contract. Quinn counter-sued and won. It was really peculiar, because everything got pulled but *The FBI.* You don't say that somebody is not doing their job, and then keep something. It was really strange. That was when Quinn became non-exclusive to ABC."

"Quinn called *Law of the Land* his *Streets of San Francisco* in the Old West," laughs the movie's costumer, Steve Lodge. "Jim Davis played a sheriff. He had all these young deputies working under him." "We did that in Columbia, California, close to Yosemite," adds director of photography William W. Spencer. "In order to make it look authentic, they had to layer the main street, which was paved, with dirt. We had to cover about a block and a half of the street with artificial snow too." "We built a whole Western street on the back lot at CBS [the old Republic street] which tied in with the town in Columbia," elaborates Lodge. "They completely refurbished the back lot—it was basically a street that had not been there. It was the *Gunsmoke* street. I remember when we did the shot of the wagon train coming into town [director] Virgil Vogel set up this one-hundred and-eighty degree shot, panning from right to left, from the road out of town all the way into town, which because it was night meant you had to light the entire town, plus the road outside of town. Every piece of electrical equipment was used. It must have taken three, four hours to light this thing, and the production managers were upset. But after they saw it, they said, 'Virgil, it's the most beautiful thing we've ever seen. Forget what we said earlier.'"

One year later, John Wilder's Porsche was burned for dramatic value in the QM pilot *The City* (1-12-77, NBC). The car was later rebuilt. Two days before filming began, pilot star Robert Forster was hit by Bell's Palsy. "I called Quinn," remembers

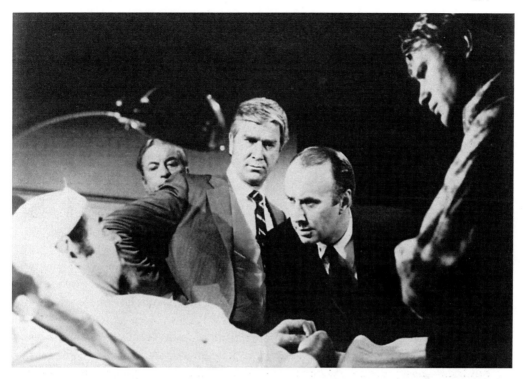

From second from left: **Ken Lynch, QM favorite Leslie Nielsen (as Lt. Brubaker), Richard Kiley (as Robert Harmon) and Christopher Connelly (as Jeff Marshall) talk to an injured David Opatoshu (in bed, as Herschel Rosen) in the February 28, 1971, ABC-TV movie-pilot,** *Incident in San Francisco.*

Forster, "and told him what I had. I said 'You can replace me, you can hold the production if you want, or I'll come in and do it.' Quinn said, 'Don't worry about it. Favor the other side when you're looking into the camera.' So I did." After two weeks, Forster's Bell's Palsy was gone.

Quinn Martin's two other series pilots for 1977 were the May 3 secret-agent adventure *Code Name: Diamond Head* (starring Roy Thinnes) and the November 28 crime drama *The Hunted Lady*—Donna Mills in Martin's remake of *The Fugitive.* Recalls the latter's producer William Robert Yates, "Quinn and I were talking about doing a woman on the run show, and the network loved the idea; so Quinn asked me to write the pilot." "Quinn was disappointed that *The Hunted Lady* didn't sell because he thought it was pretty good," adds Muffet Martin. "I think the network asked for that show. Quinn never liked to copy himself."

Despite what others may have thought, Quinn Martin was not remaking *The Invaders* when he did *The Aliens Are Coming* in 1980. After scaring Fred Silverman half to death with *Aliens,* Martin and series creator-producer Philip Saltzman thought they had a guaranteed sale. *Escapade,* with Martin's hand-picked star Morgan Fairchild, seemed a good bet too. So much so that Philip Saltzman wrote a number of scripts for both *Aliens* and *Escapade.* Neither show went anywhere. At least these pilots made it to the air. The Marty Katz comedies, *Sex and the Secretary,* and *Love and Marriage* didn't even get that far. "Marty Katz was always having these two minute meetings over at CBS," laughs Saltzman. "Katz was a hustler. He'd run off, have these meetings with the network, come back and say, 'I think I've interested them in *Mount Shasta.*' Quinn would turn to me. He'd say, 'Keep an eye on this guy. Help him out.'"

Other pilot concepts never even making it to the filmed pilot stage were *A Man Between, Coast Guard, Monster,* and *Ladies' Man.* The latter was to star Efrem Zimbalist, Jr. "That one was discussed for several years," recalls Muffet Martin. "Even after Quinn died, Efrem was asking for a treatment. It never even made it to script." *Ladies' Man* was presented to Zimbalist shortly after *The FBI*'s cancellation. "It was beautifully written," states Zimbalist. "Quinn wrote it himself. Unfortunately no one wanted to do it. It was a good idea. The protagonist is a lawyer who takes only women as clients. It was a lovely idea, but perhaps ahead of its time."

Lynda Day George's idea for the planned QM Western *Chisum* (developed by Philip Saltzman in August 1978 at Martin's urging) would more than likely have excited Quinn Martin. "If they were planning to do that as a series," muses George, "the only way they could have done it would have been to show John Chisum from the back, because you cannot replace John Wayne!" John Wayne had played *Chisum* in the 1970 Warner Bros. feature of the same name; Lynda Day George and her husband Christopher George also appeared in the movie. "Showing John Chisum from the back would have been tough," says the actress, "but it could have been done, and Quinn Martin is the only one who could have done it. Quinn Martin is the only producer in this business who could have made that work!"

Fred Silverman shared Lynda Day George's high regard for Quinn Martin. Soon after the cancellation of *The FBI,* Fred Silverman approached Quinn Martin with an interesting proposal: "Let's do a series of TV movies based on actual FBI cases." Quinn Martin liked that idea.

Chapter 20

BASED ON A TRUE STORY

It was a real departure for Quinn to do that. He put a lot into that.
A Home of Our Own *assistant director Kenneth Gilbert*

All four of the TV movies Quinn Martin did that were based on real-life incidents were departures. *Attack on Terror: The FBI Versus the Ku Klux Klan* (February 20, 21, 1975, CBS) was the biggest departure of them all. *Attack* was a four-hour TV movie. With the exception of the April 29 and 30, 1974, six-and-a-half hour TV movie, *QB VII*, nobody had ever done a TV movie as big as *Attack on Terror*. Very few people made TV movies as big as *Attack on Terror* after the film aired. The second in a series of FBI-TV movies, *Attack on Terror: The FBI Versus the Ku Klux Klan*, was the favorite FBI-TV movie of all concerned. There were three FBI-TV movies in all. As Philip Saltzman had done such a good job during the four years he'd produced *The FBI* TV series, he was the logical choice to produce the three planned FBI-TV movies. All of the TV movies were to be two hours. Thanks to Philip Saltzman, *Attack on Terror* was given a four-hour slot.

Recalls Saltzman, "Once we'd made the deal, Quinn and I flew to Washington to meet with Clarence Kelly, who had taken over as the bureau's director after J. Edgar Hoover's death. We were going to do a movie about the kidnapping of the Lindbergh baby; Kelly asked us how we felt about it. I said, 'I don't think it would make a very good story because the FBI didn't have that big a role in the case. What I'd rather do is the FBI solving the death of the three civil rights workers in the South. It's much more up to date. It's a much better chapter in the FBI's history.' Kelly said, 'I'm so glad you said that because I didn't want to do the Lindbergh show either. I would love to do things like the civil rights case.'" (In 1964, three civil rights workers were murdered by members of the Ku Klux Klan in Mississippi. Through their hard work and investigation of the crime, the FBI identified the killers.)

Continues Saltzman, "The reason why he was so excited was because the first

199

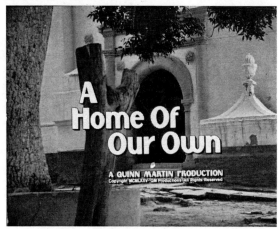

Title card for the four-hour February 20, 21, 1975, CBS TV movie, *Attack on Terror: The FBI vs. The Ku Klux Klan*. And title card for the October 19, 1975, CBS TV movie, *A Home of Our Own*.

show we did (*The FBI Story: The FBI Versus Alvin Karpis, Public Enemy Number One*, 11-8-74, CBS) was a rip-roaring '20s thing where Hoover made the arrest himself. It was a very good movie, but they didn't want to do the Roaring '20s. Kelly says, 'I'm sick of the '20s and '30s, sick of all that with the machine guns.' So, by saying we wanted to do the civil rights case, we got Kelly to approve the whole package of movies, and because of that, Silverman gave us four hours on the civil rights show. *Brinks: The Great Robbery* (3-26-76, NBC) was the last one we did. It was good, but everyone felt that the movie series was kind of played out by then."

"Quinn was very proud of the Ku Klux Klan show," states Muffet Martin. "They had to shoot some of it in San Antonio. The KKK was still kind of a touchy subject when they were shooting in the South." Adds *Attack* star Marlyn Mason, "The movie wasn't rerun for a long time, which was strange because the movie got very good reviews. Well, apparently there was a lawsuit that had been brought against the producers by some of the Klan. They couldn't run the show until it got settled. Once it got settled, they started showing it again."

A Home of Our Own (10-19-75, CBS) wasn't as lucky. The movie didn't get much play after its initial broadcast. Originally entitled, *Who Will See to the Children*, *A Home of Our Own* starred Jason Miller as Father William Wasson—the director and founder of a Mexican orphanage for children. Benefiting from the technical expertise of Father Wasson himself, *A Home of Our Own* was for assistant director Bob Jeffords "a life experience. One of the things that made it so was that we were in an actual orphanage in Mexico, working at times with seven-hundred-and-fifty orphans," explains Jeffords. "Mexico has never had great respect for orphans who are homeless. If they do anything wrong, they just get thrown into prison with adults, which was why Father Wasson started this organization for boys. Eventually he included girls."

Filmed on location in Mexico, *A Home of Our Own* was one of QM's most difficult productions. "It was very polarized," says Jeffords. "The highs were high, and the lows were low. They had what they call the Syndicato in Mexico, which is their equivalent of our unions and guilds. You had to take their people, have a standby cameraman, standby operator, standby assistants. In most cases, those people were not expected to work at all. They had a censor on the set too. They didn't want you filming anything that represented Mexico poorly. Some of the Mexican crew were great. The head make-up lady, the assistant prop-man, the second grip were all excellent. The production staff, the unit production manager, and the location people were all disasters."

"Our director, Robert Day, was very adept at working with children, and most of the children were Mexican. The children were in their own surroundings, and the people the children normally worked with helped us too. There was a supervisor named Al, who was just superb. He had come through the orphanage himself. The language was a challenge throughout that show. It was mostly Robert Day who worked with the interpreter. Robert Day was very creative, very organized. He was a very decisive director, an excellent director."

Father Wasson was very happy with the completed film. "He gave me an antique fan which I still have framed in my powder room," says Muffet Martin. "Somebody had donated the fan to his cause. Quinn was very pleased with that movie, but it didn't get replayed that much because Quinn insisted on telling where the place was. The network was really opposed to that. They felt that was soliciting donations. It wasn't. It was just telling where the orphanage was."

Almost a year before the broadcast of *A Home of Our Own*, ABC had aired QM Productions' most difficult fictional TV movie, *Panic on the 5:22*. The second of three fictional QM TV features, *Panic* had neither the sweeping locations of the 1971 San Francisco–based mystery, *The Face of Fear*, nor the period flavor of the Depression-era 1978 Western, *Standing Tall*. *Panic on the 5:22* was something really different for QM Productions. It was a one-set stage play filmed with motion-picture values!

The QM Players Present: Panic on the 5:22

Quinn always saved Harvey Hart for the special shows.
QM Production manager Howard Alston

None were more special than *Panic on the 5:22* (11-20-74, ABC). Starring (in alphabetical order) Ina Balin, Bernie Casey, Linden Chiles, Andrew Duggan, Dana Elcar, Eduard Franz, Lynda Day George, Laurence Luckinbill, Robert Mandan,

Title card for—and QM favorite Lynda Day George playing narcissistic super-model Mary Ellen Lewis in—the QM Players' "filmed stage-play": the November 20, 1974, ABC TV movie, _Panic on the 5:22_. (Lynda Day George did more series pilots and TV movies for QM Productions than any other QM Player.)

Stewart Moss, and Dennis Patrick as the passengers of the 5:22's private railroad car, _Panic on the 5:22_ was the story of how these passengers behave when what _Panic_ producer Anthony Spinner calls "three dumb stick-up men" (Reni Santoni, James Sloyan, and Robert Walden) break into the car to rob it. Because this plot-line was so similar to the 1967 motion-picture _The Incident_, many critics saw _Panic on the 5:22_ as an inferior rip-off of _The Incident_. As usual, the critics got it wrong. Unlike _The Incident_, which was simply about two thugs terrorizing people, _Panic on the 5:22_ was a study of the rich and the poor. Moreover, it was a character study. Preceding the robbery with brief character sketches of the passengers, the movie then showed the true character of the passengers as they dealt with their suddenly unexpected situation. Interestingly, showing the most defiance at the very beginning were cosmetics business-woman Countess Hedy Maria Tova-rese (Balin) and her super-model spokeswoman Mary Ellen Lewis (George).

Like its testing of these two women, and its other fictional char-acters, _Panic on the 5:22_ was also a test for its cast and crew. Though San-toni, Sloyan, and Walden all traveled to New York for some location shoot-ing, and the passenger characters' scenes were shot right outside of the train, or at the depot, or elsewhere—Balin's was at her business, Mandan's at a hospital—most of the action in _Panic_ took place on one set. There were more than fourteen characters on that one set. "It was a tiny little set," says George, "and it was very hot and uncomfortable on that set. There were a whole bunch of us. There wasn't a whole lot of room." "It was rather difficult," adds Anthony Spinner. "We had a big cast, and we had lots of problems like where do you put the camera so you don't get claustrophobic? We had a lot of stuff like that."

"That was one of the toughest shows we ever did," remembers director of photography William W. Spencer. "I think we had more than two weeks shooting time on that show. It was so confined. We had this mock-up train car, lots of rear projection. The minute you changed angles, it affected everything else. Our lamps were so close to the people that if they walked near the hot lights, they could have burned up. You had to have a lot of control. You had to shoot a lot out of continuity. That was very difficult for the director, Harvey Hart. Harvey kept a good mood on the set. That's why I enjoyed doing that movie. Harvey's attitude had a lot to do with why that movie worked."

"Harvey Hart was a person who was *extremely* well organized!" enthuses George. "To me he seemed like a person who had a map in his head of everything he wanted on the show. Not only did he have that map, but he had a picture in his mind of how it needed to look through each shot. I thought he was really clear. He had a really, really great command of the script, forwards, backwards, inside out." "Harvey Hart was a wonderful director," agrees Spinner. "He should have gone further than he did. We had an interesting script for that show. The writer Eugene Price was a novelist who had never done a television show; so he started out with a long, novelistic treatment. I had to work with him throughout the script. It was sort of like being a professor. We had a very good cast in that show."

A cast with a very good attitude. Realizing that they were in a very special production, and wanting to make it as good as it could be, the entire cast of *Panic on the 5:22* willingly rehearsed an entire week without pay. They wound up getting paid in the end, however. After the shoot was completed, someone in the cast lodged a complaint with the Screen Actor's Guild, claiming they had not been paid.

At the beginning of the movie, the adulterous, narcissistic Mary Ellen was, "a pain in the behind," laughs George. At the end, she was its heroine. It was Mary Ellen who'd quietly led the passengers to victory against their assailants in *Panic on the 5:22*. She did it through an act of compassion for the most pathetic of the three robbers, Emil Linz (Santoni).

"At that point in the piece I needed to be that person," says George. "The turning point for that character was when she stood up and defied the robbers. That was the turning point for that character, and the turning point for the audience with that character. I was hoping that was what it would be. It was also some kind of a turning point in the experience of the film. You had to dislike Mary Ellen at the very beginning so you could experience the growth she had out of that unpleasant experience. Growth always comes about through the difficulties and the unpleasantness we experience in life. Those are the things that give us character, that help us make our move to the next place."

The next place Quinn Martin wanted to move to was motion pictures. That was why he started "Quinn Martin Films."

Chapter 21

THE QM LEGACY

It was a real home. The business was never like it was when we worked for Quinn
Martin. It's never been like it was in those days. That was a true family. Because
the shows went for so many episodes, so many years, to this day, we've stayed
together, stayed in touch.

QM production coordinator Karen Shaw

Karen Shaw couldn't believe it when she was hired to work on *Cannon* in 1973.
Cannon was a Quinn Martin series. Quinn Martin was Karen Shaw's favorite TV
producer. Being hired to work at his company was a dream come true for Karen Shaw.
Many of the people at QM Productions felt the same way. "Everybody at QM got along
great," remembers location manager Robert Goodwin. "It was like a little family."
"When the Marty Katz people came in, that family feel disappeared," says production coordinator Debbie Yates Marks. "Marty Katz redecorated. He got a Porsche,
new carpeting, new painting. It seemed like an awful lot of money was being spent."
"When Marty Katz came in," laughs Shaw, "he had all the furniture scaled down, and
the doorknobs lowered because he was really really short. I remember Fred Ahern
was in the restroom one day. When he turned the light off, he couldn't find the door
handle."

"Quinn liked Marty Katz initially," says Philip Saltzman. "Marty was all over the
place. We got a lot of projects going very quickly; then Quinn became disenchanted
with him and suddenly Marty was out." So was Quinn Martin. Advised by his lawyer
Merrill Karpf (business manager, personal attorney, and CEO for QM Productions)
to keep in the background, Martin eventually got out of television. Still, Martin and
his producer Philip Saltzman did discuss QM sitcoms like the William Windom pilot
Quick & Quiet before Saltzman left QM. With *Quick & Quiet*, it looked as if Quinn
Martin would finally realize his dream of having a successful sitcom. Throughout his
career, Quinn Martin had wanted to do situation comedies. George Eckstein remembers the pilot he did for the producer at some point in the mid–1960s. "It was called

S.W.A.M.P.," laughs Eckstein. "It was about these inept heavies that are trying to take over the world. It was so over the top and so out of character for him he sparked to the idea." "He was always trying comedy," says Muffet Martin. "Every year they let him make a comedy pilot. They never put it on the air."

In the late 1970s and the early '80s that changed, at least with the William Windom ghost of a dead private eye sitcom pilots, *Landon, Landon, and Landon* and *Quick & Quiet*. Windom first played the ghost in *Landon, Landon, and Landon* (June 14, 1980, CBS); he reprised the role more than one year later in the August 18, 1981, CBS remake, *Quick & Quiet*. Guest-starring Warren Berlinger, Henry Jones, and Lynda Day George as the villainess of the piece (Quinn Martin discussed the part with George about a month before filming), *Quick & Quiet* never made it to series. "It was too bad," says Windom. "It was a pretty good idea."

By August 1981, Quinn Martin had a new business venture going, Quinn Martin Films. Debbi Lahr Lawlor who had joined QM Productions in 1978 was the secretary he picked for his new company. "He was trying to get financing for a film company," remembers Lawlor. "It didn't fly for some reason. *Cannabis Jones* was a film we had in development. It was a comedy, a departure from the things he'd done in his career. We had another thing called *Checkpoint Charlie*. It was about moles from Germany in our midst. It was kind of intriguing. There was another thing about alligators." Nothing got made.

Although Quinn Martin was by this time using a limousine once owned by Richard Nixon and driving what Lawlor calls "a beautiful white Aston-Martin, with a cream interior," he never lived the kind of life of his competitor Aaron Spelling. When Spelling later moved into the QM offices, QM downsized and moved with its new owners, Taft Broadcasting, to Westwood, California. Once Taft Broadcasting disbanded, the remaining people at QM pretty much left the company. "All of the files disappeared," remembers Lawlor. "We had scripts, information on the casts and crews; we had extensive files, stored in the storeroom downstairs. Those files technically belonged to QM productions. They probably moved to Taft."

As for Quinn Martin, he and his wife Muffet moved to Rancho Santa Fe in the early '80s. The producer spent the remaining few years of his life racing his horses at Hollywood Park in Santa Anita, speaking occasionally at classes at different colleges, and serving on the agricultural board in Rancho Santa Fe. Ironically, at the time of his death, Quinn Martin, who throughout his life had never wanted to copy his previous efforts, was helping someone to do just that. "He had a deal with Warner Brothers," recalls Muffet Martin. "They'd asked him to see if he could get *The Fugitive*. He was in the process of doing that when he died. He had a heart attack. It was so sudden. One doctor thought a virus might have attacked his heart."

Quinn Martin's mother Anne outlived her son by nine years. Anne Cohn died at the Motion Picture Home in 1996. She was one-hundred-and-one. Debbi Lahr Lawlor was one of the QM employees who attended her former boss' funeral. "I was pregnant at the time," says Lawlor. "There weren't tons of actors at the service. Quinn wasn't really Hollywood. He had a grandness to him, but it wasn't real Hollywood.

It was based in reality. He had an aura when he walked. He had a presence." Enough of one to generate an impostor. "There was actually someone who went around imitating him," reveals Lawlor. "He'd go to these places and pretend to be Quinn. He'd sign checks and do all of that. It was kind of silly, and kind of disturbing."

As Quinn Martin's friend John Wilder knew, there was only one Quinn Martin. "When I did my movie, *Norman Rockwell's Breaking Home Ties* in 1987, Quinn died while I was preparing that," remembers Wilder. "I called ABC immediately and said I wanted to put a dedication on the film. I was told, 'No, we don't do that.' I lost it a little bit, and told them, 'I want to speak to someone higher up.' So they let me, and I told the people who were higher up, 'You know. At one point in time, Quinn Martin was ABC. I owe this to him. You owe this to him.' They allowed me to put it on. They wanted me to put it on the end credits. I said, 'No. I want it on the last frame of the film.' So that's where it went."

When Quinn Martin died on August 6, 1987, at his home in Rancho Santa Fe, California, he left behind two legacies. One was the many television series and movies which showed how good prime-time television could be. The other was the fond memories of the many people who worked for him and knew him. "Quinn Martin was a really wonderful and decent man," says Lynda Day George. "He always made you feel like it was important to him to talk with you. That was really wonderful. That was really a neat thing. Whenever I had an opportunity to meet with him, it always felt good. I liked Quinn Martin a lot. Quinn Martin was very special to me. To me, he was an icon."

Many of the people at QM Productions share those same feelings. In the end, that is Quinn Martin's true legacy.

Appendix I

QM PRODUCTIONS— TELEVISION SERIES

The New Breed: October 3, 1961–September 25, 1962, ABC

The Fugitive: September 17, 1963–August 29, 1967, ABC

12 O'clock High: September 18, 1964–January 13, 1967, ABC

The FBI: September 19, 1965–September 8, 1974, ABC

The Invaders: January 10, 1967–September 17, 1968, ABC

Dan August: September 23, 1970–August 25, 1971, ABC

Cannon: September 14, 1971–September 19, 1976, CBS

Banyon: September 15, 1972–January 12, 1973, NBC

The Streets of San Francisco: September 16, 1972–June 23, 1977, ABC

Barnaby Jones: January 28, 1973–September 4, 1980, CBS

The Manhunter: September 11, 1974–April 9, 1975, CBS

Caribe: February 17, 1975–August 11, 1975, ABC

Bert D'Angelo, Superstar: February 21, 1976–July 10, 1976, ABC

Most Wanted: October 16, 1976–April 25, 1977, ABC

Tales of the Unexpected: February 2, 1977–August 24, 1977, NBC

Operation: Runaway: April 27, 1978–May 1978, August 1978, NBC

The Runaways: May 1979–September 4, 1979, NBC

A Man Called Sloane: September 22, 1979–December 1979;
June, July 1980—September 12, 1980, NBC

Appendix II

QM PRODUCTIONS—
TELEVISION MOVIES

The House on Greenapple Road: January 11, 1970, ABC—pilot for *Dan August*
Incident in San Francisco: February 28, 1971, ABC—pilot
Travis Logan, D.A.: March 11, 1971, CBS—pilot
Cannon: March 26, 1971, CBS—pilot
The Face of Fear: October 8, 1971, CBS
The Streets of San Francisco: September 16, 1972, ABC—pilot
The Manhunter: February 26, 1974, CBS—pilot
Murder or Mercy: April 19, 1974, ABC—pilot
The FBI Story: The FBI Versus Alvin Karpis, Public Enemy Number One:
November 8, 1974, CBS
Panic on the 5:22: November 20, 1974, ABC
The Abduction of Saint Anne (a.k.a. *They've Kidnapped Anne Benedict*):
January 21, 1975, ABC
Attack on Terror: The FBI Versus the Ku Klux Klan:
February 20, 21, 1975, CBS
Crossfire: March 24, 1975, NBC—pilot
A Home of Our Own: October 19, 1975, CBS
Most Wanted: March 21, 1976, ABC—pilot
Brinks: The Great Robbery: March 26, 1976, NBC
Law of the Land (a.k.a. *The Deputies*): April 29, 1976, NBC—pilot
The City: January 12, 1977, NBC—pilot
Code Name: Diamond Head: May 3, 1977, NBC—pilot
The Hunted Lady: November 28, 1977, NBC—pilot
Standing Tall: January 21, 1978, NBC
The Paradise Connection: September 17, 1979, CBS
The Aliens Are Coming: March 2, 1980, NBC—pilot
The Return of Frank Cannon: November 1, 1980, CBS—pilot
T.R. Sloane (a.k.a. *Death Ray 2000*): March 5, 1981, NBC—pilot

Appendix III

QM PRODUCTIONS— TELEVISION PILOTS

Intertect: March 11, 1973, CBS
Winner Take All: April 1, 1977, CBS
Escapade: May 19, 1978, CBS
Colorado C.I.: May 26, 1978, CBS
Landon, Landon, and Landon: June 14, 1980, CBS
Quick & Quiet: August 18, 1981, CBS

Title card for the one-hour 1977 April 1, 1977, CBS TV-series pilot, *Winner Take All*.

In addition to these aired pilots of one-hour dramas and situation comedies, QM Productions also had completed pilots that never aired, and had series ideas in development. These include "Anthony Spinner's Crisis Clinic"; "The Hunters," a World War II adventure similar to *The Guns of Navarone*; and the Martin Short sitcom "White and Reno." QM Productions also made a documentary called "Universe," narrated by William Shatner.

INTERVIEW SOURCES

Howard Alston—2001, 2002
Richard Anderson—2000, 2002
Alan Armer—2000, 2002
R.G. Armstrong—2000
Mrs. Stuart Bowie (Muffet Martin)—
    2001
Don Brinkley—2002
Richard Brockway—2001
Robert Butler—2002
Michael Caffey—2002
James Callahan—2001
Richard Church—2002
Oliver Crawford—2001
Robert Day—2001, 2002
George Eckstein—2001
John Elizalde—2001
Robert Forster—2002
Martin Fox—2002
Harold Gast—2001
James Gavin—2002
Lynda Day George—1994–2002
Kenneth Gilbert—2001
Jonathan Goldsmith—2002
Robert Goodwin—2002
William A. Graham—2001
Walter Grauman—2000
William Hale—2001, 2002
Ken Howard—2002
Robert Huddleston—2001
Robert Jeffords—2001
Debbi Lahr Lawlor—2001
Steven Lodge—2001

Sally Richman Manning—2001
Debbie Yates Marks—2002
Marlyn Mason—2001
Gerald Mayer—2001
Lee Meriwether—2002
Paul Monash—by mail—1999
Meryl O'Loughlin—2002
Barry Oringer—2000
Philip Pine—2000
Michael Preece—2002
Peter Mark Richman—2001, 2002
Carol Rossen—2002
Philip Saltzman—2000, 2002
Jacqueline Scott—2002
William Self—2001
Ralph Senensky—2001, 2002
Karen Shaw—2002
Hank Simms—2002
William W. Spencer—2001
Anthony Spinner—2001
Roy Stork—2002
Sam Strangis—2002
Duane Tatro—2002
Joan Van Ark—2002
Paul Wendkos—2002
David Whorf—2001, 2002
John Wilder—2001, 2002
William Windom—2000
Lois Winslow—2002
Paul Wurtzel—2001, 2002
William Robert Yates—2000
Efrem Zimbalist, Jr.—1999

INDEX

Numbers in italics refer to pages with photographs